SOVIET FOREIGN POLICY TODAY

SOVIET FOREIGN POLICY TODAY

Gorbachev and the New Political Thinking

Robert F. Miller

UNWIN HYMAN
London New York

Published by the Academic Division of Unwin Hyman Ltd
15–17 Broadwick Street, London W1V 1FP, UK

10 East 53rd Street, New York, NY 10022 USA

Published in Australia by
Allen & Unwin Australia Pty Ltd,
8 Napier Street, North Sydney, NSW 2059 Australia

Library of Congress Catalog Card No: 90-62229

A CIP record is available from the British Library

ISBN 0 04 445997 1 (hardback)
ISBN 0 04 445998 X (paperback)

Printed by SRM Production Services, SDN BHD, Malaysia

To my friend and colleague
HARRY RIGBY

Contents

Preface

The hazards of writing a book on contemporary Soviet foreign policy in the era of *perestroika, glasnost* and 'new political thinking' are obvious. Nevertheless, the magnitude of President Mikhail Sergeevich Gorbachev's endeavours and the importance of understanding the changes he has introduced and what lies behind them have impelled me to undertake the challenge. Everything in the socialist world appears to be in flux. Gorbachev is continually changing not only the substance of Soviet policies but also the rules governing their determination. In March 1990, he successfully had himself designated as a French–style executive president. Since then he has enjoyed greater formal legal power to set the national agenda and carry it out than any of his predecessors, who had hardly suffered for want of power to do what they wanted through their dominance of the Communist Party machinery.

Gorbachev, however, has been increasingly less willing to accept the constraints of the traditional Byzantine mode of party decision–making, obviously conscious of the fact that circumstances in the USSR and the world have changed and that the power and legitimacy of the Communist Party itself have seriously declined (at least partly as a consequence of his own actions). In seeking to build for his country a new image of legality and respectability in order to obtain its acceptance as a full partner in world economic and political processes, Gorbachev has recognised the need to abandon — for the indefinite future, if not forever — the traditional Soviet commitment to create an integral 'socialist world', capable of defeating in mortal combat the forces of 'world imperialism' and to renounce much of the ideological underpinning on which this apocalyptic image of struggle rested.

In presenting the rationale for Gorbachev's 'new political thinking', Soviet foreign policy spokespeople and scholars (the line between the two is not always clear) have accordingly found it necessary to drop many of the old ideological formulations and justifications for Soviet actions. They now concede that foreign hostility was as likely to have been a reaction to Soviet policies as it was to 'objective factors' immanent in the nature of world imperialism. In short, the Soviets themselves are now admitting that conventional Western interpretations of Soviet actions were more often than not correct. That is why, in locating the changes under Gorbachev in the context of the traditional goals and practices of the Soviet foreign policy, I have not paid what some readers may regard as due heed to 'revisionist' interpretations. I have never believed that the blame for East–West hostility must be shared equally, let alone accepted predominantly, by the West. Now there is increasing evidence from the Soviets themselves that they were often the major culprits. This is a book of interpretations, which seeks to understand the present in terms of the past. It takes a position, but it tries to be fair and objective in considering the evidence. Some of the interpretations may seem controversial; they are the result of almost 30 years of observations of Soviet foreign and domestic politics and of countless discussions with scholars and governmental experts in Australia, the United States and Europe. I have tried to present enough factual background to enable readers to draw their own conclusions. If the book stimulates them to seek alternative arguments and to challenge the positions I have taken, then I shall have accomplished a large part of my purpose.

Dr Robert F. Miller   *Canberra, Australia*
                                                                April 1990

Acronyms

APR	Asia–Pacific Region
Arcos	Anglo-Russian Commercial Society
ASEAN	Association of South–East Asian Nations
AUCP(B)	All–Union Communist Party (Bolsheviks)
CC CPSU	Central Committee of the Communist Party of the Soviet Union
CEH	Common European Home
CMEA	Council of Mutual Economic Assistance
COCOM	Co-ordinating Committee for Multilateral Export Controls
CPSU	Communist Party of the Soviet Union
DGI	Dirección General de Inteligencia
EC	European Community
ECCI	Executive Committee of the Communist International
EEC	European Economic Community
FRG	Federal Republic of Germany
GDR	German Democratic Republic
GLCM	Ground Launched Cruise Missile
GRU	Glavnoe razvedyvatel'noe upravlenie
HSP	Hungarian Socialist Party
HSWP	Hungarian Socialist Workers' Party
ICBM	Intercontinental Ballistic Missile
IMF	International Monetary Fund
INF	Intermediate Nuclear Force
IRBM	Intermediate Range Ballistic Missile
JSP	Japanese Socialist Party
KGB	Komitet gosudarstvennoi bezopasnosti
KPD	Communist Party of Germany

LDP	Liberal–Democratic Party (of Japan)
MNR	Resistência Naçional Moçambicana ('Renamo')
NATO	North Atlantic Treaty Organisation
NEP	New Economic Policy
NPT	New Political Thinking
OPT	Old Political Thinking
SDI	Strategic Defence Initiative
START	Strategic Arms Reduction Treaty
UN	United Nations
UNITA	Uniao Nacional para a Independencia Total de Angola
WPC	World Peace Council
WTO	Warsaw Treaty Organisation

Part I The setting of Soviet foreign policy

It is said that Lenin's thesis that imperialism inevitably generates war must now be regarded as obsolete, since powerful popular forces have come forward today in defence of peace and against another world war. That is not true.

Stalin

1 Introduction

The 'old' political thinking and the 'new'

Soviet President Mikhail S. Gorbachev has not only made major changes in the directions of his country's foreign policy, but he has also fundamentally altered the ways in which it is thought of and talked about. Within the armoury of new concepts and slogans accompanying his major program for restructuring the Soviet system — including words such as *perestroika* and *glasnost*, which have already entered the lexicon of Western political discourse — none has more far reaching importance than the concept of **new political thinking** (NPT) (*novoe politicheskoe myshlenie*). Its significance and that of concepts associated with it, such as **freedom of choice**, are especially great in the area of foreign policy, to which they were originally dedicated, although their reverberations in the domestic political arena have also spread widely. The essence of the NPT is a fundamental reappraisal of traditional Soviet perceptions and ideological assumptions about the outside world and how to deal with it. At issue are the basic ideological and political rules of the East–West conflict formulated first by Lenin and his Bolshevik Party stalwarts following their victory in the Great October Socialist Revolution. In fact, some of them antecede the seizure of power in 1917.

The idea of a political system guided in its international conduct by a specific code of ideological and operational principles rather than by short- or medium-term notions of state 'interests' is often difficult for Westerners to understand. Most observers would agree that the complex of goals, strategies and tactics comprising the official doctrine of Marxism–Leninism have had some impact on the conduct of Soviet foreign policy, although there are serious disagreements over how much and for how long this ideological influence has continued to be a salient factor. For example, the policy objective behind George F. Kennan's famous 1947 article setting forth the rationale for what became the 'containment policy' was expressly to compel the Soviet Union to abandon ideological modes of thinking and to become more pragmatic and accommodating. Kennan sought to achieve this by confronting Soviet leaders with geostrategic realities which made the analyses and policies derived from the ideology appear unpromising and inexpedient.[1] A major assumption behind the containment strategy was that a 'normal', that is non-ideological, Soviet Union would be much easier to deal with in the postwar era, when continued East–West co-operation would make the requirements of reconstruction and international security that much easier to achieve. Kennan himself eventually came to question the salience of the ideological factor.

Other observers, such as the late German ex-communist Franz Borkenau, consistently denied that ideology had any material impact on Soviet foreign policy, at least from the time of Stalin's accession to power in the late 1920s. According to this interpretation, the Soviet Union, almost from its inception, acted as an imperial power, merely continuing the expansionist policies of its Tsarist predecessor; revolutionary ideology was merely legitimising window-dressing for what was in reality a policy of geostrategic opportunism.[2] The Nazi–Soviet Non-Aggression Pact of 1939 was Borkenau's favourite illustration of this proposition.

The late Hugh Seton-Watson, writing on the very eve of the Gorbachev era, nicely characterised the ongoing Western debates over the wellsprings of Soviet foreign policy as a product of what he calls 'either–or fallacies':

> The most widespread is the controversy between those who see 'ideology' as the main force behind Soviet policy, and those who give this place to 'security'. It is our case that the two are inseparable, and there is no need to repeat the argument. Arising from this misleading 'either–or-ism' is the dispute, perhaps even more widespread, as to whether Soviet policy is 'expansionist' or 'defensive'. It is both. Obsession with protection of frontiers and of strategic position leads to expansion, and each successful expansion creates new positions to defend.[3]

My own position in this debate is very close to Seton-Watson's. Ideology has always been an important factor in Soviet foreign policy formation, but certainly not the only one. And its impact has more often than not been indirect rather than direct. That is, instead of directly prescribing policies, it has acted to shape the frame of reference and expectations of Soviet decision-makers, as well as their perceptions of such ostensibly non-ideological considerations as 'security', 'defence' and the conditions for 'peace'. The ideological effects being discussed here, as in the passage quoted above from Seton-Watson, refer quite clearly to the 'old political thinking' (OPT) that is now under attack by Gorbachev. In order to understand the nature of his challenge and of the changes he is attempting to introduce in the NPT—not least in the role, if any, of ideology — it is necessary to trace the development and effects on Soviet foreign policy of the OPT. Part I of this book is concerned with an analysis of the basic ideas and operational principles associated with the theory and practice of Soviet foreign policy and its historical evolution under successive leaders up to the Gorbachev era. It also considers the complex question of the influence of domestic economic and political factors on foreign policy. Part II is devoted to an application of these various thematic and historical patterns to the development of recent Soviet policy in the three main geopolitical arenas of Soviet activity — the West, the communist world, and the Third World — particularly with respect to the emerging impact of Gorbachev's 'new political thinking'.

The role of ideology

The meaning of the term ideology itself is a matter of some dispute, not to mention the nature of its role in political and other state decision-making. One American scholar defines ideology as 'a preconceived set or structure of beliefs, including both values and propositions about the way the world is thought to be. Thus, an ideology is a "world view" with judgment and action implications.'[4] In this conception, ideology is a universal phenomenon, bound to influence not only the general members of a given society, but also its decision-making elite in the choice of methods and policies considered appropriate for dealing with the society's problems. Contrast this conception with the discussion of the same general phenomena in a standard textbook on Marxist philosophy of the 1960s:

> In a class society social consciousness, whatever form it assumes, inevitably takes on a *class character*. The sum-total of political, legal, moral, artistic and other views and ideas of a definite class comprise its *ideology*...
>
> Since ideology always bears a class character, can it give the truth? Does it not distort reality to suit class interests? The revisionists claim that ideology and truth are incompatible, that ideology

sacrifices the truth to the interests of one class or another. Marxism, however, demands that ideology be viewed from a concrete, historical angle in order to establish the interests of *what* class, progressive or reactionary, it expresses...

Marxist–Leninist ideology is scientific and true to the end, because the class interests of the working class and the objective course of history always coincide and therefore the ability of the Marxist–Leninist ideology to reflect truth is preserved at all stages of its development.[emphasis in original][5]

And on matters of direct relevance to our topic, the author, V. Afanasyev, goes on to assert several pages later:

Two opposing political ideologies—of the working class and the bourgeoisie—are now at grips in the world. The political ideology of the working class is the ideology of proletarian internationalism, friendship of the working people of all countries, unity and co-operation of all the progressive forces in the common struggle for peace, democracy and socialism. It is expressed most fully and from every angle in the Marxist–Leninist theory, in the Communist parties' programmes and the socialist countries' constitutions. This ideology proves the need for the class struggle of the working class and all the working people against the bourgeoisie, for the victory of socialism and communism. It serves the working class and its party as a guide in the political struggle, the highest form of the proletariat's class struggle.[6]

The differences between the two conceptions are striking. For the one side, ideology is a distorted picture of reality which conditions the way individuals perceive the world and act upon it; in short, it is essentially an impediment to rational decisional activity. Ideology is clearly inferior to 'theory', which is regarded as soundly grounded in empirical reality, basically value-neutral and susceptible to objective comprehension and verification.[7] For the other, the Soviet, side, ideology *is* theory. There is no such thing as value-neutrality in human cognition; but Marxism-Leninism, as the ideology of the historically more 'progressive' class, the proletariat, is by definition always closer to the truth than the ideology of its bourgeois class opponent. In the hands of the vanguard of the proletariat, the Communist Party, Marxism-Leninism is thus regarded as a powerful instrument for apprehending the dynamics of change and formulating appropriate policies to benefit from them.

It should be emphasised here that this was the manifest ideological basis of the old political thinking and that Soviet practitioners of the foreign policy art showed increasing signs of paying mere lip-service to the *doctrine* in the last years of the Brezhnev era. That is, ideological formulations became essentially *ex post facto* legitimising rationalisations for policies devised on basically pragmatic, opportunistic grounds or simple inertia. It is important to emphasise the functional distinction here between ideology as legitimating *doctrine* and as an *analytical tool*. What Gorbachev professes to be attempting to achieve under the rubric of the NPT is to discard the dogmatic, doctrinal incrustations which had accumulated around the ideology (at least) since the beginning of the Stalin era and to restore its utility as a tool and method of analysis. It would be profoundly wrong to assume, as most Western observers, unaccustomed to dealing at close hand with a category of politicians committed to a theoretical understanding of policy issues, appear to be doing, that he is jettisoning Marxist–Leninist ideology *in toto*.[8] Gorbachev understands, as well as any of his conservative opponents, that Marxist-Leninist ideology is one of the principal foundations, if not *the* principal foundation, of the Communist Party's *raison d'être*. Without it there would be no legitimate reason for the party's retaining its monopoly of political power in communist societies.[9] By 1990 Gorbachev's new thinking had progressed so far as to encourage him to accept the end of the party's monopoly of power, yet he was not yet willing to give up on the project of rejuvenating ideology itself as a tool of analysis and a useful way of viewing the world in which Soviet foreign policy was constrained to operate.

At the same time, it is clear from the Afanasyev book that a major demolition and reconstruction job would be required. The ideology had become so incrusted with dogmas and pseudo-scientific certainties that very few of the existing doctrinal canons could serve as a basis for the kind of theoretical analysis that Gorbachev envisages. For example, the entire question of the obsolescence of the bourgeois–capitalist 'social formation', and hence the truth–value of its intellectual and institutional basis, is now open to debate and even to partial emulation. I shall have more to say about this in subsequent chapters.

For the moment, we are more concerned here with the evolution of the ideology and its component elements under the OPT. Although Lenin himself was not free of dogmatic proclivities, many of his arguably once viable ideological formulations came to be distorted and set in concrete, as it were, in Stalin's hands. One of the major reasons for these distortions was the tendency in Marxist social-democratic circles — not only in Russia — for ideology to be used as a polemical instrument against political opponents within the movement. Marx himself often resorted to this practice (for example, in his polemics with Ferdinand Lassalle and in his *Critique of the Gotha Program*), and Lenin would prove to be a past master of the technique. Given the authority of such figures in the movement, it is perhaps not surprising that many of the mere debating points they made in the heat of verbal conflict against opponents came to be enshrined as Holy Writ at the hands of their less intellectually fastidious acolytes. Marx once said, in response to the parroting of some of his more extreme and contradictory statements by his followers, that he was not a 'Marxist'. Lenin, as a practising politician, perhaps with an eye to the usefulness of his status as ideological 'high priest' of Bolshevism, apparently never felt the need or had the intellectual candour to make an analogous confession.

Thus, from the outset, the application of Marxist–Leninist ideology became adulterated with extraneous dogmas and short-term political expedients. To be sure, this is not a particularly unusual development in the history of world political practice. In the context of a movement imbued with the importance of systematic theoretical grounding for correct policy formulation, however, this otherwise natural tendency acquired a more ominous significance. It tended to lock its practitioners into frequently untenable and unrealistic perceptions and led them to try to impose their distorted impressions upon those portions of reality that were susceptible to their control. The recent patterns of political and economic development in 'post-communist' Eastern Europe, which their erstwhile party leaders have attempted vainly to reconstruct, are a good illustration of this process and its unpredictable consequences.

Domestic factors in Soviet foreign policy

By now there is already a fairly extensive literature on the so-called 'domestic determinants' of Soviet foreign policy. Most contributions represent compilations of essays on specific structures and processes of the internal Soviet system which are generally considered relevant to the formulation and conduct of foreign policy. As such they are useful for understanding aspects of the linkage between foreign and domestic policy, but there have been few successful attempts to discern a patterned relationship between the two spheres, for example, between an aggressive line in foreign policy and domestic repression. That is not surprising, because the relationship has never been very clearcut, even in Stalin's day, when more or less explicit connections were sometimes enunciated.

Despite the evident pitfalls, it is useful to examine some important cases, if only to illustrate the complexities of the interrelationships among the major potential factors in Soviet foreign policy formation — ideology, security, domestic politics, economics and international issues *per se*.

The obvious place to begin is the Revolution itself. In Marxist theory capitalism was inherently an international social formation, destined by the logic of international commerce, investable capital and the spread of scientific and technological knowledge to encompass the entire world. Thus, when the 'forces of production' had reached a stage of perfection and universal saturation where they had outgrown the 'relations of production' established by the capitalist system itself, the universalised proletariat would rise up in an essentially worldwide socialist revolution to bring the relations of production into conformity with the potential of scientific and technological development, making the material benefits of that development available to all of mankind.[10]

Lenin was not the first of the critics of capitalism to understand that the above predictions were not being realised.[11] In the midst of the First World War he presented his analysis of the causes of this failure of history to follow Marx's predicted path. He published his ingenious amendment to the original theory in 1916 in *Imperialism, the Highest Stage of Capitalism*.[12] Lenin accounted for the failure of the proletariat to rise up against their capitalist masters by the ability of the latter to buy them off with the 'super-profits' they were earning from colonial exploitation. The development of the capitalist empires was not a sign of strength, however, for capitalism in this highest, and presumably last, stage was inherently unstable. The 'law of uneven development of capitalism', which Lenin coined in this work, foreshadowed precisely the kind of inter-imperial rivalries which were then being clearly manifested in the First World War. Further, he postulated, the chain of imperialism would snap, not at its strongest links, the advanced capitalist countries, but in the newly industrialising countries, such as Tsarist Russia, where exploitation of the working class was greatest, since the domestic capitalists did not have the wherewithal to bribe the working class leaders — the 'aristocracy of the proletariat'. Proletarian revolution, Lenin argued, would break out first, therefore, in relatively backward countries like Russia. Moreover, such revolutions, by smashing the nexus of international capitalist exploitation, would in turn induce revolutions in the advanced countries. Hence, following Trotsky and Parvus, Lenin was arguing against more orthodox Russian social-democrats, like G. V. Plekhanov, his erstwhile mentor, that the revolution in Russia should not be delayed until the general outbreak of world revolution; rather, it was a necessary condition for that revolution and an obligation on Russian revolutionary Marxists. Implicitly endorsing Trotsky and Parvus's theory of 'permanent' or 'uninterrupted' revolution, Lenin was confident that the revolution in Russia, ostensibly premature in conventional Marxist theoretical terms, would be assisted in the development of its productive forces by the victorious proletariat in the advanced countries as the revolution swiftly spread to them.

The sweep of this intellectual synthesis was breathtaking. It had an immense impact on left radical critics of the war, both explaining its causes and offering an optimistic, action-oriented solution. Victor Serge, the one-time Comintern official and prominent Trotskyite, described its effect at the time: 'The first thing which this work accomplishes is immensely to broaden and expand the horizon of all events.'[13] There can be little doubt that *Imperialism* is one of the most important revolutionary tracts ever published, regardless of the patent inaccuracies of its predicted linkages and operational corollaries. It provided a consistent theoretical exegesis of the dynamics of the anticipated decline and fall of capitalism. It attuned communist revolutionaries and their sympathisers throughout the world to the importance of revolutionary activities in what would come to be called the Third World. And it gave Third World revolutionaries a sense of hope and a seemingly 'scientific' justification for participation in the world revolutionary process through revolutionary action in their own regions. As such it remains one of the basic foundations for the ideological doctrine of **proletarian** or **socialist internationalism**, the obligation of all socialist parties and movements to give each other material and moral support. Incidentally, the so-called 'Brezhnev Doctrine' was merely a latter-day corollary of socialist internationalism.

During the 1920s, after Lenin's death, the formulations in *Imperialism* were used by the various factions to buttress their arguments over foreign and domestic policy in the struggle for supreme political power. Stalin, the ultimate victor, was particularly astute in using Lenin's linkage hypothesis to justify his espousal of the possibility of building 'socialism in one country' against the more internationalistically inclined faction headed by Trotsky. For Lenin it had been clear by 1921 that the world revolution was not imminent. The assumption of immediate 'fraternal assistance' for socialist development in Russia by the victorious proletariat in advanced Western countries, on which the Bolshevik seizure of power had been ideologically justified, had obviously been incorrect. Consequently, the country faced a considerable period of pre-socialist economic construction before the forces of production could be prepared for the transition to socialism. Foreign communist assistance was still considered necessary and was expected by Lenin and many others, but it was no longer an imminent prospect, and something had to be done in the meantime.

The New Economic Policy (NEP) was conceived precisely as a pre-socialist program, in which the economic laws of capitalism would largely continue to hold sway. In foreign policy it implied a search for accommodation with the main capitalist powers in order to break their 'hostile encirclement' and win a 'breathing space' for domestic economic recovery and the consolidation of political control. The Rapallo Pact with defeated Germany in 1922 was a good example of this strategy in action, providing a source of trade and technological assistance and at the same time preventing the formation of a unified anti-Soviet coalition of capitalist powers. Lenin and many of his closest supporters, particularly Nikolai I. Bukharin, expected that when the 'revolutionary tide' welled up once again, the Soviet state would be in a better position to benefit from it. But a fully fledged program of socialist construction was not yet on the agenda.

Stalin, by contrast, played upon the Russo-centric, self-reliant and implicitly xenophobic sentiments of the rapidly swelling party membership in promoting a tacit reinterpretation of Lenin's theory. He used it to castigate the more internationalist, revolutionary position of Trotsky, who had argued that backward Russia was in no position to develop, unassisted, any type of system that was remotely consonant with accepted norms of socialism. And in what would become characteristic Stalinist practice, he systematically manipulated the thesis of hostile capitalist encirclement to justify internal repression and the highly coercive model of economic development which came to characterise the Soviet system down to the Gorbachev era.[14]

Under Stalin, then, ideology and — to a certain extent — even concrete domestic and foreign policies were regularly used as instruments for the acquisition and maintenance of personal political power. This fact — and the existence of conceivable alternatives to the Stalinist model in the crucial period of its formation — is coming to be understood by the new Soviet leadership itself. That is one reason for the upsurge in political and scholarly interest in a reassessment of Soviet history in the 1920s and 1930s, particularly in the rehabilitation of Bukharin and his political and economic ideas.[15] Here it is useful simply to register this new-found recognition of Bukharinism as an alternative model to Stalinism and a new source of legitimation *via* restoration of linkages to the Leninist past. The implications and possible limitations of this aspect of the NPT will be explored further later in the book.

At this point it is possible to make a few tentative observations on the relationship between ideology and foreign and domestic policy in the pre-Gorbachev period. Ideology provided, first of all, the language of discourse for participants in the debates over policy. It furnished the categories and analytical frame of reference within which the debates were carried on, identifying the main enemies and potential allies in the revolutionary struggle for power and the building of socialism and defining, however unclearly, the parameters of the goal of socialism itself. It also satisfied the Marxian desire for legitimising theoretical consistency in policy making by providing the framework for explaining how the given policy contributed to the victory of socialism worldwide and to the construction of socialism at home. In the process it provided a way of linking the constraints and opportunities of the international situation to domestic developments, suggesting ways in which domestic progress could be facilitated by foreign policy.

But as 'holy writ', which it soon became in the struggle for personal power even in Lenin's day, it degenerated into a rather blunt instrument, of often dubious value as a tool of analysis. It was very useful as a catechism for the recruitment and maintenance of a corps of disciplined, 'right-thinking' party faithful. In the form of 'the party line' it indicated to the party rank and file what they should be thinking about particular issues of foreign and domestic policy. Changes or authoritative reinterpretations of the party line were often used by Stalin and his henchmen to get rid of individuals and groups who were suspected of real or imagined ('objective' or 'subjective') disloyalty to the cause.

Concepts and operational principles of Soviet foreign policy

Among the important effects of ideological influences on Soviet foreign policy-making has been the generation of an arsenal of standardised concepts and operational principles which gave a peculiar cast to Soviet international conduct during the first four decades of Soviet rule. Of particular importance in this connection were the operations of the Third, or Communist, International (Comintern), founded by Lenin in 1919. Until its dissolution in May 1943 the Moscow-based Comintern served as the headquarters of the world network of Communist Parties, which by the late 1920s had become a highly disciplined auxiliary arm of Stalin's foreign policy. Under the so-called 'Twenty-one Conditions' for membership promulgated at the Second Comintern Congress in 1920, the member parties functioned not as autonomous political parties, but as 'sections' of the Comintern, which was regarded as a single revolutionary movement.[16] The Executive Committee of the Comintern (ECCI) was popularly referred to as the 'Headquarters of the World Revolution'. Some of the early atmosphere of enthusiasm for the Comintern is captured in the following passage written by Victor Serge in the 1930s:

> The Third International of the early days, for which men fought and many died, which filled the prisons with martyrs, was in reality a great moral and political force, not only because following the war the workers' revolution was on the ascendant in Europe and was very nearly victorious in several countries, but because it brought together a multitude of passionate, sincere, devoted minds determined to live and die for communism. The mountebanks and petty adventurers hardly counted in the ensemble. Where are all these men today?[17]

From its foundation until the last decade of its existence the Comintern was headed by prominent Soviet communists, first Zinoviev, next Bukharin, then two of Stalin's closest supporters, Molotov and Dimitrii Z. Manuilskii. Its final head was the loyal Bulgarian Stalinist, Georgii Dimitrov. Under the Twenty-one Conditions and the Statute of the Comintern, member parties were unconditionally bound to follow the directions of the Soviet leadership, through the ECCI; in fact, the members of each 'section'-party were subject to the same rules of **democratic centralism** that applied in the Soviet Communist Party — that is, once a decision had been made, unconditional obedience was required. This rule eventually cost the Comintern many foreign members, but those who remained constituted a worldwide reservoir of extremely dedicated agents for the promotion of Soviet interests.

The existence of the Comintern allowed (some early critics would say forced) the Soviet leadership to carry on a dual-track foreign policy. One track, directed through the People's Commissariat (from 1946, Ministry) of Foreign Affairs, addressed itself to dealing with foreign governments, using more or less normal diplomatic techniques; the other, channelled through the Comintern, was concerned with the revolutionary overthrow of these same governments. Until Stalin's victory in the late 1920s, which effectively 'Bolshevised' the Comintern — that is, fully subordinated it to Soviet interests — the two organisations frequently worked at cross purposes. Comintern activities often seriously hampered Soviet diplomatic efforts to establish normal relations, for example, in Germany and Great Britain. Later, under Stalin's firm control, an effective division of labour was worked out, with the Comintern in a definitely subordinate position.

During the early period a number of important strategic and tactical concepts were elaborated. Among them the notion of the **correlation of forces** between socialism and capitalism and the often related idea of **peaceful coexistence** between countries 'with a different social system' were particularly significant and proved to be long-lived. The former consisted of a calculation of the military, political and socio-economic forces at the disposal of the Soviet Union and its opponents at a given historical juncture. When the correlation of forces appeared to be unfavourable and likely to remain so for an indefinite period of time, the indicated response was to seek a **breathing space** (*peredyshka*) and to emphasise normal state-to-state relations. Foreign Communist Parties were instructed by the Comintern to play down revolutionary activities and to foster policies in their respective political arenas favouring peace with the Soviet Union. The preferred tactic for doing so was the use of the various types of **United Front — from below** (that is, trying to win over the membership of left-wing parties and movements to follow the leadership of the local Communist Parties) or **from above** (trying to form alliances with the leaders of other, mainly left-wing, parties in pursuit of policies favourable to the USSR). In the late 1930s, in the face of the increasing anti-Bolshevik aggressiveness of Germany, Italy and Japan, the united-front tactic was pushed to its logical extension in the form of the **Popular Front** (the formation of alliances with all parties of whatever political coloration willing to stand up to Nazism and Fascism).

These various 'fronts' have continued to surface under an array of different titles during periods of perceived danger, when the 'correlation of forces' has not seemed particularly favourable to Soviet interests, often under the rubric of the **struggle for peace** — a typically loaded ideological concept denoting support for the Soviet Union against hostile imperialist counteractions. Another, similar ideological derivation is **democracy**, which has historically had the connotation of pro-Soviet behaviour both domestically and in foreign relations. Thus, 'the struggle for peace and democracy' in a country not ruled by a Communist Party implied a campaign by sympathetic local groups and organisations in support of specific pro-Soviet foreign policy objectives and the legalisation of the local Communist Party and other, associated, left-wing elements.

One of the earliest diplomatic techniques coined by Lenin and Trotsky, the first of the Bolsheviks' Foreign Commissars, was what they called **demonstrative diplomacy** — speaking over the heads of the foreign diplomats with whom one is nominally negotiating directly to the people of the country in question or to 'progressive forces' in the outside world at large, with the idea of enlisting their assumed sympathies to pressurise

their own governments to accede to Soviet requests. Not since the days of
Foreign Commissar Maksim Litvinov in the 1930s have the Soviets had a
leader as skilled in the use of 'demonstrative diplomacy' as they have now
in Mikhail S. Gorbachev. Virtually every one of his speeches on foreign
policy is a clear example of the technique. He has been remarkably
successful in using it to apply pressure on his Western opposite numbers.

Perhaps the most important ideological concept associated with the
'old political thinking' and the *leitmotif* of at least the rhetoric of Soviet
foreign policy-making until the most recent period is the notion of the
class basis of the political behaviour of states and statesmen. The
essence of this notion, as illustrated in the quotation from the Afanasyev
textbook earlier in this chapter, is that political actors are constrained by
their class position, or the 'social formation' of the society they represent,
to perceive reality and to behave in a specific way. Imperialist statesmen
cannot help but to defend their system and its way of life and, *pari passu* ,
to act in a manner hostile to socialism. Here the interesting concepts of
subjective and **objective** hostility enter the picture. Even if an
opponent is 'subjectively' favourably inclined to Soviet interests in a given
situation, if the 'objective' circumstances of the situation are unfavourable,
his assistance must be rejected. (Only a Communist Party member can
reliably be expected to possess sufficient class-consciousness for his
subjective assessments to be viable and fully dependable in such
circumstances.) It is incumbent on the Soviet policy-maker to discern just
what the 'objective' requirements of the given situation are. The insights
afforded by the 'scientific' analytical techniques of Marxism–Leninism are
supposed to provide the necessary tools. All of these factors were to come
into play in Stalin's shift from the Popular Front policy with the West to
his alliance with Hitler in August 1939, which will be discussed in further
detail in chapter 2.

Before concluding this brief inventory of concepts and operational
principles I should like to mention some additional corollaries to Lenin's
theory of imperialism and its doctrinal concretisation under Stalin: the
notion of **revolutionary momentum** and what I shall call the twin
principles of **socialist patrimony** and **security of tenure**.
Ironically, it was Trotsky who drew the logical conclusions from
Imperialism that the shortest road to revolution in Europe under conditions
of temporary stability on that continent lay through Asia. (In a secret
report to the party Central Committee in August 1919 he expressly
mentioned India.)[18] The principle implied was that maintaining
momentum was all-important for the goals and continued health of the
revolutionary movement. The corollary was that when revolutionary

progress was stymied in the West, opportunities could profitably be sought in the East, hitting the imperialist homelands through their colonies and hence squeezing the resources with which the latter could continue to bribe their domestic working classes.

Under Stalin this principle of momentum acquired a somewhat more mundane coloration in terms of the concept of the 'correlation of forces'. That is, in the 'zero-sum-game' thinking behind this concept, the simple detachment of a colonial area from the imperialists' sphere of influence was regarded as a net gain for the forces of socialism. Moreover, as Robert C. Tucker has pointed out, in Stalin's thinking, international war came to be perceived as 'organically connected' with the spread of communist revolution.[19]   This conjunction of the concepts of momentum, revolutionary opportunities in the Third World and the utility of war as an instrument of revolution reached its consummation in the runup to the Second World War and its aftermath and ultimate climax under Brezhnev. In the West, Soviet penetration of the Third World was generally interpreted as merely a question of picking off 'targets of opportunity'. It was certainly that, but it was something else as well. The ideological justification for such policies in terms of the concepts discussed above provided an important impulse to aggressive behaviour, which more pragmatic considerations of longer-term Soviet interests, domestic as well as international, might have shown to be counter-productive. Gorbachev's 'new political thinking' has involved precisely such a reassessment.

 Under Stalin and his successors through most of the 1980s, these expansionist concepts had two further operational corollaries that are now also being called into some question.   The **patrimony** principle, sometimes referred to in the West as the 'ratchet principle', has prescribed that any territorial accretion to the socialist side of the international power balance must be permanently retained and defended.   It became part of the Soviet socialist 'patrimony' (*votchina*), to be handed over to the next generation of leaders as a sign of achievement and a symbol of the ideological and geopolitical skill of the present generation.   The Baltic Republics and the South Kurile Islands, as well as the Eastern European communist states acquired as a result of the Second World War and Cuba, obtained by the conscious adherence of Fidel Castro — all of which the Soviets expressly committed themselves to defend, by military force if necessary — are obvious examples of the principle.

There have, of course, been some striking exceptions which amount, in a sense, to proof of the rule. Two of these were the return of Finnish territory around the naval base of Porkkala and the withdrawal from the

Soviet occupation zone in Austria. Both of these apparent aberrations occurred in 1955, when the new post-Stalin leadership was trying to refurbish its image in the West and to secure a 'breathing space' for domestic economic and reform and political consolidation.[20] The question immediately arises of whether Gorbachev's withdrawal from Afghanistan and his pressure for his Cuban and Vietnamese allies to withdraw from southern Africa and Cambodia respectively represent analogous exceptions to the rule or an abrogation of the patrimony principle itself. His handling of the demands for independence of the Baltic Republics represents the acid test, not only of the patrimony principle but of the overarching concept of 'freedom of choice' which he is seeking to make the cornerstone of international relations in the post-Cold War world. These are obviously vital questions for what was once considered the very heart of the Soviet empire, Eastern Europe, and for the continued survival of the USSR itself in its present form and of Gorbachev as its leader.

Finally, in this section it is worth mentioning one other operational concept directly related to the patrimony principle and several other elements of the ideology and clearly reflecting the tendency toward 'ossification' under Stalin and his successors: the concept of **security of tenure**. Reduced to its simplest terms, it denotes the Soviet preference, developed in the period of mature Stalinism and carried on by his successors, for foreign alliances with countries ruled by genuine Communist Parties and susceptible to direct military pressure from the Soviet armed forces. Only such countries — where the leadership was directly subject to Soviet political tutelage and the Soviet Army was in a position to intervene militarily if necessary — could be considered reliable allies. This preference became especially germane in the course of the USSR's growing involvement in the Third World and was presumably an important motivating factor in the development of Soviet overseas force-projection capabilities, particularly the Soviet Fleet's blue-water navy. The enunciation of the Brezhnev Doctrine in 1968, after the Warsaw Pact invasion of Czechoslovakia — the doctrine that the Communist Party of a given socialist country was responsible not only to its own working class, but also to the socialist community as a whole (i.e., to Moscow) for the security and progress of socialist achievements in that country — clearly reflected the operational concerns of the security of tenure conception. It was the doctrine of proletarian, or more accurately, **socialist internationalism** (proletarian internationalism as applied to relations between Communist Party-ruled states) drawn to its extreme logical conclusions.

The impasse of the 'old political thinking' in the Brezhnev era

The Brezhnev era, like its predecessor, began with the search for a breathing space in foreign relations while certain domestic problems were being sorted out. Particularly important were the major economic reforms introduced in 1965 by Brezhnev in agriculture and by Premier Aleksei Kosygin for the economy as a whole. Although the military buildup, begun under Khrushchev after the Cuban missile crisis, continued unabated throughout the latter 1960s, the basic thrust of foreign policy was to avoid confrontations with the West. Several initiatives were undertaken in the areas of nuclear non-proliferation and disarmament, and the foundations of what would come to be called **detente** began to be laid.

However, the ostensible preoccupations of the new Soviet leaders with domestic concerns and particularly their promotion of liberalising economic reform unleashed pent-up pressures for even wider ranging reforms in parts of their East European empire. These came to a head in Poland and Czechoslovakia in 1968, just at a time when Brezhnev and his conservative colleagues in the USSR were already becoming uneasy over the political and social side-effects of economic liberalisation at home.

The invasion of Czechoslovakia in August 1968 in the name of the doctrine of 'limited sovereignty' of socialist countries — the Brezhnev Doctrine — was in many ways a turning point in Soviet foreign policy perceptions. The crushing of the 'Prague Spring' movement generated a wave of protest among foreign communists and gave rise to the elaboration of an alternative ideological and political synthesis, known in the West as **Eurocommunism**, which called into question the Soviet model of socialism itself and rejected the right of the Soviet Union to dictate ideology and policy to the international communist movement. It led to an abrupt worsening of the already strained relations with the Chinese People's Republic, with which armed clashes soon erupted on the common border between the two countries in the Far East.

The danger of a two-front controntation (with China and the West) led to intense diplomatic efforts to revive detente with the West and to isolate China. Perhaps surprisingly, Brezhnev quickly succeeded in doing so, first of all by regularising relations with the Federal Republic of Germany in 1970. Arms control agreements with Washington soon followed, and by the mid-1970s detente had seemingly become a stable, long-term feature of East–West relations.

In the meanwhile, Soviet ideologists had been cobbling together a response to the Eurocommunists in the form of a set of sterile formulas which came to comprise the concept of **real socialism,** also known as **developed socialism.** They attempted to demonstrate the Panglossian position that the model of socialism and the pattern of socio-economic relations existing in the USSR and the other countries most closely bound to it were the only valid and viable embodiment of the socialist ideal at the current stage of historical development.[21] Given the increasingly evident stagnation in the development of Soviet society in the latter 1970s and early 1980s, any effort to portray it as an ideal social formation — the best that history had to offer — was bound to have a hollow ring and to depreciate the currency of the ideology in general.

On a more practical plane, a combination of factors — including the sluggish performance of the Soviet economy, the achievement of essential strategic nuclear parity with the United States, the continuing buildup of Soviet conventional forces and the capacity to project them overseas and, finally, the growing disenchantment with detente in a Washington that was increasingly turning inward in bitter recriminations over the defeat in Vietnam and the Watergate scandal — was producing subtle changes in Soviet perceptions of the content and meaning of the new 'correlation of forces'. The string of what seemed at the time to be relatively easy Soviet victories in the Third World, most notably in Africa, but also in the Middle East and even in Latin America, using Soviet military forces directly or through surrogates, evidently convinced Brezhnev and his colleagues that the revolutionary tide was in the ascendancy once again.

In short, brute military strength came increasingly to be regarded, perhaps even more than in Stalin's day, as the most effective and reliable instrument of Soviet foreign policy and, *ipso facto*, of world revolution (if, indeed, Brezhnev still thought in such terms). Moreover, against the background of declining momentum in domestic development and accumulating social, political and moral problems, the military seemed to be the only positive performer among major Soviet institutions. The apparent inability of the United States to mount an effective challenge to Soviet military assertiveness beyond occasional rhetorical flourishes further inflamed Soviet sensibilities by demonstrating Washington's refusal to be 'realistic' and to concede Soviet demands to be accepted as co-equal determiner of the world's fate. Despite the evidence of the increasing costs of military expansion at a time of declining general economic performance, Brezhnev clearly felt that the military still represented the best investment for the extension of Soviet power. The installation of SS-20 mobile intermediate-range ballistic missiles in Europe, adventures in Africa, the invasion of Afghanistan and the rapid expansion of the Soviet Pacific Fleet were the ultimate embodiment of this militarisation of Soviet global policy.

The strategy of the United States after 1980 under President Ronald Reagan of challenging Soviet policy in its own terms proved to be remarkably effective. The elements of this strategy included a massive counter-buildup of US conventional and strategic forces, the active sponsorship of 'counter-revolutionary' challenges to Soviet client regimes in the Third World (most notably in Afghanistan, Angola, Grenada and Nicaragua) and a major ideological counter-offensive dedicated to undermining Soviet credentials as an acceptable partner in international dialogue. By the end of the Brezhnev era in 1982, we can now see from hindsight, the Soviet game was effectively up. The military were already being told by 1981 that they could no longer expect as before to receive a blank cheque for the new weapons systems that military experts were declaring necessary to keep up with the West.[22] But it would take a totally new leadership, with a radically new way of looking at Soviet national interests and at the nature of international relations in the changing climate of the final years of the twentieth century, to break the impasse of the Stalinist legacy reflected so poignantly in the conduct of Soviet foreign policy under Brezhnev.

2 The evolution of Soviet foreign policy: Major historical phases

Introduction

The aim of this chapter is to identify certain major phases in the evolution of Soviet foreign policy. The successive phases reflect important shifts in Soviet perceptions of the international situation and the world 'correlation of forces', in the requirements of the domestic economy or in the power position of various groups in the domestic political struggle — or some combination of these factors. The discussion seeks to provide selective historical illustrations and interpretations of the complex links, noted in chapter 1, between ideology, *realpolitik* and domestic policy issues in Soviet foreign–policy decision–making up to the Gorbachev era. It is evident that the policies associated so far with Gorbachev's 'new political thinking' represent just such an important shift, perhaps a sea change, in the direction and substance of Soviet foreign policy. Nevertheless, for Western policy–makers and concerned citizens alike, a number of vital questions remain — no less vital for being so obvious. Among them are just how much of a change is involved and how stable the new line is likely to be. To what extent are the shifts contingent on the current shortcomings of the Soviet socio–economic system and the apparent relative strength of the Western capitalist adversary, and how much do they reflect genuine changes in the basic worldview of the Soviet leadership? How much do they depend on the personal perspectives of one person, Mikhail S. Gorbachev, and how much are they dictated by the 'objective' circumstances, by 'life itself', as the Soviets like to say? These questions are, of course, impossible to answer with any degree of certainty at this historical juncture. We shall have to wait and see. But in the meantime an awareness of Soviet behaviour in past periods of external and domestic stress will help us at least to pose the right questions and look for the relevant evidence.

The Comintern phase

The establishment of the Comintern in March 1919 was a supremely revolutionary act. It was inspired by a mixture of motives. A spirit of revolutionary opportunity seemed to be sweeping Europe amidst the chaos and despair resulting from the war, particularly in the defeated Central Powers. Indeed, barely two weeks after the adjournment of the First Comintern Congress, a Soviet Republic was proclaimed in Budapest by the Hungarian communist leader Bela Kun, and similar less successful uprisings were soon erupting in Germany and Austria.

One of the immediate aims of the founding of the Comintern, or Third International, was to pre-empt the restoration of the Second, or Socialist, International, which had failed so dismally to unite the international working class against the 'imperialist' World War and had instead fractured along national, patriotic lines. Lenin and his colleagues felt, with probably good reason, that little assistance for the struggling Soviet state, riven by civil war and threatened by foreign intervention, could be anticipated from that quarter. As we noted in chapter 1, the outbreak of the world revolution was expected to be a direct consequence of the revolution in Russia; this had been a primary justification for undertaking the Bolshevik coup in the first place. The dire circumstances facing the new regime made the spread of revolution appear all the more imperative. The international proletariat, represented by their revolutionary vanguard, the foreign Communist Parties, were thus looked upon as the only reliable allies of the Soviet republic. But firm, 'internationalist' leadership was required. Leon Trotsky, the quintessential 'internationalist', and hence a bitter opponent of the 'socialism-in-one-country' line espoused by Stalin from 1923, was still arguing as late as the middle of 1928:

> . . . for us, the policy of the Comintern dominates all other questions. Without a correct international policy, all the possible economic successes in the USSR will not save the October Revolution and will not lead to socialism. To speak more exactly: without a correct international policy, there can be no correct policy in internal affairs either, for the line is one . . .[1]

By the time this prophetic assertion was being uttered, however, it was already out of date politically. Stalin and his acolytes, including Nikolai

Bukharin, successor to Zinoviev as head of the Comintern since 1926, had chosen a different path, one which destined the Comintern for a much less prominent role in the hierarchy of Soviet foreign policy institutions.

In the beginning, Lenin and his colleagues had had no pretensions to domination over the Comintern. They confidently expected that the headquarters of the new world revolutionary organisation would be promptly transferred from Moscow, most probably to Berlin, once the revolution had spread to Western Europe. The Bolsheviks then saw no possible contradictions between the interests of the Soviet state and those of the world revolutionary movement: the survival of the former depended on the latter. Indeed, Trotsky, the first Soviet Commissar of Foreign Affairs, had declared shortly after the seizure of power that his first official act would be . . . to issue a few revolutionary proclamations to the peoples of the world and then shut up shop.'2 Lenin's decision to accept the German terms for peace at Brest Litovsk in February 1918, on the grounds that only thus could the fledgling Bolshevik regime survive, had been bitterly condemned by many of his high–spirited allies, most notably Bukharin.3 But even in the midst of this capitulation to the imperatives of *realpolitik*, Lenin had evidently not discarded his belief in the imminence of the world revolution.

Although the early achievements of the Comintern proved to be disappointing — the Hungarian Soviet republic lasted only a few months, and other revolutionary attempts in Central Europe and the Balkans were even more speedily suppressed — the organisation undoubtedly did contribute to Soviet survival. For example, Comintern influence in the seamen's and waterside workers' unions impeded Western efforts to supply war materiel to Poland during the Russo–Polish War of 1920. The very existence of the Comintern magnified the myth of Bolshevik power in Western establishment thinking and led to over–reactions to what was usually merely rhetorical subversion by local communists. This in turn increased sympathy and support among significant elements of the working class for local communists as well as for the Soviet state. Local Communist Parties were often successful in fomenting strikes in capitalist countries and their colonies, actions which were endorsed, not to say abetted, by Moscow as favourable to Soviet interests.

Soviet politicians during the early 1920s treated the leaders of important Communist Parties in the Comintern as equals. The latter enjoyed more genuine autonomy and prestige *vis–a–vis* Moscow than they would ever do again. They were accorded the status of representatives of a significant international force and as important sources of information on the revolutionary situation in their respective countries. However, as the international situation settled down and the Soviet Union faced the prospect of an indefinite period as an isolated island of proletarian virtue in a hostile capitalist sea, as Moscow began the tasks of domestic reconstruction and consolidation with the introduction of the New Economic Policy (NEP) in 1921, and as the Kremlin developed other sources of information more directly under its control (namely, Soviet diplomatic and secret police networks abroad)[4], the nature of relations with the Comintern subtly altered. On the one hand, the interests of the Comintern as a militant revolutionary organisation came into conflict with the need for a 'breathing space' and with the institutional interests of the evolving Soviet diplomatic establishment under the more professional leadership of Georgii Chicherin, Trotsky's successor as Foreign Commissar. The Genoa Conference and the Treaty of Rapallo with Germany in 1922 had given the Bolsheviks confidence in their ability to deal with the hostile capitalist powers and to keep them off balance by playing them off against each other (known in ideological terms as 'splitting the hostile capitalist encirclement').[5]

On the other hand, the Comintern was ineluctably drawn into the internal struggles over power and policy in the Soviet party leadership after Lenin's disabling stroke in May 1922. Grigorii Zinoviev, the first head of the Comintern and soon to be one of Stalin's main allies in the drive to head off Trotsky for the accession to Lenin's mantle, began to manipulate the policies of the Comintern as a way of enhancing its international visibility and, hence, his own prestige. As the struggle for succession gathered momentum following Lenin's death in January 1924, others (most notably Stalin himself) followed suit, and the Comintern became increasingly a mere pawn in the deadly game of Soviet elite politics. Indeed, during the late 1920s and through most of the 1930s Soviet foreign policy itself not infrequently suffered a similar fate.

The so–called 'March Action' in Germany in 1921 was a good illustration of the emerging conflict between the interests of Soviet diplomacy and those of the Comintern. Just at a time when Lenin's government was seeking a 'breathing space' for domestic and international consolidation — through the introduction of NEP at home, the conclusion of a trade agreement with the United Kingdom and the establishment of formal diplomatic relations with a range of neighbouring countries, from the Baltic states and Finland in the north to Persia and Afghanistan in the south and east — the Communist Party of Germany (KPD) chose to attempt to overthrow the hard–pressed Berlin government. The chaotic conditions in Germany in early 1921, rocked by demands for war reparations, armed actions by bands of disgruntled ex–servicemen vigilantes and a wave of employer resistance to trade–union militancy, created the appearance of revolutionary opportunities in the eyes of some KPD leaders, encouraged by Zinoviev and the Comintern leadership. Against the opposition of KPD leader Paul Levi, who denied the existence of a revolutionary situation, the activist majority of the KPD leadership decided to press ahead. The uprising was soon suppressed, and Levi was expelled from the party for 'factionalism', with the full endorsement of the Comintern Executive (ECCI).[6] It was later revealed that neither the Soviet Commissariat of Foreign Affairs nor even the chief Comintern expert on German affairs, Karl Radek, had been made aware of the decision to initiate the 'March Action'.

The so–called 'October Action' in Germany in 1923 was virtually a reprise of the earlier debacle. French occupation of the industrial Ruhr Valley to enforce demands for reparations payments had created another wave of popular unrest and widespread strike activity. Working–class support for the KPD had increased in reaction to an upsurge of right–wing violence, epitomised by Hitler's abortive 'beer hall putsch' in Munich that same month. The Comintern leadership in Moscow, itching to demonstrate its revolutionary fervour, put into action a hastily contrived plan for armed uprisings throughout Germany. The 'Action' never spread beyond Hamburg, however, owing to local timidity and poor co–ordination and logistical preparation by the Comintern, and the German Army was able to crush it within three days. Trotsky subsequently attributed the failure of the uprising to both the vacillating, ineffectual leadership of the KPD and the inflexible, dogmatic tactical guidance emanating from Comintern headquarters under Zinoviev and Stalin. In Trotsky's interpretation a golden revolutionary opportunity had been lost, perhaps indefinitely, for want of timely, resolute support. He made full use of the debacle to castigate his political opponents in the Soviet party.[7]

For the Comintern as an institution the defeat was a further demonstration of its ineffectiveness as a co–ordinating mechanism for world revolution and inevitably diminished its suitability as a power base for ambitious Soviet politicians. This is not to say that the Comintern did not remain a useful instrument of Soviet foreign policy. The existence of a network of foreign Communist Parties formally independent of the Soviet Union but actually subservient to its will was undoubtedly of substantial benefit to Soviet external operations. Embarrassing adventures by Comintern agents could be repudiated by Moscow on the grounds that it was not responsible for the actions of foreign citizens. Nevertheless, the Comintern's attractiveness as a rallying point and its capacity for autonomous action in pursuit of its professed aim, the promotion of proletarian revolution, steadily declined under Stalin's increasingly totalitarian style of leadership .

The dismal failure of Comintern policy in China under the direction of Stalin and Bukharin, who had taken over as Chairman of the ECCI from Zinoviev in 1926, proved to be another, even more decisive blow to the Comintern's autonomy and authority. A dogmatic application of the Marxian concept of revolutionary 'stages' had compelled the Chinese communists to continue to support Chiang Kai–shek and the Kuomintang in the face of ample evidence that Chiang was turning against his erstwhile communist allies. Chiang's crushing of communist–led uprisings in Shanghai and then Canton in the course of 1927 represented the total failure of the Comintern's strategy of seeking to manipulate what had been characterised as a 'national–democratic' revolution. There can be little doubt that the insistence of Stalin and Bukharin on persisting with this strategy in spite of clear evidence of its failure can be attributed primarily to their desire not to be seen to accept Trotsky's analysis of the situation and the activist doctrine of 'permanent revolution' on which it was based. It was better to acquiesce in the destruction of the Chinese comrades than to yield to Trotsky in the internal power struggle. Not that Trotsky's prescriptions were necessarily correct. The Chinese communists would probably have failed in any attempt to seize power directly at that time, but a judicious separation from the Kuomintang might have allowed more of them to live to fight another day, in the next 'revolutionary upsurge'.

In the event, at its Sixth Congress in July 1928, the Comintern claimed to perceive in the defeat in China and the recent rupture of diplomatic relations between Great Britain and the Soviet Union a sharpening of the general hostility of world imperialism against the USSR and the beginning of a new revolutionary upsurge. It interpreted the sudden increase in the vote for the KPD (and even more so, for the social–democrats) in Germany as a sign of this new revolutionary temper in the working class. The Soviet leaders of the International accordingly called for a sharp turn to the left by all Communist Parties. The previous policy of the 'united front' of all leftist parties against imperialism was replaced by a policy of splitting the left and winning over the workers from the social–democrats, who were now christened as 'social–fascists' and treated as 'objectively' a more dangerous enemy than the genuinely fascist right–wing parties. Bukharin is reported to have resisted this insane policy, which, it is now acknowledged, greatly facilitated Hitler's rise to power and decimated the ranks of the KPD.[8] But in the struggle with Stalin over the turn to the left of domestic economic and social policy, his days were numbered, and he was forced to accept the new general line at the Congress.

The importance of domestic policy considerations in this leftward shift of Comintern and Soviet foreign policy should not be underestimated, although it would perhaps be going too far to suggest, as Adam Ulam does, that Stalin's overt foreign policy assessments at the time were totally and consciously spurious.[9] Nevertheless, the fact remains that the shift from NEP to rapid industrialisation and forced collectivisation of agriculture at the end of the 1920s implied a high level of internal coercion of the Soviet peoples in order to exact from them the requisite economic and political sacrifices. Hence, the concoction of an external threat and the staging of 'show trials' designed to demonstrate the linkage between domestic 'wreckers' or 'saboteurs' and hostile foreign intelligence services created a suitably tense internal atmosphere to justify the repressive techniques of centralised economic and social management that Stalin envisaged. Foreign communists were ordered to do their part for 'socialist construction' in the USSR by engaging in subversive activities to thwart anti–Soviet policies in their own countries. Tactical alliances between the KPD and Nazi storm–troopers to fight against social–democratic workers in the streets of Berlin and other German cities were just one particularly bizarre example of the new strategy for safeguarding the victory of the revolution in the USSR.

The period following the Sixth Comintern Congress witnessed the elimination of the right in the Soviet Union and the thorough 'Bolshevisation' of the component national sections of the Comintern, making them totally subservient to Stalin. The organisation, which Stalin himself now spoke disparagingly of as the 'corner shop' (*lavochka*), quickly (but far from painlessly) became a pliant tool of the increasingly inward–looking, nationalistic Soviet foreign policy. Foreign communists came to operate primarily as individual auxiliaries of the growing Soviet propaganda and foreign intelligence apparatus and less as an organised force for revolution in their own countries. Stalin's management of Soviet support for the Republican side in the Spanish Civil War provides many illustrations of this change in the role and functions of the Comintern. In this sense, it can be said that the Comintern phase of Soviet foreign policy had come to an end by the late 1920s.

The Stalinist phase in Soviet foreign policy

Hitler's consolidation of power on a platform of virulent anti–Bolshevism
and his unconcealed determination to expand Germany's military power to
implement his ideas ultimately caused Stalin to change the Soviet foreign
policy line in the mid–1930s and with it that of the Comintern. At first
Stalin tried to carry on 'business as usual' with Hitler and to continue the
important industrial and semi–clandestine military co–operation between
the two countries which had for over a decade played an important part in
Soviet planning for the industrial and defence buildup of the USSR.
Hitler's aggressive anti–Bolshevism soon acquired 'objective' as well as
'subjective' characteristics, however, and further co–operation became
increasingly difficult. The ideological formulations promulgated at the
Sixth Comintern Congress had served to justify the left–wing line by
depicting Hitler and Nazism as merely the most extreme manifestation of
'bourgeois reaction' and 'objectively' no worse than British or French
imperialism. This formulation now had to be changed in the light of
irrefutable evidence that Hitler was indeed worse. The new Soviet
Commissar of Foreign Affairs (since 1930), Maksim Litvinov, had begun
sounding out neighbouring countries as well as France, concerned over the
rise of aggressive German nationalism, on some form of collective
security, commonly in the form of a non–aggression pact with the USSR.
Towards the end of 1934, local experiments of collaboration between
Communist Parties and social–democrats in anti–fascist actions took place
in a number of Western countries.[10] The culmination of this shift was the
call for a 'popular front' policy at the Seventh (and last) Comintern
Congress in July–August 1935, promoting co–operation with the Western
capitalist states against Nazism and Fascism. For the Communist Parties
of the world the new line meant extending the old 'united front' strategy
beyond the parties of the left, to include any bourgeois parties of the centre
and even the moderate right which would agree to engage in collective
action to resist Hitler and Mussolini. Litvinov skilfully used the forum of
the League of Nations, which the USSR had recently joined in September
1934, to goad the Western allies to undertake substantive measures of
collective security, first against Italian actions in Ethiopia in 1935 and
then against German and Italian support for Franco against the Republican
government in Spain in 1936. The Comintern played an important part in
recruiting manpower for the International Brigades to bolster the Loyalist
forces. But by 1937, as the Great Purge in the USSR was reaching its
climax and as an Axis victory in Spain appeared imminent, Soviet support
for the Spanish Republican cause degenerated into a vicious campaign to

purge the ranks of Soviet and foreign communists involved in Spain of persons alleged to be disloyal to Stalin.

It is clear that Stalin's purpose in shifting to the popular front line and improving relations with the West was to buy time for the preparation of Soviet heavy industry and defences for the impending world war. At home he used the temporary respite for a massive purge of potentially disloyal elements, including a large part of the officer corps of the Red Army. It was more than ironic that Stalin's reckless destruction of the Red Army leadership fostered suspicions in the West that the USSR was not a serious partner in collective security against the Axis. Western reluctance to engage in substantive military collaboration with the Soviet Union, in turn, fed Stalin's suspicions that the British and French were preparing to embroil him in a war with Hitler for their own benefit. Not surprisingly, Neville Chamberlain's hapless appeasement of Hitler at the expense of Czechoslovakia in Munich in September 1938 was bitterly condemned by the Soviet government as confirmation of Stalin's fears.[11]

By this time he had already begun sounding out Hitler on the possibilities of a major shift in their mutual diplomatic alignments. The ideological line for the international communist movement was correspondingly drastically altered to prepare for the anticipated diplomatic *volte-face*. Now the Western capitalist powers, by their failure to resist Hitler, were declared to have become 'objectively' more dangerous than the Axis to world peace and the security of the Soviet Union, because they were making war more likely and preparing to sacrifice the USSR for their own interests.[12] The shift in Soviet policy was soon given concrete form in the Molotov–Ribbentrop Non–Aggression Pact of 23 August 1939, which made the Soviet Union a *de facto* ally of Nazi Germany and gave Hitler the security he needed to attack Poland, thus initiating the Second World War.

The Nazi–Soviet alliance placed a tremendous strain on the loyalties of foreign communists. The popular front policy, the Spanish Civil War and Litvinov's collective security rhetoric in the League of Nations had greatly increased the prestige and attractiveness of the USSR and international communism as the leading force against Fascism. In Western liberal and progressive circles there emerged the phenomenon of the 'fellow traveller', and the Communist Party succeeded in recruiting many new members among young intellectuals (Philby and Blunt, for example). Stalin's abrupt turn towards Hitler had a devastating effect in the reverse direction. Only the most committed and disciplined communists accepted the tortured logic of the *volte-face* in the Comintern's ideological and political line. It is likely that only Hitler's 'treacherous' attack on his erstwhile ally in June

1941 and Stalin's full participation in the anti–Hitler coalition saved Western communism from total disintegration. Ironically, in May 1943, in order to build confidence among his Western partners that the Soviet Union had become a reliable ally and was no longer committed to their revolutionary overthrow, Stalin ordered the liquidation of the Comintern. By that time he evidently no longer considered it a cost–effective instrument of Soviet foreign policy, even in the highly manipulative manner in which he had used it since the early 1930s.[13]

The amity of the wartime alliance did not long survive the victory over the Axis; indeed, there were already signs of friction between Stalin and his Western allies even before the tide of battle had turned in 1943. In the early stages of the war Stalin had systematically played down ideological themes, replacing them with appeals to traditional Russian national and religious values in order both to rally the masses and to convince the Western allies of the 'normality' of their Soviet partner. After the turning point at Stalingrad, however, ideological campaigns were begun once again, and the party's dominant role in society was steadily reasserted. Once the war was over, virtually all previous measures to mobilise support for the war effort by fostering domestic relaxation and social harmony were soon rescinded.

Stalin made his future international and domestic policy intentions clear in a speech on the eve of elections to the Supreme Soviet on 9 February 1946, when he re–emphasised the Leninist postulate that the very existence of imperialism made war inevitable, and he signalled a concentration on military–industrial preparations for the coming conflict as the *leitmotiv* of postwar reconstruction.[14] Once again it was a matter of resorting to perceived external threats to justify the tightening of domestic ideological, political and economic controls. To be sure, the temporary American monopoly of atomic weapons undoubtedly enhanced the credibility of the threat, even if, at the time, Stalin ostentatiously minimised their significance as a decisive element in the 'correlation of forces'. Western reactions to Stalin's new policies — for example, Winston Churchill's famous 'iron curtain' speech at Fulton, Missouri on 5 March 1946, the Truman Doctrine and the Marshall Plan a year later, and the Berlin Blockade of 1948–49 — seemed to confirm Stalin's diagnosis and to justify his calls for renewed sacrifice.

Stalin's most tangible gain from the 'Great Patriotic War' was the accretion of a massive buffer zone to the west of the USSR in the form of the Communist Party–ruled states of Central and Eastern Europe. To the re–annexed territories of the former Tsarist Empire (the Baltic states, Bukovina, Western Ukraine and Belorussia and Moldavia) were now added

Poland, Czechoslovakia, Hungary, East Germany, Romania, Bulgaria, Albania and Yugoslavia. At first, to allay Western objections to direct Soviet rule over these previously independent states, the fact of Soviet domination was concealed and the completion of the monopolisation of power by the local Communist Parties was delayed.

In the uncertain atmosphere created by this fictitious semi–independence, the individual communist leaders of most of these countries began to devise indigenous approaches to domestic problems, foreshadowing patterns of internal development that were divergent from the basic Stalinist model. Moreover, their international behaviour also soon became disturbing to Stalin: most notably their tendency to engage in direct contacts amongst themselves without the mediation of the Soviet Union. Yugoslavia, under Marshall Josip Broz Tito, considered by postwar Western observers to be the most loyal of all Stalin's satellites, furnished perhaps the most striking examples of this exercise of internal and external autonomy. Tito was alleged to have gone so far as to try to embroil the USSR against the West in support of Yugoslav claims to Trieste and other territorial issues. This behaviour seemed all the more intolerable to Stalin because of Tito's skill in thwarting Soviet efforts to penetrate the Yugoslav military and security apparatus, which the Yugoslav leader had fashioned in the course of his successful partisan campaigns against the Axis.[15]

To combat this growing diversity in thought and deed Stalin found it expedient to recreate the kind of authoritative international command centre that had been lost with the abolition of the Comintern in 1943. It was evident that the International Department of the All–Union Communist Party(Bolsheviks)[AUCP(B)] Central Committee, which had taken over most of the functions of the Comintern concerning liaison with foreign communists, was unable to perform them adequately in the new situation, where nominally sovereign Communist Party states now existed. This was the origin of the Communist Information Bureau, or Cominform, which was established at a meeting of representatives of ruling Communist Parties and the large, non–ruling Communist Parties of Italy and France in the Polish town of Szklarska Poreba in September 1947. Its functions were both geographically and substantively more limited than those of the Comintern, its principal task being to issue a unified ideological and political line for the Bloc on questions of internal development and foreign policy. The main instrument for doing so was a fortnightly journal with the unwieldy title *For a Lasting Peace, For a People's Democracy*.[16] Initially, as a concession to Tito's pretensions as *primus inter pares* among Stalin's Bloc lieutenants, the headquarters of the Cominform were to be located in Belgrade. However, the festering dispute with Tito over absolute submission to Stalin's will was soon brought to a head. Ironically, the Cominform's first (and some would argue, only) major act was thus to expel Yugoslavia from its ranks and to orchestrate a Bloc–wide campaign to overthrow the Yugoslav leadership. The expulsion of Yugoslavia in June 1948 was a turning point in intra–Bloc relations and signalled an intensive tightening of controls throughout the Communist World.

Tito's ultimately successful challenge to Stalin's authority was undoubtedly a major reason for the latter's ambivalence toward Mao Zedong's victory in China in October 1949. Stalin's satisfaction over the massive accretion of Chinese power to the 'camp of peace and socialism' was thus partly tempered by the recognition that Mao was another potential challenger to his authority as the unquestioned leader of the Bloc. The relative size of China added another dimension to Stalin's dilemma. It was simply not possible, for example, for Stalin to exploit the resources of China for the reconstruction of Soviet military and industrial power in the name of 'socialist internationalism' as he was doing to the European members of the Bloc. Indeed, the length of Mao's sojourn in Moscow in late 1949 and early 1950 (nine weeks) was a sign of the intensity of the bargaining between the leaders of the two communist giants. Mao was evidently pressing his own claims for assistance under the terms of 'socialist internationalism'.[17]

The Korean War marked another important stage in the development of Stalin's postwar foreign policy. It illustrated the operation of some of the principles of Soviet conduct mentioned in chapter 1, namely 'revolutionary momentum' and its corollary of turning to the East when opportunities were temporarily exhausted in the West. Frustrated in his efforts to expand Soviet power in Central Europe by an unsuccessful land blockade of Berlin in 1948–49 and to secure the speedy removal of Marshal Tito in Yugoslavia without direct invasion (which was actually being planned), Stalin decided to take advantage of Washington's ostensible exclusion of the Korean Peninsula from the American security perimeter in the Far East by encouraging Kim Il Sung to reunify Korea by force of arms. This was the first direct attempt to expand Soviet power by the use of surrogates, in this case North Korea and, eventually, The people's Republic of China. American military intervention with UN endorsement (as a result of inept Soviet diplomacy in that body) prevented a quick victory for the North Koreans.

The extended stalemate which resulted after Chinese entry into the conflict effectively marked the end of Soviet efforts to change the map of the world during the Stalin era. The period of the Korean War saw the honing of a number of characteristic Soviet propaganda techniques to influence world public opinion against the American–led UN forces — for example the Stockholm Peace Appeal of 1950 and the spurious germ–warfare accusations promoted by, among others, the Australian left–wing journalist Wilfred Burchett. The entire Korean venture brought about a profound intensification of the Cold War and did little to enhance the diplomatic and economic standing of the USSR.

Stalin's last years were thus preoccupied with the ideological, political and economic consolidation of his increasingly idiosyncratic personal rule in the USSR and its expanded territorial empire. These years of full–blown Stalinism (sometimes called 'high Stalinism') witnessed an outpouring of ideological and political prescriptions in various fields of human wisdom — in linguistics, genetics, cybernetics, economics, literature and agronomy. They were accompanied by a crescendo of purges and secret police terror, the total effect of which ultimately severely restricted opportunities for further economic and social development throughout the Bloc.

In foreign policy, Stalin's implacable hostility toward the West and his refusal to entertain the possibility of independent activities by non–communist nationalists in the Third World, such as Nehru and Naguib (Nasser's initial front–man in Egypt), similarly foreclosed many opportunities for the promotion of Soviet security interests. In Stalin's view a third world war was inevitable. By his own actions he had made it all the more probable and ensured that the USSR would be one of its principal instigators and protagonists, especially since by the early 1950s the Soviet Union was also in possession of nuclear weapons. Stalin's death on 5 March 1953 may well have saved the world from that fate.

The Khrushchevian interlude

One of the first moves of the ruling triumvirate (Molotov, Malenkov and Beria) which had taken up the reins of power after Stalin's death was to press for an international 'breathing space' in order to consolidate their power and begin the search for ways out of the domestic and foreign impasse produced by Stalin's rigid policies. Domestically, under Malenkov's aegis as Head of Government, there was a relaxation in agricultural policies and a general change in economic emphasis to favour the production of consumer goods. Beria, as chief of a reunified security establishment, sought to alleviate some of the internal ethnic pressures by promoting a limited expansion of local autonomy in Eastern Europe as well as the USSR itself and by repudiating certain of Stalin's recent repressive campaigns, most notably the so–called 'Kremlin doctors' plot'.

Internationally, the new leaders sought a quick end to the Korean conflict and, with Foreign Minister Molotov's grudging acquiescence, took steps to extend their domestic relaxation policies to the satellite empire. One of the immediate consequences of the hiatus in Stalinist terror in Eastern Europe had been an outbreak of working–class riots in East Berlin and in Plzen, Czechoslovakia. These had been quickly suppressed by the local authorities with Soviet military backing, but an indirect byproduct was the arrest of Beria in June 1953 (and his subsequent execution six months later) under the instigation of Nikita S. Khrushchev, who was playing upon conservative dissatisfaction with the troubles in Eastern Europe and with the radical changes in domestic economic policy to thrust aside the ruling triumvirate in the Politburo. This was another clear example of the recurrent use of disagreements over policy to camouflage a struggle for political power. By September, Khrushchev was already reasonably secure as the head of the Communist Party machine, which he quickly proceeded to raise once again to the supreme position among the instruments of Soviet power. He did so by, among other things, purging the security apparatus of Beria's lieutenants and greatly reducing its potency as an autonomous political factor. Once in power, Khrushchev moved swiftly to appropriate the relaxationist policies formerly associated with Malenkov, much as Stalin had done with the Left Opposition in the late 1920s. Malenkov and Molotov were gradually eased out of their positions at the apex of the system in the course of 1955, leaving Khrushchev free to take the initiative in foreign and domestic policy, although not without periodic challenges.

However, despite his more or less firm control of the levers of power, Khrushchev would prove to be anything but a new Stalin in either the style or the substance of his policies.[18] Domestically he introduced a 'thaw' in literature and the arts and pushed through the rehabilitation and release from the camps of hundreds of thousands of former victims of Stalin, decisively transforming in the process the atmosphere of Soviet society. In hindsight, during the grey years of Brezhnev's 'real socialism' these changes made the Khrushchevian interregnum seem like a 'golden age' of freedom.

In foreign policy his vision of a new basis for Soviet leadership of the Bloc clearly illustrated his commitment to change in the sphere of communist international relations. In place of Stalin's system of direct command over the East European regimes through their institutionalised subordination to Soviet party, governmental, military and secret police

Compare + contrast the foreign policies of
Khrushchev + Gorbachev. What factors
account for the differences?

③ 91: 9 Khrushchev >
Gorbachev

THE EVOLUTION OF SOVIET FOREIGN POLICY 33

agencies, Khrushchev sought to inject a sense of participatory, corporate decision–making, based on common ideological commitment. To symbolise the new relationship, Khrushchev renamed the erstwhile 'camp' of Moscow–oriented socialist countries the 'Socialist Commonwealth'. To be sure, the Soviet Union would continue to exercise leadership as the self–proclaimed 'elder brother' with global responsibilities and years of experience in 'building socialism'. But the individual ruling Communist Parties were encouraged to supply greater input into collectively agreed positions. And under the **New Course** they would be permitted greater leeway in pursuing their own solutions to domestic problems.

Even the formation of the Warsaw Treaty Organisation (WTO) in May 1955 can be interpreted in the light of this new pattern. While on one level the WTO represented a danger to the West, a dramatic response to the incorporation of West Germany into the NATO alliance, on another level, in the context of Khrushchev's new synthesis, it represented a shift from the Stalinist bilateral mode of control over the Bloc armies to a multilateral one, where at least the appearance of consultation and collective decision–making was featured. Finally, the WTO provided a more legitimate basis for the maintenance of Soviet military leadership and the stationing of Soviet troops in the region by equating it morally with the structures and practices of NATO.

The decision to change the Bloc's attitude toward Yugoslavia (a move that was strongly resisted by Molotov and served as one of the pretexts for his removal as Foreign Minister) was an important element in the new strategy. Khrushchev evidently considered the re–integration of Yugoslavia into the Bloc as the capstone of the new architecture of communist inter–state relations. It was expected that Tito's acceptance of the altered terms of association would be seen as confirmation of its overall viability. Khrushchev's and Prime Minister Bulganin's visit to Belgrade in May 1955 only partially succeeded in achieving this objective, but considerable progress was made in normalising state–to–state relations. Furthermore, the threat of any further move by Yugoslavia towards the West was effectively removed, particularly by pledges of generous Soviet economic assistance for Yugoslav industrial development. The Soviet Union also became once again the principal supplier of military equipment to the Yugoslav People's Army.

Other examples of Khrushchev's innovative approach to foreign policy were the withdrawal of Soviet occupation forces from Austria upon the signing of a peace treaty with that country in May 1955 and the return of the Porkkala military base to Finland in September of the same year. Both these moves were clearly designed to improve the Soviets' image in the

West, even at the expense of the hallowed 'patrimony' principle. The concessions represented an important contribution to the spirit of 'peaceful coexistence' which Khrushchev was promoting as the basic principle of Soviet foreign policy *vis–a–vis* the capitalist West.

Another important ideological innovation was Khrushchev's assertion at the Twentieth Party Congress in 1956 that in the nuclear age, thanks largely to the shift in the 'correlation of forces' toward socialism, major wars between the two world systems were no longer 'fatalistically inevitable'.[19] In this and in the new, multi–dimensional intepretation being given to the concept of 'peaceful coexistence', Khrushchev was thus demonstrating a much more sensitive appreciation of both the risks and the opportunities for Soviet foreign policy in an era of impending strategic parity. In many respects his approach prefigured Gorbachev's 'new political thinking'. The need for an international breathing space in which to address critical domestic economic and social issues was similar in the two periods. However, Khrushchev was evidently much more sanguine about the capacity of the Soviet system, more or less unchanged, to beat the West at its own game of economic competition than Gorbachev would be some 30 years later.

Khrushchev's flexibility by no means implied a passive role for the Soviet Union in international relations. His interpretation of 'peaceful coexistence' envisaged intensified competition between the two systems in all areas short of direct military confrontation — ideological, economic, diplomatic and even assistance to revolutionary movements and parties engaged in small–scale 'local' wars and wars of 'national liberation'. While denying that the Soviet Union could or would ever engage in 'exporting' revolution, Khrushchev made it clear that it would provide assistance to 'progressive' revolutionary or anti–colonial movements which requested it.[20]

In practice, occasions to act upon the new receptiveness to Third World opportunities arose almost immediately. In the fall of 1955 the Soviet Union began large–scale shipments of weapons to Egypt in aid of Colonel Nasser's continuing hostility toward Israel and his growing confrontation with Britain and France over the Suez Canal. Later that year he and Bulganin made a series of state visits to India, Burma and Afghanistan, which resulted in the conclusion of agreements for massive Soviet economic and military aid projects designed to promote the state sector of their respective economies and influence their development in a socialist direction. When this general strategy was applied to Cuba in the course of 1960 and 1961 and was quickly rewarded by the accession of Fidel Castro to the socialist camp, a process was set in motion which would have fateful consequences for Khrushchev and world peace, demonstrating a reckless side to Khrushchev's flexible style that would eventually prove to be his undoing.

In fact, almost every success of Khrushchev's imaginative policies had its more or less serious negative obverse side. To counter his increasingly restive conservative opponents, he undertook a major campaign in 1956 to de–Stalinise the Soviet system by directly attacking the record of the deceased dictator and revealing his crimes to the party faithful. Thus, at one stroke, he sought to undermine the legitimacy of his antagonists and the ideological and political orthodoxy they claimed to be upholding. This was the rationale behind Khrushchev's famous secret night–time speech to selected delegates toward the conclusion of the Twentieth Party Congress in February 1956. The 'Secret Speech' not only shattered the legitimacy of his opponents by tarring them with the Stalinist brush, but it also weakened the authority of the CPSU itself as the unquestioned leader of the international communist movement. Khrushchev had undertaken his radical de–Stalinisation campaign in disregard of the advice of some of his more cautious supporters, including the Chinese leadership, who feared what it would do to the cohesion of the 'Socialist Commonwealth'.

The consequences were not long in appearing. In the latter half of October 1956, the Polish Central Committee brought Wladyslaw Gomulka back to the headship of the Polish United Workers' Party over the objections of the Kremlin. During a hasty trip to Warsaw on 19 October, Khrushchev and several close aides grudgingly allowed themselves to be convinced of Gomulka's loyalty and of the feasibility of his reform program. Four days later Imre Nagy was similarly brought back to the centre of power in Hungary in the midst of a wave of popular unrest against the old Stalinist leadership. The latter had promptly called in Soviet troops to quell the disorders. Khrushchev at first restrained the Soviet forces and sought a solution similar to the one just concluded in Poland, but events in Hungary quickly got out of control. Acting under mass pressures from the Hungarian populace and fearing renewed Soviet military intervention, Nagy appealed to the United Nations and threatened to pull Hungary out of the WTO. Khrushchev reacted, after personally travelling to the other Eastern European capitals to enlist the support of the respective party leaders, including Tito, by sending in massive Soviet forces to suppress the popular uprising and to install Janos Kadar as the loyalist pro–Soviet leader of a 'reformed' Hungarian Socialist Workers' Party. Western efforts to chastise the Soviet Union for its actions in Hungary through the United Nations were effectively neutralised by the British, French and Israeli attack on Egypt, which occurred at almost the same time and was promptly repudiated by American Secretary of State John Foster Dulles. Western disunity was undoubtedly an important factor in saving Khrushchev's position in Eastern Europe. But his success in crushing the Hungarian uprising had a number of paradoxical, often negative consequences for both his domestic and foreign policy.

On the one hand, for over six months — indeed until June 1957 — his position as supreme party leader was again seriously challenged by his conservative opponents. Even after defeating the so–called 'anti–party group' in June 1957, Khrushchev was evidently convinced of the need to rescind some of the more liberal techniques he had introduced for Soviet leadership of the Socialist Commonwealth, and he strove once again to assert Soviet political and ideological primacy. Relations with Yugoslavia predictably deteriorated. Tito was not interested in re–association with the Bloc under the more stringent terms Khrushchev now offered.[21] The Chinese, who had been lukewarm toward de–Stalinisation from the beginning, now proved to be equally unenthusiastic about the reassertion of Soviet hegemony, unless they were accorded the status of equal ideological and foreign–policy partners of the Soviet leadership. In general, the Chinese showed themselves increasingly skeptical of Khrushchev's pretensions as ideological legislator and spokesman for the Bloc. In the wake of the revelations of the Secret Speech and the brutality of the Soviet intervention in Hungary, some of the more independently minded Western European communist leaders also began to question Moscow's legitimacy as the fount of ideological wisdom. This was the origin of the doctrine of 'polycentrism' coined by veteran Italian Communist Party leader Palmiro Togliatti.[22] Two major international conferences of Communist Party leaders, summoned by Khrushchev in 1957 and 1960 to reassert Soviet hegemony, succeeded only in papering over the increasingly obvious differences.

On the other hand, the respite afforded by President Eisenhower's split with his main NATO allies over Suez made it possible for Khrushchev to explore various avenues of agreement with Washington. This began to seem particularly desirable as relations with the Chinese deteriorated markedly following the Formosa Straits crisis of 1958. By this time the Soviets had already launched their first ICBMs and shortly afterwards, the first artificial Earth satellite, 'Sputnik'. Khrushchev had rejected Mao's conclusions on the resulting apparent change in the 'correlation of forces', however, and he had pointedly refused to become embroiled on China's behalf in a potential nuclear confrontation with the United States. One of his major initiatives was a unilateral reduction in the size of the Soviet military establishment and the pensioning off of substantial numbers of military officers.

However, Khrushchev's negotiating tactics *vis–a–vis* the West were often anything but cautious and peaceful. They seem to have followed a consciously patterned alternation of threat and bluster with interludes of sweet reasonableness. The important thing for him was obviously to maintain the initiative, be it on Berlin, the Middle East or arms control. By making outrageous demands and then pulling back from the brink of confrontation — as in his threat in the fall of 1958 to nullify Western occupation rights in Berlin by signing a unilateral peace treaty with East Germany, only to agree magnanimously to allow further time for negotiations when it appeared that the West would stand firm — he sought to keep his enemies off balance and to lure them into ostensible compromises which ultimately favoured the Soviet position. The sequence of threats and blandishments leading up to the erection of the Berlin Wall in August 1961 illustrated just such a process, and the result was basically favourable to Khrushchev's main objective: to seal off East Berlin and stem the haemorrhage of productive citizens fleeing to the West.

The Cuban missile crisis of October 1962 was perhaps the most extreme example of Khrushchev's aggressive style of policy–making. Recognising that the alleged 'missile gap', which had featured prominently in the American presidential election campaign of 1960, was a fiction, and that the Soviet Union actually lagged considerably behind the United States in deliverable intercontinental ballistic warheads, Khrushchev sought to take advantage of Cuba's proximity to the United States to install a number of Soviet medium– and intermediate–range ballistic missiles and thus restore the 'balance of terror' between the two superpowers. Soviet diplomats, including Foreign Minister Andrei Gromyko, consistently denied their government's intention to install the missiles. When photographic evidence was produced to show that the Soviet program in Cuba was at an advanced stage of completion, US President John F. Kennedy confronted Khrushchev with an ultimatum to remove the missiles, backed up with a naval blockade of Cuba and a demonstrative mobilisation for full–scale military confrontation. Khrushchev's subsequent backdown was somewhat sweetened by an American pledge not to seek to overthrow Fidel Castro by force of arms and the subsequent unilateral removal of obsolescent American medium–range missiles from Turkey. As the author can attest from his personal experience as an exchange postgraduate student in Moscow at the time, the entire episode was a frightening demonstration of the dangers of military confrontation in the nuclear age.

Khrushchev understood this very well. His retreat over Cuba was followed by an instantaneous improvement in East–West relations. In the autumn of 1963 he took the unprecedented step of buying American grain to alleviate a serious shortfall in Soviet agricultural production, setting the stage for what would become a regular feature, and indeed a barometer, of the US–Soviet relationship. But while Khrushchev managed to derive considerable benefit from the Cuban crisis, the reckless way he had provoked it and the embarrassing manner by which he had had to extricate himself from it greatly complicated his relations with his allies. Fidel Castro was, of course, furious but was rather quickly mollified with additional Soviet aid.

The Chinese were another matter. They used the episode to hammer home their contention that Khrushchev was unsuitable as the leader of the international communist movement. In the last two years of his rule the Chinese mounted increasingly strident attacks on his domestic policies and their ideological foundations, particularly as set forth in Khrushchev's new 1961 party program, which they disparaged as a thoroughly 'revisionist' document. By the end of the Khrushchev era the Sino–Soviet rift had clearly become unbridgeable, and it seemed that no progress toward overcoming it could be made while he was still in power. At a hastily called plenary session of the CPSU Central Committee in October 1964, all of the negative consequences of his daring policy initiatives came back to haunt him, and his conservative enemies finally managed to unseat him. His erratic foreign policies were among the most important rallying points in the conspiracy to oust him.

The early Brezhnev phase

The early years of the Brezhnev era were marked by concerted efforts to reform the Soviet economy, while restoring the political structures of the Stalin period which Khrushchev had substantially altered. Some of these economic reform measures had been foreshadowed under Khrushchev, most notably the 'Liberman' reforms introduced by Prime Minister Aleksei Kosygin in September 1965, which sought to inject the notion of profits from sales and limited autonomy for industrial enterprises in deciding on product assortment, investments and incentive payments to labour. In agriculture, improvements were made in the terms of trade for collective and state farms, and their obligations to the state were made more predictable and profitable. For a while, most aspects of the Khrushchevian 'thaw' in literature and the arts were maintained, and efforts by conservatives to rehabilitate Stalin and his methods were rebuffed.

Attempts by the new Soviet leaders to reach a *modus vivendi* with the Chinese came to naught, however, as the Chinese regarded the economic reform program as merely a continuation of 'Khrushchevian revisionism'. All Moscow's efforts to reassert its ideological and political primacy in the movement in the name of socialist internationalism were condemned by the Chinese as 'hegemonism' and 'social imperialism'. The Chinese ideological diatribe paradoxically pushed Brezhnev towards rapprochement with the Yugoslavs, with whom relations were restored almost to the level that had been reached in the mid–1950s. Yugoslav domestic institutional 'heresies' were once again accorded the status of a more or less acceptable method of 'building socialism', and economic relations flourished. During the June 1967 Arab–Israeli war, Tito permitted the Soviet use of Yugoslav ports and air space for the military resupply of the Arab armies, and Tito joined the Bloc states (except Romania) in breaking off diplomatic relations with Israel.

The combined effects of the Soviet economic reforms, the rapprochement with Yugoslavia and the exacerbation of relations with China were to create an atmosphere of relaxation in internal affairs within the Bloc. Significant also was the wave of student radicalism and anti–authoritarianism in Western Europe and the United States, where the anti–Vietnam War movement was reaching its apogee. Reformist elements in the party and society in certain East European countries, most notably Poland and Czechoslovakia, took advantage of this atmosphere — and the appearance of Soviet distraction — to press the conservative party leadership for economic and political liberalisation.

In Poland a reform movement of students and intellectuals in March 1968 created panic in the party leadership under Gomulka, who had long ago ceased being a reformer. With Soviet encouragement, Gomulka launched a conservative reaction with strong anti–semitic overtones, labelling the reform leaders as 'Zionist' and 'anti–patriotic elements'. Thousands of Jews, whether associated with the reform movement or not, were forced out of their jobs and encouraged to emigrate. The blatantly obvious cynicism of the campaign was profoundly corrosive of the general moral climate and of the legitimacy of the party and government, undoubtedly paving the way for the subsequent breakdown in relations between society and the state in the first Solidarity period.

In Czechoslovakia, by contrast, the reform movement was led from the beginning by reformist forces within the core of the party itself. The legitimacy of economic reform had been established by the reforms that had

been taking place within the Soviet Union itself, and its necessity for
Czechoslovakia had been throughly canvassed by reputable economists like
Ota Sik. As in Hungary at this time, there was a recognition of the need
to replace many of the elements of central planning and management with
market–type relations involving autonomous enterprises. When, however,
the reformers succeeded in winning over the new party leadership under
Alexander Dubcek and began, during the 'Prague Spring', to demand
corresponding changes in the political system, including the abolition of
censorship, Brezhnev and his conservative colleagues in the Soviet Union
and the other Bloc states decided to call a halt to the entire reform project
throughout the Bloc.

The invasion by massive military forces of the Soviet Union and four
other Warsaw Pact states in August 1968 marked an historic turning point
in Soviet domestic and foreign policy and in relations within the
international communist movement. By his brazen insistence on
justifying the intervention *ex post facto* with a doctrine of 'limited
sovereignty' of communist states, Brezhnev aroused sentiments of horror
and outrage in both East and West alike. Under the so–called 'Brezhnev
Doctrine', these states and their ruling Communist Parties were held to be
responsible not only to their own working class but also to the working
classes of the Socialist Commonwealth as a whole for the preservation of
the 'achievements of socialism' in their respective countries.[23] In fact,
Brezhnev was merely making explicit what had always been tacitly
understood as the relationship between the USSR and any other
communist–ruled states that were within reach of its power at least since
the Bolshevisation of the Comintern in the late 1920s. Nevertheless, it
was the official proclamation of this truth that made the reality so
depressing.

Domestically, in the Soviet Union itself, the crushing of the 'Prague
Spring' signalled the end of further experiments with liberalising economic
reform for almost twenty years. It naturally put a stop to autonomous
economic reforms in other countries of the Bloc, particularly Hungary,
where the Kadar regime had carefully insulated the incipient economic
changes under Rezso Nyers's 'New Economic Mechanism' from any hint of
political reform. In Yugoslavia and Romania it strengthened the
determination to resist Soviet interference in domestic affairs and led to the
hasty development of new doctrines of total national defence and flexible
forms of military organisation designed specifically to resist Soviet
invasion.[24]

The Chinese, by now in the throes of the 'Great Proletarian Cultural
Revolution', reacted with predictable fury. In early March 1969 they

provoked a series of armed conflicts with Soviet troops along the Ussuri River border between the two countries in the Far East. Within a few months the prospect that an all–out war between the two communist giants had become a distinct possibility compelled Brezhnev to begin mending his fences in the West. Rumours of United States contacts with China made the need for some kind of settlement in Europe that much more imperative.[25] There followed intense negotiations with the Americans and the West Germans, which, despite the recent alarm over Czechoslovakia, resulted in a peace treaty between the USSR and West Germany in August 1970 and a Polish–West German peace treaty five months later. Another era of East–West detente had begun.

Reaction in the international communist movement to the intervention in Czechoslovakia was not so easily defused. Shock over the invasion led directly to the emergence of the 'Eurocommunist' movement, first among the influential Italian, French and Spanish Communist Parties and then in a number of smaller parties throughout the world, including the Communist Party of Australia. The leadership of these parties had come to realise that, as a result of Czechoslovakia, their 'Soviet connection' had become an insuperable obstacle to their ever achieving respectability and political credibility in their own countries. The possibility of their participation in electoral politics had risen considerably in the upsurge of left–wing sentiments throughout the Western world in the wake of the student and anti–Vietnam War movements. The Communist Parties accordingly sought to improve their image as independent, patriotic actors in their respective domestic political arenas.[26]

To combat these fissiparous tendencies and to marshal support for the Soviet position against China, Brezhnev succeeded in convoking a conference of world Communist Parties in Moscow in June 1969. He had been trying to convene such a conclave since 1966, but now the need had become urgent. Five of the fourteen ruling Communist Parties (China, North Vietnam, North Korea, Yugoslavia and Albania) refused to attend, as did thirteen non–ruling Asian parties.[27] The results were disappointing to the Soviet hosts. They had to accept the position that there could no longer be any 'leading centre of the international communist movement' and to water down their desired condemnation of the Chinese. In general, the effort to paper over the evident diversity in the movement was unsuccessful.

Thus, by the beginning of the 1970s, Brezhnev's foreign policy had reached a turning point. He had managed to re–establish control over the East European core of the Soviet empire, but Soviet influence in the international communist movement had palpably declined. He had also been successful in re–opening doors to more or less normal intercourse with the West and establishing a reasonably sound basis for future state–to–state relations with the United States and Western Europe in the framework of detente.   However, in the process of dealing with disturbances in the Socialist Commonwealth, particularly in Czechoslovakia and along the Chinese border, he had come to look upon the military factor as one of the most reliable and secure instruments of Soviet power and influence.   His obvious pleasure in receiving and conferring military decorations and in recalling and embellishing his own modest military career as a political officer in the Second World War undoubtedly contributed to this affinity for things martial.   He showed great willingness to continue the military buildup begun by Khrushchev after the Cuban crisis and to give the Soviet military–industrial complex whatever it requested for enhancing the country's military power.   Later experience with opportunities to make use of this increasing power for expansion in the Third World during the 1970s would reinforce the tendency to rely on the military to pursue the objectives of Soviet foreign policy.   In this respect the Brezhnev era represented a reversion to older Stalinist patterns of Soviet perceptions and behaviour.   Ideology, as illustrated by the official codification in the 1977 Constitution, partly in response to the Eurocommunist challenge, of 'really existing', or 'mature', socialism, became basically a conservative force.   It was used to glorify the achievements of the Soviet system and to maintain a climate of hostility towards those within the communist movement at home and abroad who would question it or seek to change it, and towards those abroad who sought to thwart its expansionist aspirations.   This was, in short, the essence of the 'old political thinking'.

" The only difference between the foreign policies of Stalin ~ Brezhnev Brezhnev was "twenty years" Disans

3 Instruments of Soviet foreign policy

Introduction

The contradictory origins of the Soviet Union as both a regular state actor on the international scene and as the self–appointed nucleus of a future world revolutionary order have had several interesting historical consequences. First, they fostered a peculiarly striated view of the nature of the outside world, placing foreign state and non–state actors into a set of categories defined by the degree of 'objective' hostility or friendship towards the Soviet Union as the 'motherland' of the world revolution. Secondly, they led to the development of a series of unusual instruments of international activity in tandem with the formal organs of diplomacy. Practice in the operation of the various types of instruments in different countries and in different periods eventually produced a form of division of labour among them, giving Soviet diplomacy a shadowy, multi-dimensional character which brought advantages, but also some disadvantages, in the pursuit of the country's foreign–policy objectives.

As we noted in chapter 2, the differences in roles and missions of the separate types of foreign policy instrument occasionally gave rise to tensions among them. It was not always easy for a Soviet ambassador in a capitalist country, for example, to carry on normal diplomatic activities when other Soviet agencies were actively attempting to subvert the government he was dealing with. Nevertheless, Soviet leaders evidently considered it expedient and beneficial, for both ideological and practical reasons, to play this dual game despite occasional embarrassments and setbacks. Recent evidence suggests that they continue to do so, even in the era of 'new political thinking'.[1] This chapter seeks to present a brief overview of the changing patterns of interaction between geopolitical and

43

institutional features of Soviet foreign policy under the old and new political thinking.

Changing geographical priorities

From the earliest days of the Bolshevik regime Soviet theorists of foreign policy envisaged a threefold classification of actors in international politics: socialist states, capitalist states and what we now call Third World states or potential states. This scheme reflected the conventional Leninist view of the three principal sources of support for the fledgling Soviet regime:

1   the community of socialist states emerging from the expected upsurge of proletarian revolutions set off by the October Revolution in Russia;
2   the working class of the capitalist states; and
3   the national–liberation movements in the colonies and semi–colonies of the major capitalist powers.

The Comintern was established specifically to orchestrate revolutionary activities in the second and third categories (primarily to foster the development of the first). Meanwhile, the USSR People's Commissariat of Foreign Affairs engaged in more or less normal diplomatic relations with as many countries as possible.

Soviet policy towards China reflected this dual approach. While having established diplomatic ties with the nominal government in Peking, Moscow used the Comintern to assist the military and political development of the Kuomintang under Sun Yat–sen and his military deputy Chiang Kai–shek in Canton in the south of the country. It was expected that this national liberation movement, politically strengthened and guided by the Comintern's representatives, would eventually extend its power nationally. In the process it would be taken over by the increasingly strong Communist Party elements in its military and political nucleus.[2] Chiang, of course, had other ideas, and in 1927, when he felt strong enough, he moved to eliminate his erstwhile communist allies. The ensuing recriminations in the Soviet Politburo and the Comintern led Stalin thereafter to distrust non–communist leaders of national liberation movements and relatively to de–emphasise revolutionary activity in the Third World.

We noted in chapter 2 that, as the tide of world revolution ebbed and as the Soviet Union gained confidence in its ability to deal with capitalist powers, direct diplomacy generally assumed priority over Comintern activities for the promotion of Soviet international interests. However, the relative standing of the two main arms of Soviet policy depended on current perceptions of the world situation, with the Comintern, functioning increasingly as a vehicle for the activities of Soviet intelligence agencies abroad, continuing to play a vital ancillary role. The prognosis of a renewal of revolutionary conditions at the Sixth Comintern Congress in 1928 accordingly led to an upsurge in militancy by the various national 'sections' of the Comintern and a corresponding relative downgrading of normal diplomatic activity — relative, but not absolute, since in the intervening years until the popular front period of 1935–39, Soviet diplomats were very active in agitating for non–aggression pacts with whoever would agree to conclude them.

The main arena of this campaign was Europe. The collapse of the effort to transplant the experience of the Bolshevik Revolution to China led to a major shift in the centre of gravity of Soviet foreign policy back to the traditional heartland of world imperialism. As in the immediate postwar period, once the revolutionary wave had passed, Soviet policy settled down to the search for accommodation with the main centres of international power, pressing for diplomatic recognition where it was not yet forthcoming and trying to consolidate economic and political relations where it was. Foreign Commissar Maksim Litvinov was particularly active, albeit often in a 'spoiler's' role, in the spate of arms reduction negotiations which occupied much of the attention of European diplomats in the late 1920s and early 1930s.[3]

The upsurge of aggressive Fascism and Nazism in the 1930s certainly assisted Soviet efforts to rally concerned liberals and radicals through the various 'front' organisations in support of Moscow's campaign for peace and 'collective security'. The proclamation of the 'popular front' policy at the Seventh Congress of the Comintern in July–August 1935 gave the campaign powerful organisational impetus. Communist Party membership throughout the Western liberal–capitalist world increased significantly during this period, and participation in aid for Republican Spain and various other anti–Fascist projects became a badge of commitment in progressive circles throughout the West.[4]

The main features of Soviet policy from 1934 to the middle of 1939 included support for popular front governments in Europe and the downplaying of revolutionary aims by local Communist Parties, against the background of intensive Soviet agitation in the League of Nations, particularly against German and Italian intervention in Spain. Mounting Japanese aggression in China during the period also occupied Soviet diplomatic and military attention. There were direct military clashes between units of the Red Army and Japanese Imperial forces in Mongolia and the Far Eastern border region, and the USSR was extremely concerned over the danger of a two–front war in the event of the collapse of collective security against the Axis in Europe. To that end Soviet diplomacy sought to enlist Western political assistance to exert pressure on Japan for a peaceful settlement of problems in the Far East. However, the primary focus of Soviet activity remained Western Europe.

The failure of the collective security policy in Europe, demonstrated by the collapse of the Spanish Loyalists, Chamberlain's sellout to Hitler at Munich and the refusal of the smaller Eastern European states to accept direct Soviet military involvement in the defence of Czechoslovakia, brought an abrupt change in the direction of Soviet foreign policy. The Molotov–Ribbentrop Non–aggression Pact of 23 August 1939 put an end to this era of more or less 'normal' Soviet diplomacy and signified another period of turning inward, again under the ideological banner of a 'new revolutionary wave' in Europe. Now the Comintern directed its subordinate Communist Parties against the Western Allies as the 'main danger' to world peace; communist agitation against the Axis powers ceased virtually over night. Western progressives were stunned, and support of Soviet policy lost most of its appeal in 'radical chic' circles, at least until the German attack on the USSR in June 1941. Soviet opportunism during the heyday of the Hitler–Stalin alliance was particularly brazen. With Hitler's grudging assent, Stalin acquired virtually all of the territories in the western borderlands of the Soviet Union that had once been part of the Tsarist Empire, and further plans envisaged Soviet participation in the division of the spoils of the British Empire in the south and east. Even Hitler was openly discomfitted by the greed of his Soviet ally, which impelled him to speed up the timetable for his long–contemplated invasion of Russia.[5]

The wartime alliance with the West saw a return of Soviet reliance on the techniques of formal diplomacy. Stalin took major steps to ingratiate himself with his allies and to increase his support at home by discarding some of the more egregious features of his regime. He de–emphasised the overt ideological promotion of its aims and institutional arrangements, for example, by removing restrictions on the Russian Orthodox Church, curbing overt anti–semitism and by invoking traditional Russian patriotism to rally his people. He joined Roosevelt and Churchill in endorsing a common commitment to democratic and humanitarian aims for the postwar world, and he warmly encouraged the operations of Western diplomatic and military missions on Soviet territory.

These concessions were born only of desperation and expediency, however. With the passing of the danger of a Nazi victory by the middle of 1943, many of the changes were gradually rescinded, and by the end of hostilities with Japan in September 1945, the seeds of the Cold War had already been sown. The death of US President Roosevelt and the unexpected political demise of Churchill in 1945 undoubtedly contributed to the dissipation of the warm, but tough–minded, spirit of co–operation which had characterised Allied relations during the war. Stalin's determination to install puppet regimes in the areas of Eastern and Central Europe under Soviet military control and his fear of the US monopoly of the atomic bomb under a less friendly American President, Harry S. Truman, certainly did the rest. In a famous remark in the spring of 1945 to Milovan Djilas, then a member of a high–level Yugoslav Communist Party mission to the USSR, Stalin expressed the view that the Soviet Union would have to begin preparations for another war with the West in fifteen or twenty years.[6]

This prospect coloured Soviet attitudes towards the relative weight of diplomatic and military–revolutionary activities in the conduct of Soviet external policies until Stalin's death. The communist coup in Czechoslovakia, the failure of Communist Party disruptions in Italy and France in 1948 and, finally, the collapse of the Berlin Blockade in 1949 signalled the end of Stalin's postwar hopes for further expansion in Europe. The series of purges of the East European satellite regimes following the ouster of Tito from the Cominform in 1948 marked the beginning of the consolidation of the European 'socialist camp', as Stalin undertook to impose the Soviet model in its original form throughout the Bloc.

The victory of Mao Zedong in China in October 1949 presented unexpected new opportunities — and problems — for Soviet global objectives in Asia. Furthermore, the outbreak of the Korean War nine months later demonstrated Stalin's willingness to take advantage of the new situation to maintain revolutionary momentum. The anticipated speedy victory in Korea was prevented by US military intervention and General MacArthur's landing at Inchon in September, but Stalin seized the opportunity to keep the United States militarily involved in a prolonged stalemate with the Chinese while he completed the reconstruction of the Soviet economy and laid the foundations for future Soviet military preponderance on a global scale. During this period the Soviet Union succeeded in breaking the American monopoly on nuclear weapons.

Unconventional instruments of Soviet foreign policy

At this point it is useful to review the types of unconventional instruments that were developed under Lenin and Stalin for the pursuit of Soviet foreign policy objectives in parallel with the institutions and practices of formal diplomacy. These and similar institutions continued to be used by their successors, with perhaps different methods and target populations and at a relatively higher level of sophistication. Individual instruments and techniques were sometimes given new objectives and operational techniques.

Some of the earliest institutions, such as the International Trade Union Council (*Mezhsovprof*), set up in 1920 and the International Workers' Aid, established in 1921, were originally designed to create a Soviet–controlled alternative to existing organisations, just as the Comintern had initially been founded to combat the revival of the Socialist International. Indeed, all of them were in fact creations of the Comintern and worked under the direction of its Executive (ECCI) as fronts for rallying specific categories of foreign citizens in support of Soviet objectives. In 1921 *Mezhsovprof* was transformed into the 'Profintern', also known as the 'Red Trade Union International', which, in 1945, was reincarnated as the World Federation of Trade Unions.

Early debates between advocates of maintaining the Profintern's international profile and its operational independence of the Comintern in order to broaden its appeal on the one hand, and those demanding its direct subordination to Moscow on the other, were quickly settled in favour of the latter point of view. The Communist Youth International, founded in Berlin in 1919 by the young German communist Willi Muenzenberg, followed the same pattern. In 1921 Muenzenberg was given a seat on the ECCI, and he duly pledged his loyalty to Moscow.[7] Muenzenberg would go on to become one of the Comintern's most successful apparatchiks and propagandists in the 1930s, before he was purged along with many other foreign communists during Stalin's Great Purge.

Another interesting front organisation established by the Comintern in October 1923, was the Peasant International, or *Krestintern*. Its objective was to organise the peasant masses of the poorer countries in Europe and the colonies, where the working class was not yet an important political factor and where Soviet leaders anticipated potential revolutionary support for its struggle against world imperialism. Important foreign peasant leaders, such as Alexander Stamboliisky, the leader of the Bulgarian Agrarian Party, and Stjepan Radic, the charismatic head of the Croatian

Peasant Party, had a fleeting association with the *Krestintern*. Their eventual break with it reflected the tension between international peasant interests and the organisation's blatant subservience to Moscow, a contradiction that was recognised in some Soviet circles as well, notably by Leon Trotsky.[8]   Stalin's increasing domination of the Soviet Communist Party, however, signified the victory of the desideratum of firm Muscovite control over concern for organisational effectiveness.

During the 1930s, especially after Adolph Hitler's ascension to power in Germany, these tensions were yet to become fully apparent. The front organisations played an important dual role in Soviet foreign operations. They provided a rallying point for foreign non–party sympathisers and a broad spectrum of anti–Fascists in the fight against Hitler and Mussolini and against right–wing political elements unwilling to take a firm stand against Fascism in their own countries. The publishing activities of the fronts received generous support from the Comintern's coffers. At the same time, along with the local Communist Parties which controlled them, the front organisations in the various Western countries served as a useful cover for the activities of Soviet intelligence agents, including the identification of potential recruits for Soviet covert operations. Given the atmosphere in Europe in the 1930s, it is not surprising that persons of an activist temperament often responded positively to opportunities to 'do something' in the struggle against Fascism. As noted above, the abrupt shift of Stalin's policy to alliance with Hitler in 1939 was a tremendous shock to these people, but the post–June 1941 collaboration between the USSR and the Western Allies quickly repaired the damage.[9]   Front organisations regularly sponsored programs to assist the Soviet war effort in allied countries.

In general, during the war, local Communist Parties found themselves in the mainstream of political life in their own countries for the first time. Some of them, in the Axis–occupied countries such as Italy, France and Greece, took a leading role in the resistance movements.[10]   The euphoria of wartime co–operation persisted into the postwar era, and many of those active in campaigns to assist the Soviet Union continued to favour a soft line towards Moscow in the early days of the Cold War. In the United States they constituted an important element in former Vice–President Henry A. Wallace's Progressive Party's challenge to Truman for the Presidency in the 1948 election.

Another organisational technique was the creation of Soviet friendship societies in most countries throughout the world. In Australia, for example, the 'Friends of the Soviet Union', established in 1930 by the

Communist Party of Australia, and declared illegal along with the CPA in 1940, reappeared once the CPA was again permitted to function legally during the wartime alliance period as the 'Australia–Soviet Friendship League'.[11] Soviet friendship societies have continued to play a role as extensions of local Communist Parties in maintaining a channel for Soviet propaganda and other pro–Soviet activities. However, their appeal has largely been limited to the 'converted' and their sympathisers. Their obvious organisational connection with the USSR has tended to reduce their potential as agencies of influence in most Western countries.

Soviet trade organisations in foreign countries have been another active instrument of foreign policy and intelligence operations. As a result of the state monopoly of foreign trade decreed by Lenin in 1918, these trade offices abroad had considerably greater importance for the organisation and conduct of trade with the Soviet Union than is usually the case in international commercial relations. Businessmen wishing to engage in trade with the USSR had to deal through the Soviet trade office in their country. This facilitated the expansion of Soviet political and intelligence activities and served as a useful cover for operations outside normal diplomatic channels. On at least one notable occasion this concentration of trade activities under the tutelage of Soviet Embassy officials led to extremely serious complications for the USSR. On 12 May 1927, Scotland Yard raided the headquarters of the Anglo–Russian Commercial Society (Arcos) on suspicion that it was operating as a cover for Soviet espionage and propaganda activities. The raid found little that was particularly sinister, but the British Government used the evidence collected in the raid as one of the principal justifications for severing diplomatic relations with the USSR two weeks later.[12] As with the case of the Comintern itself (for example, the notorious forgery of the so–called 'Zinoviev Letter' in 1924), the reputation of Soviet–affiliated institutions as centres of subversion was sometimes exaggerated by anti–communist politicians for their own domestic political purposes.[13] To be sure, other countries have also used commercial activities as a cover for intelligence operations; the Soviets and their partner states simply do so in a more systematic and institutionalised manner.

Unique among the non–diplomatic instruments of Soviet foreign policy have been the various international front organisations, such as the World Peace Council, the Christian Peace Conference, the Afro–Asian People's Solidarity Committee, the World Federation of Democratic Youth and the World Federation of Trade Unions, which have long been used to promote Soviet policies in world affairs. Most of them have their headquarters outside the Soviet Union, although they remain closely co–

ordinated by the International Department of the CPSU Central Committee and are skilfully utilised as a cover for operations of the KGB and the GRU (military intelligence). On the whole, these bodies have been remarkably successful in using the anti–imperialist rhetoric and the millenarian peace themes of Marxist–Leninist ideology, as well as the widespread fear of a nuclear holocaust, to reach a much wider audience than would be possible for organisations more overtly linked to the Soviet state.[14] The philosophy behind the massive Soviet effort to maintain these organisations was reflected in the cynical comment by Georgii Dimitrov, the General Secretary of the Comintern, in the 1930s: 'One sympathizer is generally worth more than a dozen militant communists. A writer of reputation, or a retired general, are worth more than five hundred poor devils who won't know any better than to get themselves beaten up by the police.'[15]

The World Peace Council (WPC) has been the most extensive and durable of these international front organisations and can be considered a paradigm of their structures and modes of operation. Its origins lay in the 'World Congress of Intellectuals for Peace' convened in Poland in 1948 to orchestrate pressure against the United States and its monopoly of the atomic bomb. This effort was followed the next year by the establishment in Paris of the 'World Committee of Partisans of Peace', subsequently renamed the 'World Peace Council' in 1950.[16] One of its initial actions was to organise a 'peace ballot' in France in conjunction with 'World Peace Day' on 2 October 1949, when it managed to obtain seven million signatures in that country alone. The following year it organised the 'Stockholm Peace Appeal' to enlist worldwide support for Soviet initiatives for international prohibition of nuclear weapons, which the USSR was soon to possess itself. By the end of 1950 the 'Appeal' had succeeded in obtaining some 600 million signatures, including almost 35 million in France, Italy and the USA alone. (Most of the rest were from Communist Party–ruled states.)[17]

Since the early 1960s the WPC has been headed by Romesh Chandra, an Indian communist who has made no secret of his organisation's support for Soviet foreign policy, including the invasion of Afghanistan. From its headquarters in Helsinki, Vienna (from which it was expelled for subversive activity) and, since 1977, Geneva, the WPC has been involved in the orchestration of numerous international campaigns. Its activities reflected Soviet recognition of the effectiveness of demonstrations against the Vietnam War in Western countries in hampering the US government's prosecution of that unpopular war. Especially prominent among Chandra's projects were the anti–'neutron bomb' campaign in Europe and the United

States in the late 1970s and the campaign for a nuclear 'freeze' to head off the deployment of US Pershing–2 and cruise missiles in Western Europe in response to the Soviet deployment of SS–20 intermediate–range, triple–warhead missiles in the middle 1970s. Chandra was remarkably successful in preventing the further development of the neutron bomb by the United States, and in early 1978 he was even invited to testify before members of the US Congress on the issue.[18] He was less successful in preventing the emplacement of the Pershing–2s and cruise missiles by NATO in 1983, however, despite massive protest demonstrations, including around half a million Americans who marched in favour of the 'freeze' in New York on 12 June 1982 under the leadership of prominent American peace campaigners from the anti–Vietnam War movement.

The increasingly obvious Soviet diplomatic and intelligence involvement in these campaigns and Soviet aggressive moves throughout the world eventually combined to diminish the effectiveness of front activities and demonstrated the limits of their utility for the promotion of Soviet objectives. Nevertheless, even their partial successes showed that there was a huge potential public outside the Soviet Bloc that was sufficiently uncomfortable with the often unsubtle and insensitive American leadership of the various anti–communist alliance systems to be receptive to Soviet–sponsored initiatives. Even where the local Communist Party connection and direct Soviet involvement were understood, many prominent peace campaigners from various secular and church–based pacifist movements and even 'Generals for Peace' — a group of former high–ranking NATO officers who rejected the thrust of US nuclear strategy — agreed to involvement in the activities of the fronts because the latter could provide the organisational and financial support necessary for the pursuit of their objectives. In this sense, what was often involved was a presumption of congruence of what these people considered worthy aims with those of the Soviet Union and not merely a case of the exploitation of their naivety by the USSR. Eventually the unpopularity of certain Soviet policies, such as the occupation of Afghanistan and the imposition of martial law in Poland, led many of these pacifist groups to try to keep their distance from the USSR and to avoid being completely swallowed up by its front organisations.

Ironically, the front relationships came to exert some reverse influence on at least the tactics and presentation of Soviet foreign policy and probably made them somewhat more defensive and circumspect than they might otherwise have been, particularly towards the end of the Brezhnev era. The extension of the potential mass constituency of Soviet foreign policy *via* the international front organisations was thus a two–edged sword: on the one hand, it provided widespread public support for Soviet policy and opportunities for the recruitment of 'agents of influence' and other auxiliaries for the conduct of diplomatic and intelligence activities; on the other, publicised espionage scandals sensitised many of the 'innocents' to the realities of Soviet control and eventually made the organisations themselves seem somewhat less reliable to Moscow as an instrument of its foreign policy.

New perspectives, new instruments

Effective use of uncoventional techniques became more feasible with the advent of the more imaginative and resourceful leadership of Nikita S. Khrushchev. Khrushchev's approach to foreign policy was in many ways similar to that of Gorbachev some 30 years later. He too sought to reduce confrontation with the West to gain a breathing space for addressing the accumulated problems of economic stagnation and bureaucratic sclerosis. Like Gorbachev, he perceived the opportunities of a climate of reduced tensions for expanding Soviet influence by economic, political and diplomatic methods in regions previously outside the traditional arenas of Soviet interest.

Khrushchev discarded Stalin's dogmatic two–camp approach to nationalist leaders in the colonial and newly independent countries and foresaw the potential benefits of active Soviet support for such movements. He began the process with arms shipments to Nasser's Egypt in 1955 and shortly thereafter began to extend economic and military assistance to a limited number of other target countries, including India and Indonesia — all founding members of the non–aligned movement. Khrushchev's extensive travels in Asia with Premier Nikolai Bulganin in 1955 and 1956 put him in personal contact with the leaders of this emerging movement. He perceived it as a potential adjunct to the socialist camp but was wise enough not to go beyond stressing common anti–imperialist perspectives.

Khrushchev and Mao Zedong hammered out an agreement on a geographic division of their countries' zones of paramount interest in the Third World, South and East Asia generally being assigned to the Chinese sphere of influence. In 1957, in partnership with the Chinese, he established the Afro–Asian People's Solidarity Organisation and convinced Nasser to permit its headquarters to be located in Cairo, where it reportedly became a cover for KGB operations in Africa and the Middle East.[19] The rift with China, which occurred shortly thereafter, left the Soviets in sole

control of this organisational asset. The bonanza of Fidel Castro's
accession to the Soviet Bloc in the early 1960s provided a new entree for
Soviet interests in Latin America. Under Khrushchev, the KGB developed
a tutelary relationship with the Cuban intelligence agency, the DGI, which
served as an important extension of Soviet intelligence capacity in the
Third World and, eventually, in the international terrorist fraternity.[20]
Later, under Brezhnev, Castro would become an important, relatively
autonomous force in the communist world in his own right, a force for
revolutionary activism and ideological purity that was sometimes an
embarrassment to the USSR. Fidel's attempt to bind the non–aligned
movement to the Soviet Bloc when he became its Chairman in 1977
alienated many of its most prominent figures — most notably, President
Josip Broz Tito of Yugoslavia, one of the movement's founders — and
undoubtedly reduced its cohesiveness and utility for Soviet purposes.

The climate of detente in Europe promoted by Brezhnev in the early
1970s, despite the shock of the WTO invasion of Czechoslovakia in 1968,
provided fertile soil for the development of the various peace movements in
Western Europe throughout the decade. Agreements with Washington on a
partial nuclear test ban and on anti–ballistic missile deployments and the
first Strategic Arms Limitation Treaty (SALT I) encouraged the
development of the West European peace movement, especially after
Soviet relations with the United States began to sour later in the decade
because of the expansion of Soviet military and political influence in
Africa, the Middle East and Latin America.

For a while, as we have seen, Brezhnev and his colleagues were able to
use the threat of nuclear confrontation to develop a strong peace
constituency against efforts by NATO to respond to Soviet conventional
and nuclear arms deployments in Europe. However, the contradictions
between Soviet–inspired peace initiatives and the growing weight of
military and intelligence factors in the conduct of Soviet foreign policy
towards the end of the Brezhnev era (e.g. in Afghanistan, Poland and in the
rapid expansion of Soviet military and naval power) eventually led to a
decline in the effectiveness of Moscow's peace propaganda and undermined
the efforts of the network of front organisations. This was particularly true
in the United States, where President Reagan's vociferous anti–communist
stance and his active sponsorship of armed resistance to Soviet client
regimes in the Third World effectively frustrated the efforts of the peace
movement and demonstrated its limitations as an influence on American
strategic policy.

The differences between Khrushchev's and Brezhnev's approaches were
apparent in other areas as well. Khrushchev's political and organisational

initiatives had not been limited to the non–communist world. In place of the Cominform, which he had caused to be dissolved in May 1956, partly as a concession to Tito, Khrushchev instituted the practice of convening international conferences of Communist Parties to co–ordinate their policies and assert Soviet ideological primacy in the 'Socialist Commonwealth' (largely in response to Mao's increasing challenge to Soviet hegemony). Important world conferences were held in Moscow in 1957 and 1960, at which Khrushchev tried to paper over differences with the Chinese. In 1957 he created a new department of the CPSU Central Committee for Liaison with Ruling Communist Parties and nominated Yuri Andropov, the Soviet Ambassador in Budapest in 1956, as its first head. Its primary function was to facilitate continuing Soviet supervision of the domestic and foreign policies of these parties, just as the International Department did with respect to parties and movements in the non–communist world. After the split with the Chinese, and especially after the Warsaw Pact invasion of Czechoslovakia under Brezhnev, both departments found it increasingly difficult to maintain ideological and political uniformity in the international movement, as Soviet positions became harder and harder to justify in rapidly changing world circumstances. Brezhnev's attempts, after the invasion of Czechoslovakia, to summon international conferences to gain endorsement of the Soviet line met with determined opposition from important non–Bloc parties, particularly the 'Eurocommunists', the Romanians and the Yugoslavs; when the conferences were finally held, in 1969 and 1976, the results were less than satisfactory from the Soviet standpoint.

By the end of the Brezhnev era it was becoming clear that the instruments of Soviet foreign policy and the specific policies themselves were no longer adequate for the opportunities of the new international situation. The two poles of the postwar bipolar superpower confrontation had both been losing their unquestioned pre–eminence, particularly the Soviet pole. China, a potential third superpower, was moving dangerously close to the United States; and Western Europe and Japan had become important power centres in their own right. Some of the developing countries of the Asia–Pacific region had begun to overtake the Soviet Union in their level of civilian economic development and technological sophistication. The existing institutions and practices of Soviet foreign policy, designed primarily for control over 'friends' and subversion and pressure against 'enemies', offered little hope of access to and inclusion in these dynamic world processes.

The late Foreign Minister, Andrei A. Gromyko, who had served in that post since 1957 and who had been promoted to the ruling party

Politburo in 1973, epitomised the stagnation of Soviet external policy. His membership of the Politburo had given him substantially enhanced weight, not only in the conduct, but also in the formulation, of foreign policy, and his basically authoritarian, dogmatic perceptions of the world (he was known in the West, almost affectionately, as 'Mr Nyet') probably influenced, as much as they reflected, official Soviet attitudes. Western dismissal of his ultimative handling of the INF deployment negotiations in 1983 demonstrated the unfruitfulness of his limited repertoire of diplomatic techniques in the new world situation, where the 'correlation of forces' was no longer moving in a direction favourable to the Soviet Union. Gorbachev's replacement of Gromyko by Eduard Shevardnadze in July 1985, barely three months after coming to power, was an important signal of the changes that were to occur in Soviet foreign policy. For the time being Gromyko was 'promoted' to the still largely ceremonial post of Chairman of the Presidium of the USSR Supreme Soviet, from which he was honourably retired in September 1988 to allow Gorbachev to take over that post. Gromyko died some ten months later, just before his 80th birthday.

New political thinking and new techniques

Shevardnadze, formerly party First Secretary in the republic of Georgia, had had no previous foreign policy experience. Gorbachev had reportedly been impressed by his flexible worldview and by the general political style and skill he had demonstrated in his handling of the difficult economic, social and ethnic problems of his volatile native republic. In any case, Gorbachev plainly intended to take personal charge of foreign policy. To this end he made signficant personnel and institutional changes in the machinery of party control in that area. Boris Ponomarev, the dogmatic, long–serving head of the International Department, was summarily pensioned off and replaced by Anatolii Dobrynin, the veteran Soviet Ambassador to Washington. The Department for Liaison with Ruling Communist Parties was subsequently abolished and its functions apparently transferred to the International Department.

It soon became evident that this shift in the centre of gravity of foreign policy–making to the CPSU Central Committee was basically a holding operation, designed to instil new conceptions and outline new strategies and priorities in international relations while the governmental foreign policy establishment inherited from Gromyko underwent a thorough restructuring and personnel shakeup. The organisation of the

Ministry of Foreign Affairs had remained virtually unchanged since the time of Czar Nicholas II.[21] Its geographic departments reflected a bygone era with its old patterns of alliances and political commitments. Australia, for example, was included in the 'Second European Department' along with Canada, Ireland, Malta, New Zealand and the United Kingdom — that is, mainly the old English–speaking parts of the British Empire. Communist and non–communist countries were commonly lumped together in the same department. Thus, East Germany (the GDR) was listed alongside West Germany and Austria in the Third European Department, while Bulgaria, Cyprus, Greece, Hungary, Romania and Yugoslavia were all covered by the Fifth European Department. The Southeast Asian Department grouped together Cambodia, Laos, Malaysia, Singapore, Thailand and Vietnam; while Indonesia, Japan and the Philippines were in the Second Far Eastern Department. (China, North Korea and Mongolia were under the First Far Eastern Department.)

In the latter half of May 1986, Gorbachev convened a secret meeting at the MFA attended by party and government officials involved in foreign affairs as well as the heads of all Soviet diplomatic missions abroad. Seconded by his chief ideological lieutenant and *perestroika* supporter Aleksandr Yakovlev, socialist countries liaison chief Vadim Medvedev and ID chief Dobrynin, Gorbachev is reported, among other things, to have presented a general statement of the new Soviet foreign policy priorities, prescribed changes in the style and negotiating techniques of Soviet diplomacy and ordered a cleanup of the MFA itself.[22] Major personnel changes took place at the second and third levels of the MFA hierarchy (first deputy and deputy ministers): the two serving first deputy ministers were replaced by three new people (two of whom were promoted from deputy minister); the number of deputy ministers was raised from eight to nine, of whom six were new appointees. Several major new agencies were created:

1 an Administration for Problems of Arms Reduction and Disarmament, headed by Viktor Karpov;
2 an Administration for Humanitarian and Cultural Ties, headed by Yuri Kashlev; and
3 an Information Administration, headed by Gennady Gerasimov.

Among the geographic departments, a new Department of Pacific Ocean Countries was established, covering Australia, New Zealand, the Pacific Island states, Japan, Papua New Guinea, Indonesia, Malaysia, the Philippines, Singapore and Thailand. Communist states were now grouped together under separate Administrations, for Europe and Asia (although Cuba continued to be covered by the First Latin American Department, which also included the Caribbean Basin, Costa Rica, Guatemala, Guyana, Jamaica, Mexico, Nicaragua, Suriname and Trinidad–Tobago). Canada was now assigned to an expanded Department for the United States and Canada, which had previously been devoted to the United States alone. A number of the previous geographic departments were subordinated to new regional administrations — for example, the Near Eastern and North African Countries Administration, which also contained a separate department for 'regional issues and problems' or, as in the case of the new Department of Pacific Ocean Countries, a 'Regional, Political and Economic Questions Department'. Important personnel changes were also made in Soviet diplomatic missions abroad. Roughly one–third of all Soviet Ambassadors were replaced, including half of all Ambassadors to the NATO countries and a substantial proportion of the representation in the socialist countries.[23]

The significance of these structural and personnel shifts soon became evident in the kaleidoscopic initiatives which sprang forth from Moscow to change the Soviet image in world affairs. Gorbachev was now explicitly seeking to involve the USSR in international economic and political processes from which its leaders had traditionally sought to exclude themselves and which they had once attempted to disrupt wherever possible. This meant, for example, a new, more supportive attitude toward the United Nations and the Nonaligned Movement. It also meant active assistance in the settlement of local conflicts which the Soviet Union had once helped to foment — most notably, Afghanistan, Angola and Cambodia. There was also a perceptible shift away from the sponsorship of anti–government protest movements in the non–communist world in favour of direct contacts with the governments concerned and with other organised political forces in the mainstream of political life, such as Social–democratic and Labour Parties.

In some ways, the policy was reminiscent of the popular front strategy of the 1930s, but there were important differences. For one thing, the role of the local Communist Parties was now almost totally ignored as embarrassing baggage from the past. To the extent that the activities of these parties continue to be controlled from Moscow, they are now being directed to favour centrist, and even right–wing government forces.[24] For another, instead of trying to establish alternatives to existing non–communist international bodies, such as the EC, the World Bank, the IMF and the International Confederation of Free Trade Unions, the Soviet Union has sought to join or merge its surrogates with these bodies in order to become a fully fledged participant in what Gorbachev now recognises as the centres of real action in the world. Soviet enthusiasm for membership in the emerging Pacific trade bloc currently being promoted by the Australian government is a good illustration of this change in attitude.

On the other hand, there does not seem to have been any corresponding de-emphasis of the operations of Soviet intelligence agencies. If anything, under the leadership of the new head of the KGB, Vladimir Kryuchkov, a veteran intelligence professional who was formerly in charge of overseas operations and 'disinformation' activities abroad, KGB and GRU activities seem to have increased, particularly in the most sophisticated aspects of the trade.[25] There can be little doubt that the new, peaceful and constructive image of Soviet foreign policy, which has facilitated the expansion of Soviet diplomatic and economic representation throughout the world, greatly enhances opportunities for intelligence activities. The fact that Kryuchkov was elevated directly to full membership in the party Politburo in September 1989 certainly enhances the role of the KGB in the decision-making process.[26] The upgrading of the status and activities of the KGB does not seem to have been a major consideration in the change of foreign policy orientation, merely a useful by-product; it may be related more closely to Soviet domestic events, such as the need to combat the upsurge of local nationalism and internal Kremlin politics. In any case, the uncovering of expanded Soviet espionage activities does not appear to have unduly hampered the generally favourable reception of Gorbachev's initiatives for improvement of the international climate. If these activities eventually do undermine his image-building efforts, it will be interesting to see how the contradiction between the two processes is resolved and how much of the intelligence-gathering function is sacrificed or at least reduced in intensity.

Conclusions

The revolutionary ideological origins of the Soviet state gave its leaders a potential overseas constituency that was unique in the annals of modern international relations. (One is reminded of the international popularity of revolutionary France before the rise of Napoleon.) Moscow developed a network of international front organisations, based on the Comintern, which it was able to manipulate in support of Soviet policies. In time, Soviet party and intelligence officials acquired considerable skill in managing these organisations, while concealing from their mass membership the often sordid realities of Soviet objectives and practices. Under Stalin's grim, inward-looking leadership, however, it is probably fair to say — echoing Trotsky — that the Soviet Union's revolutionary reputation and the associated non–conventional instruments of Soviet foreign policy were not used to full advantage, and many potential opportunities were lost.

As in many other areas, Nikita Khrushchev brought fresh perspectives on the scope and modalities of Soviet foreign policy. In particular, he opened up the Third World to Soviet influence and penetration to such an extent that the 'correlation of forces' in the world for a time seemed destined to shift to the advantage of socialism. But as in many other areas, Khrushchev was too impatient and frequently overplayed his hand. His successors learned perhaps too much and too superficially from both his successes and his failures. They permitted the imaginative diplomatic and political techniques he often successfully employed to atrophy, while focusing on the purely military aspects of Soviet national power and influence in the hope of avoiding the need to back away from direct confrontation in situations of opportunity after bluff and bluster had failed, as they had for Khrushchev during the Cuban missile crisis.

Moreover, Khrushchev's successors were perhaps marginally less adept than he at managing the problems of empire and adjusting to a situation where Moscow's ideological and political writ was no longer automatically accepted as authoritative in the socialist world. He had a vision of relations among socialist states in which the bonds of ideology and institutional linkages — through the WTO, CMEA and periodic international conferences — would replace the terror and unconditional subordination of the Stalin era. Khrushchev's successors evidently lacked this vision and concentrated primarily on the mechanical aspects of these institutional ties.

Throughout the period from the late 1920s to the mid–1980s, however, there were serious contradictions between the international ideological goals of the Soviet Union as the centre of world revolution and the national interests of the Soviet state as a potential and actual superpower. These contradictions were reflected in the operations of the network of front organisations. To the extent that they were universal in their appeal and aspirations, they were successful; to the extent that they were merely a figleaf for the promotion of narrow Soviet interests they were eventually unsuccessful and even an encumbrance to a country whose economy and political system were facing heavy weather in trying to maintain its superpower status in a changing world. One of Gorbachev's great merits has been his recognition of the existence of these contradictions and of the need to tailor the ideological goals and approaches of Soviet foreign policy to what he perceives as the universal requirements of the contemporary era. Judging by the international reception his worldwide initiatives have received so far, his perceptions appear to be correct. Time will tell whether he has the time and political opportunity, at home and abroad, to fashion the policies and instrumentalities to bring his visions to reality.

Part II Regional patterns of Soviet foreign policy

Economic, political and ideological competition between capitalist and socialist countries is inevitable. However, it can and must be kept within a framework of peaceful competition which necessarily envisages co-operation. It is up to history to judge the merits of each particular system. It will sort out everything. Let every nation decide which system and which ideology is better.

Gorbachev

4 The Soviet Union and the capitalist world

Introduction

Since well before the October Revolution, Bolshevik party leaders have had a peculiar love–hate relationship with the advanced capitalist world. On the one hand, they were committed to its overthrow and replacement by socialism on a world scale. On the other hand, the West represented the standard of technical and economic achievement to which the Soviet Union and its later acolytes aspired. Indeed, according to the vulgarised interpretation of Marxism employed by Lenin's successors, the Soviet Union and its socialist partners would cross the threshhold of communism only when they had 'overtaken and surpassed' the leading capitalist powers in the per capita production of certain key items — steel, for example. For a while, during the 1950s and 1960s, it seemed as if this goal was within reach; in fact, Soviet production of certain products did surpass that of the USA — but well after these items, such as steel, basic farm machinery and simple machine tools, had ceased being the determinants and symbols of technological modernity in the era of 'scientific and technological revolution'. Although the quality of Soviet products remained well below contemporary world standards, impressive quantitative advances continued to be registered.

The actual slowdown in economic growth in the latter 1970s was, consequently, a serious blow, not only to the Soviets' ability to compete economically, politically and militarily with the West, but also to their leaders' ideological self–confidence and sense of historical mission. Their authority and the correctness of their policies began to be questioned even by previously loyal elements within the socialist world, most notably the Eurocommunist parties in Western Europe and the various dissident

63

movements at home and in Eastern Europe. The immediate response was to try to insulate the regions under Moscow's control against Western liberalising influences and to seek further development within the Panglossian sheltered workshop of 'real socialism' — a system that was not really 'socialist' but was asserted to be as near to it as possible under the (largely self–imposed) constraints of 'hostile capitalist encirclement' and the still imperfectly socialised human material living under Communist Party rule.

The potency of the West in the imagination of Soviet leaders and their continuing sensitivity to its challenges were illustrated by the reactions of the post–Brezhnev leadership to US President Ronald Reagan's hard–line, anti–Soviet rhetoric and particularly to his reaction to the declaration of martial law in Poland in December 1981. Perhaps even more than his call for sanctions and embargoes and his commitment to developing the Strategic Defence Initiative ('Star Wars'), they were disturbed by his public indictments on the 'ideological plane', for example, his characterisation of the USSR as an 'evil empire' and the 'focus of evil in the modern world' and by his condemnation of Moscow for maliciously 'promoting the use of violence and subversion'.[1]

Soviet fears were given official expression in June 1983, at a Plenary Session of the CPSU Central Committee devoted to ideological questions. Prominent on its agenda was the 'ideological crusade' against socialism allegedly being mounted by world imperialism under the leadership of Ronald Reagan. At the Plenum Konstantin Chernenko, General Secretary Yuri Andropov's man in charge of ideology and the presumptive second–in–command, delivered the main address, where he said, among other things:

> The class enemy is openly declaring its intention to liquidate the socialist order. President Reagan has appealed for a new 'crusade' against communism. And imperialism sees in 'psychological warfare' one of the principal instruments for achieving its goal. It is being carried on by the West on the highest, one could say, most hysterical anti–Soviet, anti–communist pitch. The enemy has resorted to downright piracy of the airwaves. We are faced with attempts to organise against us real informational and propaganda intervention, to turn radio and television channels into an instrument of interference in the internal affairs of states and for conducting subversive activities.
>
> That is why it is essential broadly to develop aggressive *counter– propaganda work* not only in the international arena, but also within

the country. Party committees should clearly set forth: what, in what form and by what channels the enemy is trying to force upon us, and give his attacks an up–to–date and convincing rebuff. One cannot leave without a principled party judgment, also, those persons who, consciously or unconsciously, sing, as they say, with an alien voice, spreading all kinds of gossip and rumours. No communist should pass by such phenomena. . . The ideological struggle in the international arena knows no pause. We shall in the future, too, wage it actively, with dignity, without submitting to provocations. The Soviet people may rest assured: in the struggle for securing peace on earth, for the social and national rights of the peoples our party will spare no efforts. [emphasis in the original][2]

The Decree issued by the Plenum on Chernenko's report conveyed the official assessment of contemporary East–West relations in even tougher language:

It is necessary also to keep in view the fact that an acute sharpening of the struggle is occurring in the international arena between the two social systems, the two polar opposite worldviews, which is unprecedented for the whole postwar period. The historical achievements of real socialism, the growth in the authority and influence of the world communist and worker's movement, the progressive development of countries throwing off the yoke of colonial oppression, the upsurge of the national–liberation struggle, the huge scale of the anti–war movement are ever more profoundly affecting the consciousness of peoples throughout the whole world. Imperialist reaction, and first of all the ruling clique of the USA, nurturing delirious plans for world domination, are by their aggressive policy pushing the world to the brink of nuclear catastrophe. Against the Soviet Union and the countries of socialism a psychological war is being waged that is unprecedented in its scale and shamelessness. Unscrupulously employing lies and slander, bourgeois propaganda is striving to blacken the socialist order, to undermine the socio–political and ideological unity of our society. Therefore, the class toughening of the toilers and an uncompromising struggle against bourgeois ideology today acquire special importance.[3]

This was 'old political thinking' *par excellence*. Its significance was open to several levels of interpretation. The tough rhetoric displayed here and in other sections of the June 15th Decree seemed to suggest that the party leadership was profoundly disturbed by the dangerous impasse which the aggressive, military–oriented policies of the past fifteen years had produced. Confronted by a combative opponent like Reagan, who was determined to meet them on their own ground, so to speak, employing rhetorical hyperbole on a par with their own, they seemed genuinely alarmed. Their reflexive reaction was in many respects a throwback to the late 1920s: namely, to batten down the hatches for an indefinite period of defensive isolation and to prepare for the worst. During the ensuing hiatus surrounding Andropov's prolonged and ultimately terminal illness, Reagan himself noted a tendency toward 'introspection' on the part of the Soviet leaders and, in mid–January 1984, he sought to move towards some form of accommodation prior to the opening of the Conference on Confidence and Security in Stockholm.[4]

Another, equally plausible, companion explanation, not necessarily inconsistent with the first, is that the post–Brezhnev leaders were consciously using, not to say exaggerating, the atmosphere of heightened East–West tension in order to justify a restoration of tight political, economic and ideological discipline at home and in the international communist movement, reasserting their leadership while they attempted to work their way out of the increasing difficulties of the system. Chernenko, Gromyko, Andropov and the other Brezhnev holdovers in the Politburo, all heavily involved in shaping the policies which had gotten the country into the present impasse, evidently saw no other way of getting out of it. Accustomed to viewing the West as the source of all external difficulties (and most internal problems as well) and regarding their own conduct and techniques as historically justified and therefore blameless, they saw no remedy but a resort to the tried and tested methods of internal consolidation.

Gorbachev's alternatives

There were alternatives, of course. Small groups of academic analysts had begun in semi–clandestine fashion at about this time to formulate alternative diagnoses of the ills of the Soviet system and its parlous international situation and to suggest proposals for reform.[5] Gorbachev and a number of his colleagues of the post–Stalin generation found many of these unofficial analyses congenial to their aspirations for improving the performance of Soviet socialism at home and abroad. The radical implications of the academic diagnoses were evidently not at first fully understood by the new leaders; or if they did understand them, they found it expedient to conceal their thinking from their more conservative party colleagues.

The transformations Gorbachev ultimately came to endorse were radical indeed. They involved nothing less than a re–examination of the accepted model of socialism itself as a credible alternative to capitalism. Gorbachev and his colleagues dismissed the formulas of 'real socialism', which had been the main conceptual foundation for the return to ideological orthdoxy demanded by the June (1983) Plenum, as a travesty on Marxism–Leninism and mere rationale for the unimaginative policies of their predecessors. As an operating mechanism, too, they judged the institutions of 'real socialism' to be no longer capable of solving the accumulated problems of the Soviet economy and society, let alone of inspiring the admiration and emulation of the world's uncommitted masses.

The path of reform was even more tortuous than Gorbachev and his colleagues initially anticipated, however, and not only because of the obvious difficulties of grafting market elements on the centralised planning and management system, which they were at first reluctant to dismantle to any significant extent.[6] The new leaders understood that ideology was an indispensable component of the structure of legitimacy of Communist Party rule, something they had no intention of giving up. Consequently, rather than discarding socialism entirely, they committed themselves to modernising it and eliminating the dogmatic incrustations which had accumulated around it under Stalin and his successors.[7] Reform, therefore, had to be systematic and made to conform to some recognisably 'socialist' theoretical model. It soon became clear, however, that even in the best of circumstances both the theoretical and practical elements of this ambitious exercise would require a substantial amount of time to elaborate and implement; the tense international situation inherited from their predecessors was a far–from–ideal context for such an endeavour.

That is why the thoroughgoing review of Soviet foreign policy and the flurry of peace and disarmament initiatives associated with the 'new political thinking' became so much an integral part of *perestroika*. The autarchic, inner–directed model of the world of socialism was recognised as no longer valid, if it ever had been, from the standpoint of creating an attractive and viable alternative form of social organisation. It was not merely a matter of pandering to the West in order to be able to buy one's way to economic reform and technological modernisation. Rather it was a question of changing the whole society's way of viewing the outside world and the place of the Soviet Union and its socialist partners within it — and of transforming the image of the socialist world into that of a fully 'normal' and acceptable member of the international community.

The program of transformation contemplated by Gorbachev was thus a dialectical exercise in the truest sense, and it would require a good deal of sensitivity, persistence and tactical flexibility toward both the West and conservative elements in his own camp. It was based on a daring twofold gamble on Gorbachev's part:

1   that the opening to the world would facilitate the transformation of Soviet society itself and the rationalisation of relationships within the Soviet Bloc; and
2   that the process could be sufficiently controlled by Moscow to prevent the world of socialism from disintegrating into chaos and mutual recriminations.[8]

One of the crucial elements of Gorbachev's alternative concerned the role of the military in the new political thinking. As was the case with the economic and political dimensions, changes in thinking on the military emerged only gradually. In Gorbachev's first major policy speech, to the April Plenum of the CC CPSU in 1985, much of the OPT rhetoric remained in evidence. He continued to excoriate the 'aggressive' nature of NATO, the 'plundering role of transnational corporations' and especially the 'ruling circles of the United States of America', whose 'egoistic military course' was said to be evoking 'ever greater criticism and resistance in many countries'. And while holding open the prospect of improving relations with Washington, he qualified this with the warning that progress toward a revival of detente was possible 'only if imperialism renounces efforts to solve the historical conflict between the two social systems by military means'.[9] Large–scale Soviet naval manoeuvres in the Central Pacific — the largest ever seen in that region, according to United States Navy observers — continued to be held after Gorbachev's ascension to power, possibly because they were already in the 'pipeline' when he took over, but perhaps also because he had not yet fully reassessed the effectiveness of the old bluff and bluster approach.[10] Domestic economic considerations and the new, peaceful and constructive image of Soviet foreign policy that Gorbachev was trying to project converged to suggest the need for a shift from the traditionally offensive orientation of Soviet military doctrine to a more defensively oriented doctrine.[11] But there were many obstacles to be overcome before the need for such a shift could be widely accepted.

As was the case with the foreign policy establishment, where change in policy and diplomatic style was possible only after the removal of Foreign Minister Gromyko and his long–serving team of subordinates, real changes in the complexion of the military factor had to await high–level personnel shifts in the armed forces hierarchy. Because of the traditional prestige of the Soviet military establishment and its increased salience in foreign policy and the ideology of 'real socialism' during the Brezhnev years, shifts in this area took somewhat longer to arrange than in foreign policy *per se*. The retirement, late in 1985, of Admiral of the Fleet Sergei Gorshkov — the architect of, and guiding spirit behind, the massive buildup of the Soviet 'blue–water' Navy, with its increasing force–projection capability — and his replacement by Admiral Vladimir N. Chernavin, a pioneer Soviet nuclear submarine professional, had important implications for such a shift in doctrine.[12] The occasion for the removal of the 'old guard' of the Soviet Army, in the person of the Minister of Defence, Marshal Sergei Sokolov, came on 19 May 1987, with the landing in Moscow's Red Square, evidently unhindered by the vaunted National Air Defence Command, of a light plane piloted by West German teenager Mathias Rust. Sokolov was replaced as Defence Minister by an outsider, General Dmitri Yazov, who was presumably more favourably inclined toward Gorbachev's proposals for a change in military doctrine. Subsequent personnel appointments in the Ministry of Defence hierarchy also followed this pattern. The relative downgrading of the military was also facilitated, of course, by its disappointing performance in Afghanistan, which Gorbachev had characterised in his Political Report to the 27th Party Congress in February–March 1986 as a 'bleeding wound'.[13] Unlike the foreign policy establishment, it took Gorbachev the better part of three years to obtain a military establishment he could manage with a substantial degree of confidence.

So far in our analysis we have focused primarily on the introspective, basically passive aspects of the new political thinking. Given the Western media hype around Gorbachev and his famous 'initiatives', it scarcely needs saying that the NPT contains as well many positive elements that have contributed to the more agile and effective prosecution of traditional Soviet national interests. Foremost among them was a more insightful understanding of the immanent and inevitable friction between the United States and its formal and informal partners in the non–communist world. Aleksandr Yakovlev, one of Gorbachev's principal allies in *perestroika* and the NPT, was evidently a leading conduit for these perspectives. He had been a participant in the early student exchanges with the United States in the late 1950s, and from 1973 to 1983 he had served as Soviet Ambassador to Canada. During his sojourns in North America he is alleged to have developed a bitter dislike for the United States and its way of life, as well as an understanding of the opportunities for Soviet foreign policy inherent in the latent tensions in the Western alliance system.[14] Yakovlev and his fellow old North America hand, Anatolii Dobrynin, who had served as Ambassador to Washington for even longer than Yakovlev had done in Canada, were probably largely responsible for Gorbachev's keen sense of the potential of the American media as an instrument of pressure on the administration of any American president. Yakovlev was a prominent participant in the crucial May 1986 review of Soviet foreign policy goals and methods mentioned in chapter 3. His special closeness to Gorbachev as a fellow Andropov *protégé*, his extensive diplomatic experience in the West and his current position as head of the party Central Committee's Commission on International Policy have all contributed to his becoming highly influential in the formulation and conduct of Soviet foreign policy, even more so than Dobrynin, his predecessor until September 1987 as the party's chief foreign policy *apparatchik*.[15] These affinities seem to suggest that Yakovlev and Gorbachev share similar strategic and tactical perspectives, particularly on the central idea that, in both a direct and indirect sense, relations with the United States are the key to effectuating the goals and strategy of Soviet foreign policy under the new political thinking.

Soviet relations with the United States

Despite its relative economic decline in recent years, the United States remains the acknowledged leader of the Western system of political and military alliances. Consequently, any attempt by the USSR to establish regular diplomatic and economic relations in areas within the American sphere of influence — which includes most of the economically and politically significant areas of the globe — requires at least Washington's tacit consent, and preferably its explicit endorsement. Soviet foreign policy–makers have, of course, been aware of this relationship ever since the Second World War. It is the fundamental assumptions and aims underlying Soviet approaches to the USA which are new in the Gorbachev era. Before this period, the Soviets saw Soviet–American agreements as a kind of ratification of the current 'objective' East–West balance of power. They expected Washington to be able to act in the name of its part of the world, while Moscow pledged to do the same for its area — that is, until subsequent 'revolutionary' changes in peripheral areas had further improved the 'correlation of forces', setting the stage for the ratification of a new, more favourable, balance–of–power agreement. Brezhnev's foreign policies, with their reliance on the relentless expansion of Soviet military force–projection capabilities, clearly followed this strategy. It was based on the Leninist conviction that the long–term 'class' interests of the two opposing social systems were permanently irreconcilable and on the equally Leninist notion, expressed in *Imperialism, the Highest Stage of Capitalism*, that the steady chipping away of capitalist interests in the Third World would eventually lead to the collapse of world imperialism and the victory of world socialism (see chapter 1). Nuclear weapons placed certain cautionary restraints on Soviet behaviour; hence the resort to arms control agreements under Brezhnev. But the basic scenario remained unchanged.

The 'new political thinking' rejects much of this argument. Rather than seeking to expand a self–contained world of socialism, Gorbachev has been trying to open it up and expose it to mutual interpenetration with the world of capitalism. This involves a tacit abandonment of the postulates of Lenin's *Imperialism* and their impulse towards continuing class and national–liberation struggle on the periphery. In a sense, it is a reprise of the Stalinist policy from the late 1920s of subordinating the world communist movement, through the Comintern, to the national interests of the Soviet state. But Gorbachev's policies transcend Stalin's approach by working toward nothing less than a change in the overall climate of international relations. He explicitly plays down 'class' considerations in favour of what he argues are overriding global interests in peace and stability so that the Soviet Union can participate in universal processes of development and technological progress.

But that is only part of the story. Gorbachev evidently believes that a modernising socialist world can eventually flourish in such an international order. For this to happen, however, it needs a 'level playing field' — to make up for the time and opportunities lost during the period of self–inforced isolation and 'stagnation'. And that requires cutting the United States 'down to size', by effectively detaching it from its allies and dependants in the capitalist world. This strategy envisages a dual–track approach to relations with the USA and its partners: on the one hand, a continuing dialogue with Washington on strategic international political and military issues; on the other, an economic rapprochement with Western Europe, and if possible Japan, for the accelerated development of the Soviet economy. The first track is necessary for progress on the second. This strategy does not preclude intensified economic relations with the USA. Indeed, competition between the United States and its Western partners for penetration of the allegedly boundless Soviet market is seen as useful — directly, for obtaining the optimal conditions for the Soviet economy, and indirectly, by increasing friction within the Western camp.

But the main thrust of Soviet *economic* policy is toward Western Europe and the EEC, where the potential for binding economic linkages and the eventual political leverage expected to flow therefrom are considered much more advantageous for long–term Soviet interests. This is the strategic rationale behind Gorbachev's favourite slogan of a 'common European home'. In other parts of the world, such as the Asia–Pacific region, the priorities for partnerships are likely to be somewhat different. There, Japan, China, Australia and the rapidly developing smaller Asian countries are being invited to participate in the economic development of the resource–rich, but infrastructurally backward, Soviet Far East and Eastern Siberia. Political and security issues are also heavily involved there as well, as we shall see below.

Nevertheless, Western Europe clearly remains the primary focus of Gorbachev's foreign policy and the most consistent target of his famous 'initiatives'. Undoubtedly one of the main reasons for the frenetic quality of his European diplomacy is the rapid approach of 1992, when a major threshhold of integration of the European Community will have been crossed. Gorbachev clearly seeks to conclude some kind of tenancy arrangement for the USSR and its increasingly putative socialist allies in the 'common European home' before the door is locked and all dealings with it must be conducted *en bloc*, through a supranational EC bureaucracy. Before he could even expect an answer to his knock on the door, however, he had to pay a call on the American concierge.

Paradoxically, the first step toward rapprochement with Washington came from President Reagan. Immediately after the death of Konstantin Chernenko, on 12 March 1985, Reagan extended a personal invitation to Gorbachev to visit Washington and begin discussions on arms control in a letter transmitted by his representative to Chernenko's funeral, Vice–President George Bush.[16] Ten days later, at a press conference, Reagan repeated the call for a Soviet–American summit meeting in the near future. At his first Politburo meeting as General Secretary, Gorbachev said that the USSR was ready to improve relations with the West, but he set firm conditions for such a move and continued to blame Western aggressiveness for the tense state of East–West relations.[17] As we have already noted, these mixed signals — of a readiness to negotiate, but of continuing to hold the West responsible for the arms race and current world tensions — constituted the official Soviet position adopted at the April 1985 Plenum of the CC CPSU, which Gorbachev persistently hails as a decisive turning–point in Soviet history. As far as foreign policy is concerned, however, his Report to the Plenum, taken at face value, seemed to represent very little that was new, pledging only '. . . steadfastly to follow the Leninist course of peace and peaceful coexistence, which is determined by our social order, our morality and worldview.'[18] He vigorously condemned the USA for '. . . openly claiming the "right" to interfere anywhere and everywhere', and for '. . . ignoring and frequently and directly trampling on the interests of other countries and peoples, the traditions of international intercourse, existing treaties and agreements'. He went on to charge that the Americans '. . . continually create sources of conflict and military danger, heating up the situation in one region of the world after another'.[19]

Gorbachev's anti–American rhetoric and his declaratory commitment to consolidate the economic, technological and political capacity of the socialist world seemed to indicate a continuation of the defensive, isolationist phase of the the traditional Soviet foreign policy cycle, begun in the late Brezhnev era. Yet his actions suggested otherwise and indicated that his aggressive tone was directed at world public opinion and at conservative forces in his own country. At the beginning of April, President Reagan announced that Gorbachev had responded positively 'in principle' to his invitation to a summit meeting.[20] Almost simultaneously there was a tacit easing up on Jewish emigration from the USSR, as a number of 'refuseniks' were told that they could reapply for exit visas.[21]

Now it was Washington's turn to heat up the rhetoric on East–West relations. The United States expressed suspicion of the latest Soviet proposals for a moratorium on INF missiles, seeing them as a tactic to delay NATO deployments of Pershing–2 and Tomahawk ground–launched cruise missiles (GLCMs).[22] A few days later Reagan, in an interview with the *Times of London*, accused the Soviet Union of 'misrepresentation, threats and disingenuous peace gestures designed to divide the Western alliance'.[23] At the end of June he raised the issue of Soviet espionage, charging the USSR with 'stealing or buying' American military and industrial secrets and calling for a sharp reduction in the numbers of Soviet diplomats and officials stationed in the USA, alleging that 30 to 40 per cent of the 2500 Soviet personnel in the country were 'known or suspected intelligence agents'.[24] In a similar vein, Gorbachev, in a speech in Moscow on the 40th Anniversary of VE Day on 8 May, denounced US 'militarism', which he called 'a permanent negative factor in international relations' (although he did call for 'a patient and constructive dialogue with the West to check the slide into a nuclear abyss').[25]

These charges and counter–charges continued until September, while both sides undertook a review of the efficacy and appropriateness of their old modes of behaviour in the light of the new prospects for a change in their mutual relations. Significantly, a series of unpublicised official meetings was already in progress to exchange viewpoints and establish 'rules of engagement' for actual and potential points of conflict throughout the world.[26] On 2 July it was announced that the summit meeting between Reagan and Gorbachev would take place on the neutral ground of Geneva, Switzerland from 19 to 21 November 1985.[27]

The Geneva summit meeting marked a turning point in US–Soviet relations, at least to the extent that the two countries' leaders gained a first–hand acquaintance with each other's thinking on major issues and an idea of the directions in which future progress lay. The content of their deliberations was not made public, and the final communique was short on specifics, but the ice had evidently been broken, and agreement was reached on holding further discussions the following year. Gorbachev's remarks on foreign policy in his Political Report to the 27th Congress of the CPSU on 25 February 1986 reflected these changes. While continuing to criticise the US 'military–industrial complex' as the 'locomotive of militarism' in the world, he asserted that its interests were not the same as those of the American people and spoke of a general awareness that the world had grown too small and vulnerable for warfare and a policy of force.[28] And he said that he looked forward to the next summit meeting with President Reagan, where he wished two main issues to head the agenda: a complete ban on testing of nuclear weapons and a treaty on the elimination of intermediate–range nuclear forces.

As it turned out, the next summit, in Reykjavik, Iceland, on 11 and 12 October 1986, was not as successful as either side had anticipated, and both sides downgraded it rhetorically to the status of a 'pre–summit' or 'mini–summit'. [29] Although substantial progress on reconciliation of viewpoints was made initially, especially on the framework for an INF treaty, Gorbachev clearly overplayed his hand by attempting to lure Reagan into abandoning the Strategic Defence Initiative (SDI), presenting this as an integral part of the Soviet arms reduction package and then engaging in 'demonstrative diplomacy' to incite world public opinion against the United States for placing obstacles in the way of agreement.

There can be little doubt that Gorbachev got the better of Reagan in the public relations battle which followed Reykjavik.[30] This caused a certain amount of resentment in Washington and injected a note of caution in future dealings with the cagey Soviet leader, but the results were ultimately beneficial to both sides. On the Soviet side they made Gorbachev face up to the need for genuine concessions to obtain agreements with the United States, particularly as the implications of economic *perestroika* in the USSR made the necessity for such agreements all the more insistent. By the time of the Reykjavik meeting, Soviet officials were already tacitly conceding that the image of their system's economic and human–rights performance at home was exerting a powerful and unavoidable impact on its ability to operate to maximum effect abroad.[31] Some three years later, when the extent of the crisis in the Soviet economy and society was more fully evident, Foreign Minister Eduard Shevardnadze admitted to a Soviet interviewer:

> The achievements of our foreign policy would be much more impressive if we could ensure greater internal stability. The numerous misfortunes that have befallen our country recently, the critical situation in the economy, the state of ethnic relations and natural calamities are reducing the chances of success in our foreign policy.[32]

On the American side, the international pressure on Washington produced by the deluge of well publicised initiatives from Gorbachev made it very difficult to delay for long the presentation of concrete responses and the conclusion of specific agreements, even where the terms offered by the Soviets were considered sub–optimal by some in Reagan's entourage. It seemed clear from these early encounters that Reagan wanted arms–control and other agreements, although perhaps not quite as much as Gorbachev did.[33] To achieve his broader foreign–policy objectives, and to establish the USSR's new image, Gorbachev thus had to meet Reagan more than halfway. The stakes were evidently considered worth the risk, and the gamble has obviously paid off handsomely in many respects.

The thinking reflected on the pages of Gorbachev's much publicised book *Perestroika* (written for Western readers in response to an invitation by an American publisher) suggests that, as of the autumn of 1987, when the book first appeared, the full extent of the concessions needed for the Soviets to gain acceptance in Western 'polite society' was just beginning to dawn on the Soviet leader.[34] Although the Soviet media still found plenty to criticise in Western, and particularly American, conduct of foreign policy, the official line became that the Soviet Union itself had not been blameless for the persistence of tensions in East–West relations. One of the most significant aspects of *glasnost* in the area of foreign policy was Gorbachev's demand that the 'blank spots' of Soviet history, especially in the Stalin era, be filled in by historians in order to present a complete picture of the internal sources of Soviet foreign behaviour which had led to the paranoia and self–imposed isolationism of the world of socialism under Stalin and his successors. Gorbachev himself delivered a foretaste of this reassessment, albeit a relatively bland one, in his address on the 70th anniversary of the Bolshevik Revolution. One of Gorbachev's leading *perestroika* advisers, Professor Georgii Shakhnazarov, a prominent political scientist, referred to his patron's 70th anniversary speech as a model of such historiographic *glasnost*. In expanding on the need for 'real Soviet socialist patriotism', which he said, 'has nothing to do with nationalist self–delusions', Shakhnazarov concluded, 'Nothing elevates a people . . . so much in the eyes of other peoples as an ability to look at past mistakes objectively and courageously.' He also declared:

> [I]t would be hypocritical not to add that along with the excellent internationalist qualities of our society there is evidence of negative things which are due to years–long propaganda in glowing terms suggesting that our country is always and perfectly right as regards its actions on the international scene and to incomplete, often biassed information on the response of this or that section of international opinion to Soviet foreign policy moves.[35]

More radical and concrete examples of the process of historical reassessment were to follow, prompting Western observers to recall the old adage that under socialism it is easy to predict the future; what is impossible to predict is the past.

The objective of this dramatic exercise in rewriting Soviet history was two–fold: first, to indicate to the outside world that the Soviet Union had, indeed, come to grips with its past and its earlier dogmatic conception of socialism's place in the world and was now prepared to act as a normal, co–operative member of the international community; and secondly, to justify these changes to its internal constituency — officials and rank–and–file members of the CPSU and the 'fraternal parties' of the Bloc, as well as Soviet citizens in general — by establishing that the previous foreign policy orientation had been wrong because it was based on erroneous ideological and practical assumptions. This was a calculated, but dangerous risk, for it was bound to sow much confusion in the ranks of the faithful. Indeed, far from all of the latter responded with good grace to the changes and the rationale behind them.[36]

What Gorbachev needed was a quick payoff in foreign policy to demonstrate the correctness and efficacy of the new approach. Fortunately for him, such a payoff was soon obtained, and from its most desirable source, the Reagan administration in Washington. At a summit meeting in the US capital in early December 1987, Gorbachev and Reagan signed the INF Treaty that had escaped them a year earlier in Reykjavik. To achieve this landmark agreement and render operative the longer–term strategy for penetrating the American sphere of influence in Europe,

Gorbachev had to discard his previous insistence on linking an INF agreement to the abandonment of SDI. Nor were he and Reagan able to agree on other major bones of contention, such as strategic arms reduction, Afghanistan or human rights. Nevertheless, both sides recognised the INF Treaty as a breakthrough in their relations. Gorbachev saw the negotiating process which brought it about as 'a kind of agenda for joint efforts in the future' which would put 'the dialogue between our two countries on a more constructive footing'. Reagan, for his part, described the summit itself as a 'clear success', adding that 'We have proven that adversaries, even with the most basic philosophical differences, can talk candidly and respectfully with one another, and, with perseverance, find common ground.'[37] Although the INF Treaty disposed of only about 4 per cent of the nuclear arsenals of the two superpowers, there were indeed grounds for optimism that a turning point had been reached in East–West relations.

Further progress on arms–related issues continued to be an important feature of US–Soviet relations during the remaining year of the Reagan Administration. A solid foundation for a future treaty on strategic arms limitation (START) was laid, but the negotiations were not brought to speedy consummation as Reagan had hoped. An important obstacle remained the basic philosophy behind the negotiating positions of the two sides. The Soviets continued to press for dramatic, but vague, across–the–board reductions, which would have had the effect of sharply reducing the diversity and salience of the American position in the Western alliance. The Americans remained cautious and firm in their attention to the details of what could be sacrificed without reducing the essential deterrent capacity of their nuclear arsenal.

American thinking at the beginning of the Bush Administration was set forth in an address by Reagan's chief arms negotiator, Paul H. Nitze, to the Nobel Institute in Oslo, Norway on 6 February 1989. He said that it was necessary to keep in mind the 'proper role of arms control', which should enhance security but 'cannot be a substitute or replacement for adequate defense'. A START treaty should make it easier to improve the survivability of strategic deterrence forces. It would 'provide the leeway needed to undertake the force modernization necessary to redress these problems [of force survivability — RFM] and would make the job easier by reducing and bounding the Soviet threat'. If it does these things, he concluded, the projected START treaty 'fully satisfies the proper objectives for a good arms control agreement'.[38] Nitze went on to recommend a mixture of 'patience and determination' on matters of principle and 'creativity' in matters of detail and techniques of negotiations. These qualities, he insisted, had borne fruit in the INF Treaty, despite persistent

Soviet attempts to 'split the alliance and turn our publics and parliaments against us'.[39]

Nitze's remarks indicated the depth of the differences between the public stances of the two superpowers on disarmament issues. Soviet commentators tended to ridicule the American preoccupation with deterrence and 'the Soviet threat'. For example, in a remarkably even-handed article on improving Soviet–American relations, which appeared at the end of 1988, Professor Genrikh Trofimenko, the leading specialist on US foreign policy at the USSR Academy of Sciences' Institute of the USA and Canada, had the following to say about the kind of thinking reflected in Nitze's remarks:

> The tenet of one side's foisting upon the other some rules of behaviour in the world arena has still another unexpected aspect: if in some instance one side has failed to foist these rules for any reason, this gives the other side reason to portray the situation as its own victory or a defeat for the other side. For example, the fact that we were unable through stern demarches to prevent the deployment of American intermediate–range missiles in Western Europe initiated in 1983 and that the USSR ultimately went to the negotiating table with the USA, basing itself on the 'zero option' the Americans had advanced in their time, gives grounds to some American Sovietologists to speak of Soviet foreign policy as a 'policy of weakness'.
>
> In other words, they are seeking, in pursuit of their selfish aims, to pass off the policy of realism grounded in the new political thinking as weakness, although I am certain that they understand full well that the USSR would hardly have agreed to so radical a solution of the problem had the former leadership remained at the head of the Party and the state. . .[40]

There is much in Trofimenko's article with which an objective Western analyst would find it difficult to disagree: for example, on the need to preserve deterrent capabilities on both sides while the necessarily slow process of confidence–building proceeds. In general, there is considerable evidence that behind the extravagant rhetoric of new political thinking, the Soviets, too, are concerned with the specifics of defence and deterrence. Once the Bush Administration had decided to join the rhetorical game of sweeping arms reduction proposals, the Soviets themselves began to urge caution. In response to President Bush's offer of drastic conventional force reductions by the two superpowers in Europe by the end of 1989, for instance, Soviet Defence Minister Dmitri Yazov told British Prime

Minister Thatcher that he considered the timetable much too ambitious, and the number of Soviet troops to be permitted to remain in Central Europe too small.[41] Within a few months, however, Bush and Gorbachev were busily engaged in trying to outdo one another with concrete proposals for conventional force and troop ceilings in Europe. By the (northern) spring of 1990, Bush had clearly developed a stake in Gorbachev's survival as leader of the Soviet Union and was willing to overlook his occasional regressive lapses — for example, in the forcible rejection of Lithuania's demand for independence — in order to preserve the new harmonious relationship with Moscow.

By the middle of his fifth year in office, Gorbachev had thus obviously scored major successes in one of the key areas of reconstructing Soviet foreign policy: relations with the USA. Mutual suspicion remained on both sides, but Gorbachev had succeeded in convincing Reagan and Bush of the *bona fides* of his commitment to change in Soviet foreign policy and to reliance on peaceful means for its implementation. For Reagan and then Bush, these changes at times seemed to be something of a mixed blessing, since they exposed the myriad cracks and stresses in the Western alliance system the United States headed. However, on balance, their net assessment ultimately had to be positive, if only because the United States also had solid financial reasons for desiring relief from the arms race. The main problem for Washington was to control the pace and direction of the changes in its own bailiwick in response to Moscow's skilful diplomatic manipulation of the new Soviet image. In the end, after a prolonged review of the state of US–Soviet relations, the Bush administration decided on a diplomatic challenge of its own in Eastern Europe as the best response to the Soviet diplomatic offensive in Western Europe. This, in turn, forced Gorbachev to seek to manage the pace and direction of change in his own sphere of influence; his inability to do so effectively has had totally unanticipated consequences which have literally changed the course of history on the European continent and beyond. In the next section we shall consider the rapid development of Soviet relations with Western Europe both before and in the immediate aftermath of these changes. The transformation of Soviet relations with the erstwhile empire in Eastern Europe will be discussed in chapter 5.

Soviet relations with Western Europe

Soviet policy toward Western Europe underwent an evolutionary process similar to that toward the United States. At the outset it is worth noting that the habit of treating Western Europe as an entity is of rather recent provenance for the Soviets. For ideological and other reasons they did not really take the processes of integration in the European Community very seriously until well into the 1980s and preferred to try to play one West European country off against the others — and all against the USA — in the conduct of economic and political relations. There was always the hope of 'Finlandisation' — of being able to dominate a fragmented Western Europe after an eventual decoupling of the United States, in military and political terms, from continental affairs. Meanwhile, it was expected that the 'objective' laws and contradictions of capitalism predicted by Lenin would impede economic and political integration. An article in the foreign policy monthly *International Affairs* in March 1979, for example, ridiculed the efforts of Western European social–democratic 'reformists' toward integration as misguided and destined to fail for 'objective' class and structural reasons. 'Indeed,' wrote the author, V. Pankov, 'Reformist projects for transforming bourgeois society in the spirit of "democratic socialism", which amount in fact to a modernized version of state–monopoly capitalism, are closely bound up with the development of the EEC.'[42] Among the factors militating against integration, in Pankov's opinion, were the disparate levels of development of the member states, something he compared unfavourably with the situation in the counterpart Soviet–led organisation, CMEA (the Council of Mutual Economic Assistance), which he confidently expected to be more successful in achieving integration![43] Needless to say, this assessment would change drastically in a few short years.

The high point of detente and of Soviet relations with the Western European countries in the Brezhnev era were undoubtedly the Helsinki Agreements of July–August 1975. At Helsinki the Soviets traded a number of (for them) marginal concessions in the area of human rights ('Basket 3' of the Final Act) and an agreement to hold regular, follow–up meetings ('Basket 4') for a recognition of the inviolability of the territorial arrangements in Europe established by the Yalta and Potsdam Agreements of 1945 ('Basket 1') as well as a commitment to increased East–West economic and technical co–operation ('Basket 2').[44]

Brezhnev had good reason to be pleased with the results of the negotiations at Helsinki. In his statement on the eve of signing the Final Act he praised the agreements as having given 'specific material content' to the process of detente, characterising it effusively as a result of 'accommodating the views and interests of each and every one and with general consent'. He added:

If there are compromises here, then these compromises are well grounded and of the kind that benefit peace without obliterating the differences in ideologies and social systems. To be more precise, they represent an expression of the common political will of the participating states in a form that is feasible today, in conditions in which there exist states with different social systems.[45]

As events would quickly show, however, Helsinki represented for Brezhnev merely a registration of the existing 'correlation of forces' between the two systems, which he saw as moving inexorably in favour of world socialism. Within two years detente was in disarray, as the Soviet Union took advantage of favourable opportunities to extend its power in Africa and Asia. The increasing repression of domestic dissidents, moreover, amply demonstrated Brezhnev's contempt for 'Basket 3'.

In the meantime, the USSR continued to try to expand economic relations with individual Western European states.[46] France was a particular focus of Soviet attentions. Playing upon the determination of the French to demonstrate their independence of the United States and NATO, fostered by President Charles de Gaulle since 1966, the Soviets placed great stress on reciprocal summit meetings with French leaders to bolster this 'special relationship'. The visit by French President Valery Giscard d'Estaing to Moscow in April 1979 was the tenth such meeting since 1966. Indeed, the exiled Soviet dissident Andrei Amalrik, to whom Giscard steadfastly refused to accord a hearing and who was outraged by the latter's attitudes on human rights, pronounced the French President a Soviet 'Trojan Horse' in the West.[47]

French, as well as West German and British, officials were in fact far less inclined than the Americans to belabour the Soviets on human rights and other social issues for fear of impeding detente and the development of East–West economic relations. Giscard consistently refused to raise human rights issues in his meetings with Brezhnev. The French government also pointedly rejected American requests not to supply computers to Moscow for coverage of the 1980 Olympic Games.[48] French, West German and British firms were largely supported by their respective governments in evading Washington's demands for an embargo on the shipment of technology for a Soviet natural gas pipeline to the West. Nor did they pay much heed to American arguments on the danger of dependence on the USSR for energy supplies.

On the whole, then, detente placed great stresses on the Western alliance. The Soviet policy of forging economic links with individual countries created a stake in the maintenance of better political relations in a number of countries. This was particularly true of some of the smaller NATO countries, like Greece and Denmark, where there were significant social groups in favour of disarmament and greater economic and political independence of the USA. The coming to power of Andreas Papandreou in Greece in 1981, largely on a pledge of removing NATO installations, exemplified this tendency, although the special circumstances of the conflict with fellow NATO member Turkey over Cyprus were an additional factor in Greek behaviour. Even after the declaration of Martial Law in Poland in December 1981, the Greek government refused to join the general Western condemnation of the Soviet Union and continued to pursue an expansion of economic and political relations with the Soviet Bloc.

Had Gorbachev come to power even five years earlier, it is conceivable that relations on the continent would have developed far differently. As it was, the Soviets, emboldened by their increasing military strength in Europe and elsewhere, overplayed their hand and frightened the NATO countries into re–establishing alliance solidarity. The rapid Soviet deployment of new, advanced SS–20 missiles merely provoked West German Chancellor Helmut Schmidt to request American counter-deployments. The NATO decision in December 1979 to move toward the installation of Pershing–2 IRBMs and Tomahawk cruise missiles evoked a storm of Soviet protests and threats, accompanied by a wave of 'peace' demonstrations that were largely, but not solely, orchestrated by Moscow (see chapter 3 above).[49] The Western decision was accompanied by a parallel offer to begin immediate talks with Moscow on eliminating the entire spectrum of intermediate– and medium–range nuclear missiles prior to the beginning of actual NATO deployments (scheduled for the end of 1983). However, Brezhnev and his two short–lived successors could not bring themselves to give up what they considered a highly advantageous weapons system and preferred to try to preserve it by a policy of threat and bluster, accusing the West of increasing the danger of nuclear catastrophe by its intransigence over the Pershing–2s and Tomahawks.

The entire exercise was a prime example of the 'old political thinking' which held sway during this period. There were many other illustrations as well. Foreign Minister Gromyko threatened Spain with the prospect of becoming a nuclear target if it went ahead with plans to join NATO; and Brezhnev was reported to have heatedly warned Chancellor Schmidt not to support Spain's membership during the latter's visit to Moscow in June 1980.[50] Spain entered NATO shortly thereafter, nevertheless. Similar insensitivity brought Moscow into conflict with other small Western countries as well. In 1982 and 1983 the Swedish government protested loudly over the incursion of Soviet submarines and reconnaissance units into Swedish territorial waters, and for a while there was even some talk of Sweden's abandoning its traditional neutrality for the security of alignment with NATO. Finally, the early months of 1983 witnessed a significant upsurge of expulsions of Soviet diplomats and other officials from a number of West European countries for espionage and other hostile acts (for example, from Switzerland for involvement in the local peace movement).[51] Whether these expulsions reflected a genuine increase in Soviet intelligence activity or were simply being manipulated by Western counter–intelligence services, acting on information from recent high–level KGB defectors, to keep the new Andropov administration off balance, the numbers involved suggest a rather cavalier attitude on the part of Moscow toward the security concerns of Western Europe.

Afghanistan, Poland, intransigence in arms control negotiations (despite the inflated Soviet rhetoric of impending nuclear catastrophe) and brazen intelligence activities all reflected a mode of thinking whose major result had been to lead Soviet foreign policy into an impasse in virtually all parts of the world, communist as well as non–communist. And nowhere was this more evident than in Western Europe, where the potential economic, political and military payoff from improved relations was greatest. By the end of the Brezhnev era there were already some signs of a recognition of the need for change. But before Brezhnev's successors could bring themselves to accept the necessity of a genuine shift in their policies, they had to come to grips with the full gravity of their predicament. Andropov's and Chernenko's continuing endorsement of the Brezhnevian concept of 'developed socialism' (also referred to variously as 'mature', 'real' or 'really existing socialism') did not help matters, since it engendered complacency and a belief in the unimpeachability of existing structures and practices. These attitudes were reinforced by a blinkered ideological view of conditions in the opposing camp, which made their own seem 'objectively' superior. In the words of General Secretary Yuri Andropov at a Central Committee Plenary Session in June 1983:

> As far as the world of capitalism is concerned, we are witnesses to a significant deepening of the general crisis of that social system. The methods by which capitalism has been able to maintain relative stability in its development in the postwar period are increasingly losing their effectiveness. It is becoming ever clearer that imperialism is incapable of coping with the social consequences of the unprecedentedly deep and broad scientific and technical revolution, where millions and millions of toilers are doomed to unemployment, to poverty.

> Imperialism has become embroiled in internal and inter–state antagonisms, shocks and conflicts. This is reflected deeply, but differentially, in the policy of the capitalist countries.[52]

Andropov went on to distinguish between the aggressively oriented imperialism of the United States and the allegedly growing number of 'more realistic' elements in the capitalist world, who understood the impossibility of turning the clock back to a time when imperialism was dominant. Socialism (presumably of the 'really existing' variety) was destined ultimately to prevail, he asserted. However, he reassured his audience and the outside world that, although fundamental antagonisms would remain as long as capitalism existed, there were still many issues which peoples from both camps could tackle together, such as environmental and space problems and tapping the resources of the World Ocean. After pledging to maintain and strengthen the military might of the Soviet armed forces to deter the aggressive plans of imperialism, he announced that the USSR would be happy to see the strategic balance mutually reduced to a significantly lower level, which would be 'a great benefit for all countries and peoples'.[53] In short, by 1983 there were already signals which prefigured a number of Gorbachev's later initiatives. However, the basic changes in attitude and self–perceptions which underpinned the 'new political thinking' were not yet present. The Soviet leaders were still arguing from what they considered a position of economic, military and ideological strength.

Those illusions apparently persisted for at least several months after Gorbachev's accession to power. Such perennial chestnuts of traditional Soviet thinking as the sanctity of 'unity and cohesion' in the socialist world, the need to promote splits between the United States and her European allies and the duty to support the Third World against imperialism continued to echo in his rhetoric.[54] However, subtle conceptual and substantive changes soon appeared. The growing importance of Western Europe in Gorbachev's thinking was reflected in his call in June 1985 for a resumption of the talks on formal relations between the EEC and CMEA which had been broken off in 1980 in protest over the Soviet invasion of Afghanistan. He had also accepted with alacrity invitations to visit France, West Germany and Italy by the representatives of those countries at the funeral of Chernenko. At this stage, however, the main instrumental focus of Soviet policy in the region remained the peace movements and left–wing forces involved in the campaign to pressurise Western governments against the INF deployments. West Germany was a particular target of attacks by the Soviet media on this issue.

An article by the economist A. Bykov in the journal *International Affairs* in January 1986 was a good illustration of the old political thinking which still predominated in the first year of Gorbachev's rule. The author blasted the United States on a number of counts:

1   for accelerating the arms race;
2   for forcing her NATO allies to shoulder a larger part of the alliance's military spending in order to keep them dependent on the US economy by weakening them economically and isolating them from the socialist market; and
3   for keeping the Third World in thrall economically through 'technological neocolonialism' and the actions of the 'transnational monopolies'.[55]

Bykov went on to warn the West Europeans that they risked losing out in the race with the United States and Japan for technological advancement, as well as missing the chance to solve their problems of domestic unemployment and social unrest by failing to take advantage of the opportunities offered by the allegedly expanding and modernising CMEA economies.[56] Given the increasingly obvious decline of those economies and their growing technological backwardness, such arguments were bound to be unconvincing to their nominal target audience in Western Europe. In any case, they were probably intended primarily for consumption by a domestic and Bloc readership which was still presumably receptive to this kind of self–justificatory whistling in the dark.

To a considerable extent this vestigial reflex of old political thinking and its associated diplomacy was probably attributable to the continued tenure of Andrei Gromyko as Minister of Foreign Affairs, although the ideological caste of Gorbachev's own statements during the period also largely reflected many of the old stereotypes.[57] The germ of the new political thinking began to appear only with the appointment of Eduard Shevardnadze as Gromyko's replacement in July 1985. However, it took more than two years for the ideas associated with the NPT to crystallise and perhaps another year more for appropriate modes of implementation to be adopted.[58] As was the case with domestic *perestroika*, Gorbachev showed himself willing to be governed by practical results and the reception of his initial ideas by various target audiences for the final shaping of operational concepts and concrete policies.

The successful conclusion of the INF Treaty in Washington in December 1987 was undoubtedly a major stage in the process of Gorbachev's policy development. It demonstrated the viability of summitry with leading Western politicians as a method of achieving breakthroughs on major East–West issues and the importance of direct contacts in promoting the *bona fides* of the new Soviet approach to international relations. Gorbachev and his two closest supporters in foreign affairs, Foreign Minister Shevardnadze and party foreign policy chief Aleksandr Yakovlev, undertook a series of meetings with Western European leaders in the ensuing two years to continue the the desired process of dialogue. Shevardnadze established the practice of regular consultations with officials of virtually every EEC country, from Britain, France and West Germany to Spain and Luxembourg, to explain Soviet viewpoints and to accustom his hosts to dealing with the USSR as a regular and normal member of the European community of nations.[59]

A symbol of the increasing importance of the 'common European home' and the 'general European process' — code words for the shift in Soviet strategy toward engagement in the processes of economic and political integration in Western Europe — was the establishment in April 1988 of a new Institute of Europe in the USSR Academy of Sciences. It was headed by Dr Vitalii V. Zhurkin, formerly Deputy Director of the Institute of the USA and Canada (ISShAK) of the Academy, one of the most important 'think tanks' on policy toward the USA and, incidentally, an alleged front for both the KGB and the International Department of the CPSU Central Committee. ISShAK's academic status has provided its members with easy access to North American scholars and policy advisers.[60] If these allegations are true, and the new Institute were assigned a similar role, its operations would have more than merely academic and informational significance, although one should probably not exaggerate the salience of this aspect of its activity. The broader significance of its establishment is the implicit recognition of the special nature of Western Europe as a part of the capitalist world and the utility of this type of organisation as a bridge to the European community of 'influentials' and as a supplier of expertise to Soviet policy — makers. Zhurkin is a specialist on armaments issues, and arms control has certainly figured as one of the principal points of entry for the systematic dialogue with Western Europe which Moscow is currently banking on to bring about attitudinal changes favourable to Soviet involvement in European developments.[61]

The rapid evolution of the internal Soviet discussions of relations with Western Europe has covered a broad spectrum of issues, from military developments within NATO to economic, political and cultural aspects of the 'general European process'. In general, the tone and content of the discussions of the opportunities and limitations of the Soviet position have become increasingly realistic and perceptive. On recent tendencies toward Western European military integration, for example, there are arguments that such a development is a normal outgrowth of changes within NATO. The United States is said to be consciously fostering greater autonomy among its European partners so as to leave itself free to attend to its own interests in other regions of the world.[62] To the extent that these tendencies are associated with a reduction in East–West tensions, that they remain linked to an overall NATO strategy — fully involving the US — of reducing confrontation, and that they lead to a decline in the purely military orientation of the NATO partnership, they are regarded as not necessarily inimical to Soviet interests.[63]

However, neither are they greeted with as much enthusiasm as one might have expected — that is, as evidence of the decoupling of the United States from Western Europe. For one thing, the Soviets have few illusions about the likelihood of an interruption or reversal of the trans–Atlantic character of the integrative processes in Western armaments production: they are recognised as part of the general tendencies toward technological integration among the Western economies. For another, Gorbachev has increasingly come to regard a continuing US presence on the continent as a useful factor of stability and as a guarantee of the maintenance of some element of symmetry in the relationship within and between the opposing blocs, at least until more favourable, possibly 'bloc–free', conditions can be established for Soviet involvement in the 'general European process'. During his state visit to France in July 1989, Gorbachev was notably cautious in playing upon his hosts' traditional coolness toward Washington. Indeed, he went out of his way to emphasise the importance of keeping the United States fully involved in the development of East–West relations.[64]

Military considerations necessarily remain paramount in these still largely exploratory stages of Soviet rapprochement with Western Europe. As Eberhard Schulz has pointed out, the development of Soviet military thinking on European security issues (most notably among civilian specialists) has increasingly tended to play down the danger of military confrontation on the European continent and to encourage the broad acceptance of such concepts as 'reasonable sufficiency', a 'defensive military doctrine' and 'non–aggressive defence' as desirable modes of military planning and organisation for both sides of the East–West divide.[65] To be sure, there are still opponents of these shifts, and not only among the Soviet military. The chief of the Soviet MFA's administration for arms control and disarmament affairs, Viktor Karpov, was still maintaining — in an interview in May 1988, for example — that in opposing Soviet disarmament proposals 'the USA places its egoistic interests above the interest of European security'.[66]

Gorbachev himself tends to eschew such accusations as fruitless 'point–scoring', which serves only to put his Western negotiating partners on their guard. He is quite conscious of the fact that the Western Europeans are well aware of their own security and other interests, and it is precisely this consciousness of 'interests' that he is banking on, with a sometimes astonishing faith in rationality, to bring success in his quest for the inclusion of the USSR and its allies in what he sees as the major processes of economic and political integration taking place in Europe and the (capitalist) world as a whole.[67] These processes are now generally viewed as progressive and objectively determined. In contrast to the disparaging views expressed a decade ago by commentators like Pankov, cited in the beginning of this section, a series of 'Theses on The European Community Today' promulgated by the Institute of the World Economy and International Relations of the USSR Academy of Sciences in December 1988 gave the following evaluation of the EC, which was by this time accepted as involving more than simple economic integration:

> The EC can become an active participant of the restructuring of the entire system of mutual political and economic linkages on the European continent. Integration processes in Western Europe reflect a basically progressive tendency toward the strengthening of the mutual dependence of states, toward an ever greater bringing together of the nations and peoples inhabiting them, to a peaceful solution of inter–state contradictions and thus to an elimination of the underlying causes generating military conflicts and confrontations.[68]

There is increasing awareness that the Soviet Union must make haste to conclude formal economic linkages with the EC to avoid the danger of being left outside after the 1992 target date for integration. However, there is also growing recognition that the present structure and capabilities of the Soviet economy offer few opportunities and inducements for large–scale participation in EC commercial and production affairs.[69] One of its principal problems is the non–convertibility of the Soviet ruble; another is the lack of sufficient hard currency reserves for technological imports; a third is the glaring lack of infrastructural development to induce the investment of foreign capital; a fourth are the legal and administrative structures of the Soviet system, which are not yet compatible with the demands of rapidly changing modern technology; a fifth problem are the Soviet linkages with the CMEA countries, for which Moscow still claims some responsibility and the pace of whose participation in the EC it is (vainly) seeking to control. All these problems have been under consideration by Gorbachev and his colleagues, and many of them are specifically included in the program of domestic *perestroika*. Gorbachev would like to enlist the help of the Western Europeans, as well as the Americans, Japanese and other advanced capitalist countries, in solving them, but he has little bargaining leverage beyond the dramatic visions of regional and world integration and interdependence which figure so prominently in his statements to foreign audiences. By persisting with these rhetorical pronouncements he is obviously hoping to set the tone and conceptual framework for future East–West relations and to direct them along paths congenial to Soviet interests. So far, at least, the goals he has enunciated seem unobjectionable and even generally desirable, but he has come up against a good deal of skepticism from his more pragmatic negotiating partners. In response to Gorbachev's letter to Mitterand during the G–7 meetings in Paris in July 1989, for example, US President Bush, while welcoming Soviet movements towards accommodation with the Western capitalist market system, said that the Soviet economy was 'not yet ready' for full participation in the West's decision–making forums.[70]

In confronting the prospects of fundamental rapprochement with Western Europe, Gorbachev thus finds himself facing a dilemma. On the one hand, the Soviet economy desperately needs the kinds of technological and managerial assistance and capital investment that the advanced capitalist economies alone are capable of supplying. Its existing planning, administrative and financial systems were designed for a model and structure of priorities that are entirely different from those prevailing in the West and which have patently failed to satisfy the developmental and welfare requirements of its people. The structure of its foreign economic relations is recognised as more akin to that of a Third–World economy than of a superpower.[71] The increasing awareness of these facts and Gorbachev's willingness to change them has led to a remarkable shift in Soviet foreign policy attitudes towards the West and particularly towards Western Europe, which he regards as the most promising and most desirable source of the co–operation and assistance he needs. There is a price to be paid for Western Europe's acceptance of his bid for tenancy, or 'co–ownership', as Francois Mitterand has called it, of the 'common European home',[72] and Gorbachev is evidently prepared to go a considerable way towards paying it, although both sides are still obviously dickering over the precise terms and conditions of cohabitation. The decision to import a massive $86.6 billion worth of food and consumer goods to honour pledges made to end the wave of miners' strikes in the summer of 1989 may have more than merely commercial significance.[73] The size of the purchases, which undoubtedly included substantial commercial credits, implies not only a recognition of the seriousness of the domestic economic situation at the present stage of *perestroika*, but also a radical reappraisal of the Soviet Union's traditional attitude towards hard–currency indebtedness. (By mid–1990 it seemed to have gone perhaps too far in this direction.) On a different plane it also reflects a recognition of the psychological potential for removing barriers to Soviet inclusion by involving Western European firms in large–scale production for the Soviet market. The implications of this dramatic shift in Soviet policy as a sign of commitment to the Western European strategy remain to be seen, but they may well be substantial.

On the other hand, while increasingly ready to accommodate the interests of his prospective fellow inhabitants of the 'common European home', Gorbachev clearly has some vital interests of his own which may prove extremely difficult to reconcile with theirs. He explicitly intends to preserve his country's commitment to socialism, however elastic that concept may eventually turn out to be in practice. One element of his strategy is to establish cordial relations with Western European socialist and social democratic parties, which he expects to be more receptive to his visions of a future integrated Europe with large elements of the 'socialist project'.[74] In this connection it is interesting to note that in his remarks to President Mitterand at the close of his visit to Paris in July 1989, he tried to convince his host that 'the multivariability of development, both within the systems and in states belonging to different systems is a positive factor. And all this should be considered with all the more caution and attention in politics.'[75]

His original intention was thus to enter into any future arrangements with the EC with guarantees for the preservation of the Soviet Union's basic systemic commitment and to insist that this condition apply to the countries allied with it as well. He wished, if possible, to have CMEA and the EC negotiate *en bloc*, so to speak, and to act also in the name of his junior partners. But that was before the dramatic events of the (northern) autumn of 1989, when most of his Eastern European allies one by one left the orbit of direct Soviet control and effectively ceased being ruled by Communist Parties. The Soviets continue to maintain considerable leverage over the Eastern European economies, as we shall see in chapter 5, but Moscow no longer accepts responsibility for their economic wellbeing or for the terms under which they are to be included in the Western market system.

Before the rush toward German reunification in February 1990, Gorbachev was basically supportive of the efforts of the individual Eastern European countries to reach accommodation with the EC, since CMEA was obviously moribund and their success would presumably facilitate eventual acceptance of Soviet inclusion in the broader processes of integration. Since then, particularly after the victory of the conservatives in the East German elections of 18 March, Gorbachev and his colleagues have shown a good deal more ambivalence over the direction events seemed to be taking. This was reflected in the mixed signals emanating from Moscow over the question of the relationship to NATO of a reunified Germany. Gorbachev had assured FRG Chancellor Helmut Kohl on 11 February that he had no objections to German reunification, leaving the latter with the impression that the conditions brought back from Moscow a week earlier by the then East German (communist) Premier Hans Modrow — that reunification must proceed by stages and that a reunified Germany be neutral and demilitarised — no longer applied.[76] Shortly thereafter it became clear that Kohl was incorrect in assuming that the Soviets would permit NATO membership for a united Germany. But a few weeks later Foreign Minister Shevardnadze let it be known that German participation in a different European security framework or a different kind of NATO might be another matter.[77]

Gorbachev's adaptation to the rapidly changing situation in Central and Eastern Europe was yet another illustration of his great talent for 'lateral thinking' and his ability to make the best of an unexpectedly bad situation. If he could no longer maintain the existing institutional balance between NATO and the WTO, as a result of the altered political relationships underlying the security arrangements in the latter organisation, then he would seek to reduce the cohesiveness of the former. The debacle in East Germany would be turned to Soviet advantage by luring the reunified, FRG–dominated Germany out of its central position in NATO, in the process building on the evidently growing fears of a revived German colossus in both Western and Eastern Europe to change attitudes toward the Soviet Union as a central feature of an eventual European security system. In a sense, the USSR would in large measure replace the United States as the principal guarantor of stability in Europe, although a continued, if somewhat reduced, presence of North American forces on the Continent would be welcomed by all parties. He received unexpected support for this scenario from, of all persons, Lord Carrington, the former NATO Secretary–General and erstwhile British Foreign Secretary.[78] Other Western leaders were decidedly less responsive to Gorbachev's initiatives to change the structures of the alliance system, but he continued to ride the crest of the wave of radical change in East–West relations. It would remain to be seen just how seriously his efforts to handle internal developments in the Soviet Union, namely the demands for autonomy of the Baltic States and other unwilling members of the Soviet Union, would affect the reception of his overtures to the West.

Moreover, there were also other aspects of Gorbachev's ideological commitments which tended to complicate the accommodation process, namely his insistence on continuing to act as a spokesman for Third World interests in pushing the so–called 'North–South' dialogue as a companion process to East–West negotiations. His sponsorship at the United Nations or the 'new international economic order' and his bombastic, visionary rhetoric of globalism and universal interdependence were likely to dismay his more pragmatic, concretely orientated Western negotiating partners. Somewhere along the line, Gorbachev would have to establish his priorities and decide which of the broad, visionary goals of his rhetoric were to be sacrificed to the more immediate requirements of formal engagement in capitalist Europe and how much of a tribute he was willing to pay on global issues to gain entry into the world market decision–making club.

Soviet relations with the Asia–Pacific Region

As in the case of Soviet relations with the United States and Western Europe, relations with the Asia–Pacific Region (APR) are a composite of military, economic and political elements, and as with Western Europe, the position of the United States is a major factor in the equation. However, the weighting of the various elements and the lineup of contending forces both tend to be quite different, as are the Soviet perceptions of priorities and opportunities. To be sure, the inclusion of this extensive region in a discussion of Soviet relations with the capitalist world may seem problematical. Many of its states clearly belong economically and politically in the category of Third World countries, whose status *vis–a–vis* the USSR will be discussed in chapter 6. However, the important points for our purposes are that the Soviets themselves now consider the region as an integral whole, the 'ATR' (*Aziatsko–tikhookeanskii region*) and that they implicitly accept it as a region of developed or developing capitalism.

It is only very recently that the region has attracted much attention among Soviet policy– makers, and it is important to keep their newfound interest in proper perspective. Indeed, now that relations with China have been more or less fully 'normalised' and the Chinese military threat effectively removed, the APR has returned to its former status as a region of relatively lower priority than, say, Western Europe or the Middle East in

Soviet geopolitical thinking. However, this is not to say that the APR is not intrinsically important to the Soviets. As Gorbachev's well known speeches in Vladivostok in 1986 and Krasnoyarsk in 1988 clearly showed, the Soviets are well aware of the growing economic and political importance of the region and are determined to play a role in the shaping of its future. But the demands on Soviet resources at home and elsewhere in the world dictate that policy toward the APR be conducted on a relatively low–cost basis, which necessarily limits the possibilities of major Soviet moves in the region. For the short term, therefore, Moscow is concentrating on diplomatic and piecemeal economic initiatives to establish its regional credentials and prepare for more substantial engagement some time in the future.

The situation looked far less benign to Moscow two decades ago. Clashes with the Chinese in the eastern regions of their common border in the spring and summer of 1969 created a sense of urgency in a Soviet leadership which was still nervous over Western reactions to the invasion of Czechoslovakia the previous year. The prospect of hostilities on two fronts undoubtedly paved the way for Soviet intitiatives in the West, leading to the conclusion of the peace treaties with the Federal Republic of Germany by the USSR and then Poland in 1970. Detente in the West was thus at least partly a product of tension in the East. To address the eastern problem, Brezhnev began, in the summer of 1969, to float the idea of a 'general Asian collective security agreement', which has figured in Soviet strategy toward the APR, in one way or another, ever since. Originally the scheme had a twofold purpose: to isolate and encircle China, building up the military forces of selected regional countries, if necessary on a bilateral basis; and to take over what it perceived as the essential elements of the American power position in the region, which it saw as declining in the wake of the Vietnam War.[79] However, in the face of US objections and a general fear of greater Soviet involvement among non–communist powers in the region, only India, which had its own grievances against China, seemed mildly favourable to the project. Meanwhile, the Soviet Union began steps to increase its long–term naval presence in the area by establishing semi–permanent mooring facilities in the Indian Ocean on a unilateral basis, presumably with Indian acquiescence.[80] The Indo–Pakistani War of 1971 and the subsequent rapprochement between China and the United States the following year strengthened Moscow's bilateral relationship with India, but the broader Asian collective security project languished.

One of the more important consequences of the worsening of relations with China was to concentrate Soviet attention on the economic development of Eastern Siberia and the Soviet Far East. The possession of this territory, traditionally the basis of Soviet claims to be considered an Asian, as well as a European country, has always brought both benefits and problems to Moscow. Under Brezhnev the sparse population and lack of infrastructural development, particularly of roads and railroads, along the Sino–Soviet border came to be regarded as a strategic weakness and an undesirable attraction for alleged Chinese expansionist ambitions. Hence the 1970s witnessed an upsurge of interest in developing the resource potential of the region and its ability to attract and hold an enlarged Soviet population. For both economic and political reasons the Soviets sought to enlist Japanese help in financing and organising this development, hoping thereby also to build a Japanese stake in the furtherance of Soviet interests in the region.

However, the reluctance of the Japanese to undertake more than a limited commitment of resources proved to be a constant source of annoyance to Moscow, especially when they began to play a political game of their own by raising the issue of the four Kurile Islands (in Japanese parlance, the 'northern territories') seized by the USSR as part of the post–Second World War settlement.[81] As Robertson has pointed out, the entire scheme to lure Japanese and other investments to the Soviet Far East has always foundered, despite its reportedly fabulous untapped riches, on the rock of the difficult climatic conditions of the region and its lack of infrastructural facilities, as well as on the inability of Soviet political and economic structures to absorb and effectively utilise the technologies introduced.[82] The general slowdown of the Soviet economy in the 1970s and the rapid rise in the costs of resource extraction in Siberia and the Soviet Far East inevitably diminished the economic attractiveness of these regions for foreign investors. This was particularly true of the Japanese, for whom the prospect of tying up substantial capital on the product–'compensation' terms offered by the Soviets became increasingly unattractive in comparison with available alternative investment and commercial opportunities. To the dismay of Moscow, Japan's trade with China, following Mao's death in 1976, soon outstripped that with the USSR.[83] Worse still, the Japanese showed a growing tendency to use their trade leverage with Moscow for political purposes, namely for a reversal of the Soviet position on the 'northern territories'.[84]

The peculiar vulnerability of the Soviet Far East, owing to the high costs of developing its potential, has thus turned out to be a source of both strengths and weaknesses for the Soviet position in the APR. Paradoxically, Brezhnev's growing tendency to rely on a buildup of military strength as the primary manifestation of Soviet power in the region ultimately served mainly to accentuate the weaknesses of the Soviet position by evoking countervailing responses from the United States and regional non–communist states. Gorbachev has assiduously attempted to convert these weaknesses into an asset by a radically different approach to the creation of a general Asian collective security system, based on a substantial reassessment of Soviet interests and capabilities.

To understand these changes it is necessary to look briefly at the military and political situation of the Soviet Union in the APR at the close of the Brezhnev era. The Soviet invasion of Afghanistan and its support for the Vietnamese occupation of Cambodia, continuing sponsorship of communist guerilla movements in the Philippines and Thailand,[85] and the rapid buildup of the force–projection capabilities of the Soviet Pacific Fleet all combined to frighten the states of the region into consolidating their forces and strengthening their ties with the only power deemed capable of effective resistance, the United States. These sentiments were exacerbated by the extension of Soviet naval and airforce operations into the Indian Ocean and the South China Sea (through access to long–term basing facilities in Camranh Bay), which seemed to place Soviet power right in the heart of the region. Although the primary purpose of this expanded Soviet outreach was probably to contain the Chinese, about whom most of the regional states, particularly the members of ASEAN, had few illusions, the principal effect was to increase the perceived threat from Vietnam, which, in ASEAN eyes, represented by far the clearest and most present danger to their security. Moscow was particularly incensed at the Chinese for playing upon these fears to turn ASEAN against the Soviet Union and undermine its various peace initiatives in the region.[86]

By the early 1980s the only 'friends' the Soviets had in the entire APR were the Vietnamese (and the latter's Cambodian and Lao clients) and the non–communist Indians. US President Reagan's massive naval counter-buildup in the Pacific was already underway, accompanied by a change in the doctrine for its application which seemed distinctly threatening to the Soviet Far East itself. Moreover, Sino–American military co–operation seemed to be rapidly approaching the status of an alliance, and Soviet commentators had begun to speak of a 'Washington–Peking–Tokyo triangle' and an 'American–Japanese–South Korean axis'. In 1982 Brezhnev sent out peace feelers to the Chinese, hoping to relieve some of the growing pressure on his regime, but he was met with demands for major changes in Soviet policy that were still unthinkable. In mid–1984 Konstantin Chernenko condemned the emerging 'geometrical' groupings of non–communist forces as inimical to Soviet interests in the region: 'We are against such geopolitics, against all kinds of "spheres of influence" and "zones of interest", against closed military groups in general and in the Pacific Ocean in particular.'[87] By the early 1980s, the Soviets were clearly well aware of the dangerous impasse into which they had been placed by their previous policies in the Asia–Pacific Region, but they seemed to have little idea of how to get out of it.

Gorbachev was more imaginative. Confronting the dilemmas, inherited from his predecessors, of growing Soviet military strength with no net gain in security and a marked deterioration in the country's economic capacity to keep pace with the strategic challenge — all compounded by Moscow's increasing political isolation in the region — he was more willing and able than they had been to accept the changed realities of the situation and to explore possible opportunities. His first order of business was to defuse the confrontation with the Chinese. This was an especially difficult problem because it involved not only conventional great–power rivalry, but ideological disputation as well, which gave their mutual antagonisms the character of a bitter intra–family feud.

Nevertheless, a main issue of Beijing's quarrel with Moscow, as was the case in most of the latter's other political problems in the region, was the fear of Soviet military power. As a requirement for beginning the process of normalising relations, China had set three specific conditions: the withdrawal of Soviet troops from Afghanistan, the removal of Soviet forces from the Chinese border (especially in the Mongolian People's Republic where Soviet troops had been greatly strengthened in the wake of the 1969 frontier clashes) and the termination of the Vietnamese occupation of Cambodia, which the Chinese regarded as indirect Soviet meddling against their interests in Southeast Asia. Thus, as in Western Europe, Gorbachev soon came to realise that a reduction in the Soviet military profile was the key to any improvement of its political and economic prospects in the APR. This was the essence of his new political thinking for the region. The Soviet Union would have to change its image and *modus operandi* in the APR if it wished to participate in the dynamic economic and political developments of the region.

Gorbachev's speech in Vladivostok on 28 July 1986 was a major exposition of his views on the region at an early stage in the development of the new political thinking. For Western commentators the most noteworthy aspects of his message were his assertion that the USSR, as an Asian and Pacific power, was entitled to full participation in the political and economic affairs of the entire region, together with his pledge to seek a mutual arms reduction with the United States as a means of transforming the nature of superpower rivalry in the APR. However, the tone and much of the content of his remarks on both domestic and foreign affairs still largely reflected the old political thinking.[88]

On domestic issues, for example, Gorbachev maintained the traditional line that the existing structures and processes of socialism merely needed 'perfecting' (and not fundamental restructuring). He accordingly held out to the residents of the Soviet Far East bright prospects for moving away from the low–technology, primary–product orientation of the regional economy by intensifying its manufacturing and scientific and technological base. He also called for an increase in self–sufficiency in energy and food supplies. Glaring problems of consumer goods and services and other social-infrastructural facilities came far down in his list of priorities, however, which suggested that he still had an incomplete understanding of the basic reasons for the region's failure to develop and an unrealistic picture of the resources available to improve the situation.

In foreign affairs, although calling for arms reductions and increased economic and political co–operation with the United States and Japan, he still emphasised the primacy of the USSR's ties with the socialist regimes in the region and placed the blame for heightened tensions squarely on the shoulders of the 'imperialists'. Improving relations with China was at the top of his list of objectives, and he promised favourable consideration of the Chinese conditions for normalisation. But here, too, he blamed the interference of the imperialists as the primary obstacle to a peaceful resolution of the Afghan and Cambodian conflicts. In a further gesture to Beijing he committed his country to accept the long–standing Chinese demand to move the riverine boundary between the USSR and China to the centre of the Amur and Ussuri River navigation channels.

Gorbachev also presented a number of broad proposals for the settlement of the Cambodian and Afghanistan conflicts and for an improvement of Vietnamese relations with China and the ASEAN countries. In the Pacific, he called for a program of eventual de-nuclearisation and announced his support for the South Pacific Nuclear Free Zone promoted by the South Pacific Forum (and somewhat ambivalently sponsored by the Australian government). On Korea, Gorbachev, like Chernenko two years earlier, expressed concern over the security implications of the emerging 'Washington–Tokyo–Seoul triangle', and he urged the de–nuclearisation of the Korean Peninsula and moves toward re–unification of the two halves of the country — conspicuously on North Korean principles. The socialist 'Hermit Kingdom' proclivities of North Korea's Kim Il Sung did not make Gorbachev's task at all easy. Kim totally eschewed the need for domestic *perestroika* and the 'national reconciliation' approach to improving relations with South Korea that would have been required to allow Gorbachev to make much headway in creating conditions for the establishment of economic arrangements with that rapidly growing regional centre of capitalist power.

Gorbachev was unenthusiastic about regional tendencies towards formal structures of economic co–operation and towards the formation of a 'Pacific Ocean Community', but he reserved the right of the USSR to participate in these ventures on a 'non–discriminatory' basis. As an alternative he resurrected the long–standing proposal for a general Asian collective security system, calling for the convocation of a Helsinki–type conference, possibly in Hiroshima (!), to involve all the Pacific Ocean states. This was remarkably blatant opportunism, and its injection in a key section of what purported to be a major Soviet initiative did little to enhance the overall credibility of his proposals. But, as we have seen in the cases of his diplomacy toward the United States and Western Europe, it was early days yet. Gorbachev was still finding his way along the 'learning curve' of new political thinking. He evidently did not yet fully understand the hard facts of the domestic economic and political situation and their implications for Soviet foreign policy.

Nor was much of an advancement along the learning curve registered in the so–called 'Delhi Declaration' which Gorbachev signed with Indian Prime Minister Rajiv Gandhi in November 1986. Again, beyond a relatively specific appeal for the mutual withdrawal of American and Soviet naval forces from the Indian Ocean and its total de–nuclearisation, the document was long on rhetoric concerning universal human values and short on the kind of concrete proposals that might have attracted the serious attention of Western negotiating partners. The Soviets and Indians undoubtedly found common ground on the desirability of eliminating the American naval and air base on Diego Garcia (leased from the United Kingdom in response to the establishment of Soviet installations around the Indian Ocean), but they offered little to induce the United States and her allies to entertain such a proposition. The Delhi Declaration never proved to be as important a document as the Soviet media have made it appear to be, but it did serve to strengthen bilateral ties with India, thanks largely to some skilful pandering to India's universalist philosophical pretensions.[89] It also reflected Gorbachev's readiness to take advantage of the congruence of Soviet and Indian strategic interests (if not necessarily of the respective motives behind them) to let the Indians take the lead in military matters in the Indian Ocean. The subsequent decision to lease a Charlie–class nuclear–powered attack submarine to the Indian Navy and continuing sales of other advanced Soviet military equipment were concrete illustrations of the opportunism which underlay much of the peaceful, anti–nuclear rhetoric of Gorbachev's policy initiatives in the APR.

A further stage in Gorbachev's process of learning about the region was his speech in the East Siberian city of Krasnoyarsk on 16 September 1988, where he presented additional proposals for Asian security. On the whole, they were more concrete than his previous initiatives in Vladivostok and Delhi. Meanwhile, the Soviet Union had taken important steps to remove some of the main irritants in its relations with China and other countries in the region. Gorbachev had already contracted in Geneva in April to withdraw all Soviet troops from Afghanistan by 15 February 1989 and had pressured Vietnam to pledge withdrawal from Cambodia; he had also begun the transfer of Soviet troops from the Sino–Mongolian border.

Earlier, in his Krasnoyarsk speech, Gorbachev bemoaned the mediocre economic results of *perestroika* to date, particularly in the eastern regions of the USSR, and displayed both a growing recognition of the need for outside economic aid and a realisation that an improvement in the regional political climate was the key to obtaining it: 'We see much better now the problems in our mutual relationships, the current and long–term tasks which we shall have to solve together in the interests of each country and in the interests of [our]friendly states.' [90] The interests of the Soviet Union's allies in the region would continue to be taken into account, but they would no longer be allowed to stand in the way of broader agreements. South Korea would increasingly be a focus of Soviet attention, despite the hostility of the North Korean hardline leadership.

The Krasnoyarsk speech suggested a dual–track strategy in the region, similar but not identical to that being applied in Western Europe. A general security settlement would be sought with the United States and its major regional allies, at the same time as a series of flexible diplomatic and economic initiatives was being directed at the individual states of the region. The seven major proposals Gorbachev presented in the speech were designed primarily for the first track:

1 he pledged unilaterally not to increase the number of Soviet nuclear weapons in the APR and invited the USA to do likewise;
2 he called for consultations among the major maritime powers in the region to agree not to expand their naval forces there;
3 he urged multilateral talks on the freezing and eventual reduction of naval and air forces in the sensitive common border regions between the USSR, China, Japan and North and South Korea to eliminate the possibility of conflicts;

4   he offered to abandon the Soviet naval base at Camranh Bay in return for the liquidation of American bases in the Philippines;
5   he suggested the drafting of regulations to prevent accidental incidents between opposing naval and air forces in the region;
6   he demanded an international conference, to be held no later than 1990, to convert the Indian Ocean into a 'zone of peace'; and
7   he proposed discussions 'at any level' to set up negotiating mechanisms to consider suggestions by the USSR and other powers 'relating to the security of the APR'.[91]

Most of these offers were variants of the old Asian collective security scheme, although they displayed greater sophistication in terms of the mechanisms for achieving it. They still bore the character of a 'wish list' of Soviet desires and priorities in the region, however, so they had little prospect of attracting a favourable response from the United States, which clearly had other priorities. Nevertheless, in presenting them in such a reasonable and systematic manner, Gorbachev obviously hoped to increase pressure on Washington to come up with at least equally reasonable-sounding counter–proposals. The concrete steps taken on Afghanistan and Cambodia went a considerable way toward establishing a climate of greater confidence in Soviet intentions among the states of the region, and that in itself undoubtedly made it difficult for the United States to ignore his initiatives.

The Krasnoyarsk proposals were thus clearly intended for the second track as well. In the speech Gorbachev expressed his country's interest in the 'expansion of mutually beneficial, equal relations with all the states of this part of the world, regardless of their size and social order'.[92] There was already considerable evidence by then that the Soviet diplomatic offensive was having an impact in the region. Gorbachev noted that relations with Australia, for example, had undergone a 'principled about–turn' as a result of his summit meeting in Moscow with Prime Minister Hawke the preceding year, adding that the content of their discussions went beyond merely regional significance. Ties with Australia were materially strengthened by the signing of a series of agreements on fisheries and other economic and cultural matters during Prime Minister Ryzhkov's official visit to Canberra in February 1990.[93] Gorbachev also mentioned successes in his talks with leaders of the ASEAN countries, especially Indonesia, the Philippines and Malaysia. The personnel changes in the Ministry of Foreign Affairs in 1986 and the ensuing improvement in the style of Soviet diplomacy had evidently had some payoff in relations with the individual states of the region.

The second track of his approach was similar to the one being followed towards the smaller states of Western Europe. It involved the holding of periodic, high–level discussions with the officials of the individual Asian and Pacific states to present Moscow's viewpoint on regional issues and to accustom its partners to dealing with the Soviet Union as a regular participant in regional affairs. Fishing deals with the island states of Kiribati, Vanuatu and Papua New Guinea as well as with Australia and New Zealand were an early product of these talks. Their commercial benefits to the USSR were not always readily apparent, but they served as a point of entry for more intensive economic, political and other relations. As Desmond Ball has shown, the establishment of Soviet diplomatic and trade missions in the countries of the region (as elsewhere in the world) had led to an expansion of intelligence operations, which were undoubtedly calculated, at least partly, to compensate for the scheduled reduction in Soviet naval deployments.[94] It is probably no accident that the upsurge in Soviet diplomatic activity in the Philippines, which included an apparently successful request for ship–repair facilities on the island of Cebu, coincided with the Aquino Government's involvement in difficult negotiations with the USA over the future of the American bases in the Philippines. The Soviet offer was clearly designed to suggest to the Filipinos that they can survive without the income from the American military presence.[95] The Soviet decision to phase out the base at Camranh Bay in 1990 put additional pressure on the Philippines to force the United States to follow suit.

Gorbachev's policies in the region since the Krasnoyarsk speech have continued to demonstrate an increasingly realistic appreciation of the weaknesses and opportunities of the Soviet position. On the status of the Soviet Far East there is now widespread recognition that the backwardness of the territory is so great as to require extraordinary measures, such as the establishment of Chinese–style 'special economic zones' to attract the necessary foreign developmental capital. But this will require a good deal more confidence in Soviet intentions and a demonstrated commitment to make the required structural and legal changes.[96] There is an awareness of the special economic problems of the Soviet Far East, especially the absence of reserves of cheap labour, which makes the creation of special economic zones highly problematical. One solution now under discussion is the establishment of joint Soviet and foreign enterprises and of special border zones where Soviet raw materials can be combined with the surplus labour of countries in the region, most notably China, North Korea and Vietnam.[97] Australia and other capitalist countries have begun to invest in joint ventures in the Soviet Far East to develop local resources such as timber, but the negotiation process has usually proved to be extremely arduous.[98]

In general, then, the Soviets have come to realise that for the moment they have little in the way of convertible currency reserves for the type of commercial arrangements desired by the smaller economies of the APR. For the foreseeable future they will be content merely to establish their presence as a potential trading partner by engaging in relatively small–scale purchases and deals, such as the fishing agreements with the island states, and to lay the groundwork for further penetration of the region when the Soviet economy is in healthier shape. Eastern Siberia and the Far East will continue to be one of the instruments for the injection of the Soviet Union into the regional economy, but for a long time they will probably not be a very important factor in the overall Soviet approach to the region. Nevertheless, the impending conclusion of a consular agreement with South Korea suggests that continued efforts will be made to increase the economic stake of regional capitalist powers in the Soviet economy and to threaten the Japanese with being left out of the eventual development programs.

A much more important factor in setting the tone for the broader program of inclusion is the continuing stream of arms control and disarmament initiatives. Gorbachev's address to the UN in December 1988 contained for the first time some specific unilateral force–reduction proposals, which have subsequently been elaborated by Soviet military officials in line with the shift to a 'defensive military doctrine'. In February 1989, Defence Minister Yazov detailed a planned reduction, by the beginning of 1991, of some 200 000 men in the Eastern and Southern border regions of the USSR, largely by converting mechanised strike forces into defensive machine–gun and artillery units.[99] Some three months later Yazov (working from the smaller total of troops to be withdrawn promised by Gorbachev during his pilgrimage to Beijing — 120 000) explained that the program would include the elimination of twelve ground–force divisions and eleven air regiments and the removal of sixteen warships from the Pacific Fleet.[100] In a further bid to capitalise on its arms control initiatives, the Soviet government invited fifteen countries in the region to observe its Pacific Fleet manoeuvres in mid–July 1989. The United States, Japan and Australia declined the invitation to avoid pressure for reciprocal invitations to their own forthcoming exercises.[101]

With regard to China, Gorbachev evidently achieved most of what he set out to accomplish in his historic visit in May 1989. Besides signing a number of economic, scientific and technical and cultural agreements, he succeeded in re–establishing Communist Party ties between the CPSU and the CCP, which indicated something substantially closer than a mere normalisation of state–to–state relations. It will allow continual consultations between the decision–makers of the two countries on a whole gamut of ideological, domestic and foreign–policy issues and effectively signifies the end of hostilities between them. At the same time, it is clear that there will not be a return to the closeness of their relationship of the 1950s. That was based on China's implicit subordination to the Soviet Union and dependence on it for economic and political development. There is no question of a reversion to that situation, nor is it likely that either side would relish a return to that degree of interdependence.[102] The student demonstrations during Gorbachev's visit, the Beijing massacre of 4 June and the subsequent ideological and political crackdown by Deng Xiaoping were obviously an embarrassment to the Soviet leader, who had welcomed the apparently successful liberalising tendencies of the Chinese regime as legitimation of his own program of *perestroika*. The possibilities of substantial mutual economic assistance between the two countries are extremely limited; they are, in a sense, competitors for the favours of capitalist investors. Moreover, the Chinese have been highly critical of Gorbachev personally for having allowed, and indeed encouraged, the decimation of communist power throughout the world.

Nevertheless, the strategic and political gains from the formal Sino–Soviet rapprochement are immense for both sides. They give both parties increased freedom of manoeuvre in domestic development and in dealing with the capitalist world, since they no longer have to worry about a military threat from each other. In that sense, the rapprochement has radically changed the parameters of the security equation in the entire APR, placing the maintenance of the American military presence in the region in a quite different light.

These changes are bound to affect relations between the Soviet Union and Japan as well. On the one hand, they substantially reduce the value of Japan's 'China card' by alleviating the pressure on Moscow to reach agreement with Tokyo in order to lessen the danger of a Sino–Japanese anti–Soviet entente. On the other hand, they place Japanese–Soviet relations much more on a purely economic footing. Gorbachev has had remarkably little success in effecting an improvement with the Liberal–Democratic Party government of Japan, which has responded to Soviet peace initiatives with extreme suspicion. In the course of a conversation with the then Japanese Foreign Minister, Sosuke Uno, in Moscow on 5 May 1989, Gorbachev put two embarrassingly frank questions to his guest:

First, how is one to understand the fact that in conditions when the Soviet Union is implementing its principled course in the area of disarmament and reducing the level of its military potential in the eastern part of the country, Japan, together with the USA, is continuing to increase its military potential and its military activity in the region?

Secondly, how is one to explain the exceedingly cool attitude of Japan, as well as the United States, to our good intentions, expressed in the Vladivostok and Krasnoyarsk initiatives? For this is an invitation to all states of this huge and promising region to search jointly for solutions to questions that are timely and common to all. To seek with consideration for the interests of all, without discrimination, not bypassing anyone, to say nothing, of course, of such powerful states as Japan and the USA. Why are they suspicious of us here?[103]

Uno reportedly had no direct reply to Gorbachev's questions. The Japanese clearly felt that they still had the upper hand in their relations with the Soviet Union and deemed it possible to press ahead with their demands for the return of the 'northern territories' as a condition for economic and political concessions. Indeed, there were reports in a major US news weekly in August 1989 that the Soviets were about to offer to restore the four islands in question to Japan in return for massive Japanese economic aid. These rumours were quickly denied by the Soviet Foreign Ministry, but in the context of recent Soviet diplomatic moves they had seemed quite plausible.[104]

The subsequent turmoil in the Japanese government over scandals involving the LDP leadership can only have been gratifying to the Soviet Union. The sudden, totally unanticipated possibility that the Japanese Socialist Party (JSP), under its charismatic leader Ms Takako Doi, might soon be in a position to form a government raised the prospect of a radical shift in Japanese strategic policy. The JSP's traditional anti–Americanism, its abhorrence of nuclear weapons and its opposition to the development of the Japanese Self–Defence Force beyond purely local defensive needs were clearly in harmony with Soviet desiderata on Asian security.[105] Meanwhile, economic negotiations continued, and not without some notable successes. A major oil and gas development on Sakhalin Island, to be financed by the Japanese to the tune of some $US4 billion over five years, was reportedly near finalisation in mid–July 1989.[106] Clearly, some movement favourable to Soviet interests thus seemed to be occurring in relations with Japan as well. The eventual victory of the LDP in subsequent lower house elections was probably a disappointment for the Soviets, since they would continue to have to deal with essentially the same opponents with the same views on the requirements for improved relations. Nevertheless, there are signs of increased flexibility on both sides, and Gorbachev can be expected to make considerable concessions during his scheduled visit to Tokyo in 1991. Some form of accommodation on the 'northern territories' issue is highly likely.

The intensified Soviet diplomatic activity also appeared to be bearing fruit in the smaller states of the APR. Preparations for the opening of an embassy in Port Moresby towards the end of 1989 proceeded smoothly, and Soviet fishing operations were scheduled to begin shortly thereafter. Attending a session of the South Pacific Forum Fisheries Agency in April 1989, the genial Soviet Ambassador to Australia, Dr Evgenii Samoteikin, expressed the hope that the recent success in concluding a fishing agreement with Australia (which included limited shore facilities) would clear the way for similar agreements with other South Pacific states.[107] Those hopes appear to be well founded, given the willingness of the Soviets to pay a higher fee to the contracting states than do their competitors; earlier fears of Soviet intentions were evidently dissipating in the face of demonstrative Soviet support for anti–nuclear and peace movements in the region.[108]

One of the keystones of the Soviet campaign to establish closer relations with the ASEAN states was a solution of the Cambodian conflict. Moscow attempted to apply there the same 'national reconciliation' strategy that it had used to disentangle itself from Afghanistan and Angola: that is, to bring the guerilla forces opposing the pro–Soviet government into a national–reconciliation coalition, which would still be dominated by its Communist Party core, but which would adopt a non–ideological developmental policy domestically and a nonaligned policy internationally. This strategy has been partially successful in the Afghan and Angolan situations, but negotiations for an analogous solution in Cambodia in Paris in August and September 1989 eventually broke down over the refusal of the anti–Vietnamese resistance coalition to accept the pro–Vietnamese and pro–Soviet Hun Sen government as the nucleus for the projected coalition. Continued Chinese support for the Khmer Rouge, which seemed to intensify after the crackdown of 4 June, made further progress impossible, and the Soviets probably wished to avoid antagonising Beijing by prolonging the search for an agreement.

Despite the failure of their efforts in Cambodia, the Soviets evidently received good marks in the region for trying. Relations with individual

ASEAN members continued to improve, especially with Indonesia, and the visit of President Suharto to Moscow in September was hailed as a major success by both parties. Important increases in bilateral trade were expected to follow.[109] Further improvements in Soviet relations with the Philippines and Thailand also occurred during 1989, and in Soviet communications to ASEAN and its individual member states, there were indications of an increasing readiness to push the untempered Soviet line on regional security, arms reduction and nuclear–free zones without the earlier concern about antagonising the United States and dismissing its security interests.[110] The Soviets obviously felt they were making substantial progress in the region.

In reality, however, their prospects for a decisive breakthrough were limited. As Singaporean Prime Minister Lee pointed out in July 1989, the Soviets really had very little to offer the states of the region, given the parlous state of the Soviet economy. The developing economies concerned needed export markets, capital investments and technological expertise — just the things the Soviets themselves were trying to obtain from the West, and even from countries like Singapore, Taiwan and South Korea! Lee didn't expect them to be a serious participant in the economy of the APR for at least five to ten years.[111] Moreover, Lee and some other ASEAN leaders were still determined to try to maintain a major American military presence in the region — even at the expense of sharing part of the burden themselves — as insurance against possible changes in the Soviet attitude. The crackdown in China must certainly have reinforced that determination

Conclusions

Relations with the capitalist world have always been the main focus of Soviet foreign policy, first as the principal source of danger to the survival of the Soviet state, and then as the primary obstacle to the expansion of Soviet power and influence throughout the world. In the traditional perspectives of Marxist–Leninist ideology, imperialism — the final stage of capitalism — was doomed to destroy itself as a result of its own systemic 'contradictions', paving the way for the victory of socialism in one area of the globe after another. International class struggle, occasionally violent, was considered the appropriate mode of interaction between the worlds of socialism and capitalism, with intermediate non–violent periods of 'peaceful coexistence', when the 'correlation of forces' was temporarily unfavourable for the further expansion of socialism.

Under Gorbachev this scenario has explicitly been discarded, with the realisation that the world of capitalism possesses unexpected reserves of vitality, while the self–contained fortress of international socialism has proven itself incapable of sufficient technological and social progress to compete with capitalism in economic development and political influence. Even in the area of military power, the one arena where socialism did seem to be able to maintain an advantage, economic sluggishness threatened to undermine its competitive capacity. To end its isolation and stagnation, according to Gorbachev, the USSR and its allies had to join the world economy, reconciling themselves with capitalism and its rules of internal and international behaviour. That meant changing the Soviet Union's international image and its traditional modes of promoting its interests throughout the world.

By its previous conduct the USSR had managed to erect an international strategic and political coalition against itself, headed by the United States, whose relationship to its allies in various parts of the world was in most respects quite different to the USSR's own, not only in political, but also in economic terms. Even under circumstances of relative decline in its economic power *vis–a–vis* the other main centres of capitalism, Western Europe and Japan, the United States remained the linchpin of the financial and technological mechanism of the world capitalist system. In order to participate in that system, or its major subsystems, such as the European Economic Community, the Soviet Union had to gain the assent of the United States. Much of the Soviet effort to find a place for itself in the 'common European home' has, accordingly, had to be expended on reaching agreement with Washington, particularly on military issues. Although his ultimate objective is undoubtedly to replace the United States as the dominant political and economic power in Europe, Gorbachev has evidently concluded that he must reckon with a strong American presence for the foreseeable future. Indeed, with the disintegration of the Soviet satellite empire in Eastern Europe and the rise of Germany, he has apparently come to see certain advantages in the maintenance of American involvement. The costs of Gorbachev's opening to Western Europe, in terms of the disruption of traditional patterns of control over the world of socialism, have been considerable, and it is still uncertain whether the eventual payoff will prove worthwhile. He is evidently convinced that he has no realistic alternatives, however. US President George Bush's muted response to his crackdown in Lithuania in March 1990 suggests that Gorbachev's gamble has been quite successful, and that the American administration is firmly committed to his survival as Soviet leader as the key to the successful management of international relations in a post–Cold War world.

In the Asia–Pacific region, Gorbachev faces a similar situation, although the centrality of the American position is somewhat less evident. He recognises that the dynamic development of the region offers attractive opportunities for the solution of serious economic and social problems in the eastern parts of the USSR. However, even in the absence of American strategic domination, which seems likely to diminish in proportion to the decline in the perception of the Soviet military threat throughout the region, Gorbachev realises that his economy is in no position to take decisive advantage of the opportunities available. His strategy in the APR is therefore to increase the intensity of low–cost diplomatic and economic activity, while easing the United States out of its position of primacy in the region. Recent changes within China and Japan promise to make the implementation of this dual–track strategy more complex, but mean it will probably be more fruitful in producing long–term political and economic advantages for the USSR. So far, the United States and its allies have not been as receptive to Soviet initiatives in the APR as they have in Europe, but some movement toward accommodation is virtually inevitable.

Gorbachev's explicit objective in paying the high entry fee to join the world market club was to integrate the socialist countries into the world economy, not to dissolve them in a sea of capitalism. However, he has not been able to maintain control over the processes he has set in motion. In order to try to salvage as much as possible from the resulting debacle and to accommodate the stringent conditions of entry, he has even been willing to re–conceptualise the essence of socialism itself. Ironically, it may turn out that neither he nor his successors will be very happy with the result.

5 The Soviet Union and the communist world

Introduction

Undoubtedly the most radical shifts in Soviet foreign policy have occurred in relations with fellow communist states. Particularly in Eastern Europe, where Moscow's Communist Party ties have been closest and the strategic stakes have been highest, the changes taking place at the end of the 1980s, with Gorbachev's apparent acquiescence, have gone beyond the wildest Western speculation of just a few years ago. Indeed, the Orwellian prediction of the late Soviet dissident exile Andrei Amalrik that the Soviet Union itself would not survive until 1984 may have been wrong only in its timing.[1] The 'communist world' has shrunk and is still shrinking, and its remnants are perhaps more fragmented ideologically than at any time since the early days of the Comintern.

The discussion of these tumultuous changes here focuses primarily on Soviet relations with the Warsaw Pact states, since that is where the influence of Gorbachev's new political thinking has been greatest and where the impact on the Soviet Union's position in international affairs has been most striking. Consideration will also be given to relations with other socialist countries, such as China, Cuba and Vietnam, where they illustrate general issues of the transformation of Soviet attitudes towards friends and foes in the post–Cold War world.

To appreciate the magnitude of the changes that Gorbachev has introduced and/or permitted in the USSR's relationship with its Warsaw Treaty Organisation (WTO) allies requires a brief re–examination of the situation in the 1970s and early 1980s before his accession to power. If, today, we are compelled to ask whether any of these countries can still be considered allies, let alone 'satellites', of the USSR, that question could hardly have arisen in the last decade or so of the Brezhnev era. The WTO invasion of Czechoslovakia in 1968 under the umbrella of the 'Brezhnev doctrine' — the doctrine of the 'limited sovereignty' of the states of the Socialist Commonwealth (other than the USSR, of course) — had seemingly put paid to any notions of significant internal autonomy on the part of the Eastern European regimes in managing their domestic economic and social problems. And yet, as the 1970s progressed, it became clear in many of these countries that the model of 'real' or 'developed' socialism prescribed by Moscow was failing to keep pace with the requirements of economic development in an era of rapid scientific and technological change.

Detente with the West in the early 1970s had had its own economic corollaries, which seemed to contradict Soviet arguments for uniformity. The Soviet Union itself had begun to take advantage of detente to seek techological short cuts by imports from the West. It could hardly forbid its satellites from following a similar course if they insisted on doing so. Indeed, there were intelligence and commercial advantages in expanding Bloc economic relations with the West via the Eastern European countries, which were naively looked upon in some Western quarters as being less threatening than the USSR from a security standpoint. It was not uncommon for elements of sensitive technology that were under COCOM (Co–ordinating Committee for Multilateral Export Controls) or direct American embargo to the USSR to reach the latter through Eastern European channels. Moreover, Western lenders paradoxically regarded credits to Eastern Europe as a sound investment, on the implicit assumption that, under the canons of 'socialist internationalism', the Soviet Union would ultimately bail out its junior partners in case of repayments difficulties.

Ironically, it was those countries — Romania, Czechoslovakia, the German Democratic Republic and the USSR itself — which maintained the most rigid 'dictatorship over needs'[2] and largely avoided heavy foreign hard–currency debt burdens, that seemed, at first, to suffer the least disruption of traditional communist patterns of social control. By contrast, Poland and Hungary, which took greatest advantage of foreign borrowing, ostensibly to modernise their economies and improve popular living standards, suffered most heavily from the accumulation of such debts and found it increasingly difficult to satisfy the aroused expectations of their peoples. These negative consequences were not entirely the fault of the regimes. Their intentions of paying off their debts with the products of the newly modernised industries were frustrated by a downturn in the economies of their potential Western markets as well as by growing

protectionist barriers against their traditional exports. Nevertheless, much
of the imported capital was not wisely used,[3] and the very structure of the
Polish and Hungarian economies, which had retained basically the same
centralised, politically determined allocative mechanisms as in the rest of
the Bloc, was far from optimal for the absorption of the new technologies.

Patterns   of   Soviet–Eastern   European   relations   under Brezhnev

From the outset, the Brezhnev regime in the USSR had been sensitive to
the potential negative effects of Western economic and technical
penetration and had attempted to insulate its Bloc partners from them as
much as possible. Mao's charges of ideological revisionism and the direct
military threat posed by military incidents along the Sino–Soviet border
also put pressure on Brezhnev to try to consolidate still further the Soviet
position of dominance in Eastern Europe. These considerations were the
rationale behind Brezhnev's Comprehensive Program of economic
integration announced in 1971. The idea was to integrate the economies of
the Council of Mutual Economic Assistance (CMEA) member states by
establishing a division of labour among them, featuring product
specialisation and bilateral and multilateral co–operation in the production
of key technological items.[4] The Soviet Union, as by far the largest and
most diversified of the Bloc economies and as the principal supplier of
strategic fuels and raw materials, would automatically be in the driver's seat
in setting the priorities and directions of development for the projected
collective economic system. On the surface, one would have expected that
the common centralised planning and managerial structures of the member
states and the co–ordinating mechanisms of the CMEA apparatus would
greatly facilitate the process of integration.

   In fact, the reality was just the reverse. The identity of structures
actually tended to obstruct economic integration and co–ordination. Under
the mandatory Stalinist model each Bloc state's economy was organised to
achieve a maximum degree of autarky and a maximum utilisation of its
own product. Furthermore, each country's system of social and political
rewards was structured, in the absence of a market mechanism and of freely
convertible currencies, to ration scarce domestically produced goods and
services among a hierarchy of favoured groups and strata whose loyalty was
considered essential to the maintenance of the regime's power. In short,
there was little surplus for export. Apart from defence expenditures, which
were dictated by the Soviet Union through the Warsaw Pact for mandatory

inclusion in each country's annual production plan, and the clearing of annual trade balances with the USSR and other Bloc states for essential imports, most available resources were jealously guarded by the respective regimes for internal use. The non–convertibility of national currencies within the Bloc, let alone with Western hard currencies, militated against 'shopping around' within CMEA, since there was no way of knowing just how much imported goods really cost. (A sign of this anarchy of prices is the recent wave of consumer goods purchases by East European tourists in search of bargains within the region in terms of their own currencies. The resultant shortages of items for domestic consumers prompted Czechoslovakia, East Germany and Poland at the end of 1988 to decree limits on the quantities of goods available to Bloc visitors. The Soviet Union itself threatened to follow suit in January 1989.)[5]

It was commonly reckoned that exports within the Bloc represented a net loss to the domestic economy.[6] Oil imports from the Soviet Union were a partial exception to this rule until 1975, when Moscow decided to bring its prices gradually up to world market levels and later, when it decided to reduce the level of guaranteed supplies to its Eastern European partners. (In the absence of hard currency reserves the Eastern Europeans were always willing to pay for Soviet oil with their goods.) Otherwise, 'free' exports within the Bloc tended to be regarded as a residual. Whatever could not be sold for hard currency on the world market or was surplus to domestic needs was dumped on the insatiable Soviet market. Even non–Bloc member Yugoslavia became addicted to this practice, although it was conscious of the political and other dangers of becoming economically dependent on the USSR. Without alternative markets for their products the Yugoslavs found it advantageous to resort systematically to the Soviet market as a means of keeping their plants running and maintaining employment.

This is not to say that the European CMEA states did not trade extensively with one another. A major share of the foreign trade of most of these countries was with each other (See Tables 1 and 2 in the Appendix). But this was dictated primarily by the need to clear trade balances in paying for intra–Bloc imports. Bulgaria's dependence on the Bloc has been particularly striking. Poland's variable position up to 1976 and its increasing dependence on the Bloc, particularly after the proclamation of Martial Law in 1981, are graphically shown in the tables. Romania's position as the 'odd man out' is clearly reflected in the near parity between trade with the Bloc and with the advanced capitalist economies. The country's strong–willed leader, Nicolae Ceausescu, sought to preserve Romania's independence as much as possible by, among other things, restricting the proportion of Bloc–oriented imports and exports. Poland and Hungary used the same technique, but not entirely for the same reasons.   In all three cases the resultant financial and commercial obligations to the Western market economies led to considerable economic and social difficulties. Ceausescu's policy of rapidly paying off Romania's Western debts by forcing down public consumption and curbing all but essential imports was, for political reasons, simply not a viable option for Poland and Hungary. The Soviet Union itself (as can be seen in Tables 1 and 2 in the Appendix), although obviously heavily involved in Bloc trade, was economically too powerful to have been as dependent on Bloc imports or exports as its junior CMEA partners. Internal Soviet demand was large enough to discourage the export of manufactured goods to pay for essential imports (raw material and fuel exports sufficed for the latter), even if the quality of Soviet manufactures had been sufficiently high to make sales in the West a realistic alternative, which it certainly was not. By the late 1980s the supposed advantages of this traditional import–substitution strategy were being acknowledged as a long–term weakness — a symbol of the technological crisis of the Soviet economy.

The military dimension of the Soviet–Eastern European relationship was equally problematical. The WTO provided a useful international legal cover for the continued deployment of Soviet troops in the region, both as an occupation force and as a counterweight to NATO. It also served as a useful forum for the Soviets to orchestrate the foreign and defence policies of the alliance.[7] However, apart from the WTO's obvious territorial benefits for the Soviet Union — defence in depth far to the west of Soviet frontiers and room for manoeuvre and the marshalling of Soviet troops and weapons for an offensive war in Europe — there was always a question about whether the Eastern European armies in the alliance represented much of a net addition to Soviet military strength. Given Brezhnev's obvious fascination with the gross physical aspects of military power, the answer to this question tended to be considered affirmative. The WTO invasion of Czechoslovakia in 1968 and General Jaruzelski's 'auto–invasion' of Poland in December 1981 under threat of direct Soviet intervention suggest that Brezhnev regarded Soviet forces *in situ* as a powerful political and psychological, as well as military, component of Bloc unity. His grudging willingness to bail Poland out of its economic difficulties after the Jaruzelski coup indicated a recognition of the obligation to pay a price for this unity.[8] The demonstration of Soviet determination was undoubtedly designed to impress the Chinese as well.

The political relations which developed between Brezhnev and the Eastern European party leaders, particularly after the Czechoslovakian crisis, had a peculiar, Mafia–like quality. In addition to formal state visits and exchanges of high–ranking party delegations, Brezhnev introduced the custom of entertaining individual national party leaders during his summer holidays on the Black Sea. These visits acquired a ritualistic character and seemed to follow a regular sequence. Important exchanges of views and information on the internal situation in the respective countries evidently took place in the midst of conspicuous luxury, and a rough cameraderie seems to have developed between Brezhnev and most of his Bloc lieutenants. Even the highly cautious and independent–minded Ceausescu seemed to have been a regular participant in these sessions 'at court'. In many respects they were a reprise of Stalin's technique of summoning East European leaders for personal 'instructions', although the atmosphere under Brezhnev appears to have been decidedly less nervewracking and/or physically dangerous to the 'fraternal guests'. Nevertheless, it was clear that Brezhnev exercised a form of *nomenklatura* supervision over personnel appointments in the Bloc (with the exception of Romania), and appointments, if not removals, of key figures were evidently subject to Soviet veto. The replacement in Poland of Wladyslaw Gomulka by Edward Gierek in 1970 and the subsequent replacement of Gierek, first by Stanislav Kania in 1980 and then by General Wojciech Jaruzelski in 1981 after annointment by Moscow, illustrated this type of supervision.

By establishing personal relations with his Bloc satraps, Brezhnev was able to dispense with Stalin's practice of issuing direct instructions to them on details of internal policy and administration and, consequently, to avoid responsibility when things went wrong. As long as the Eastern European comrades abided by the general formulas of 'real socialism', they were free to seek their own solutions to domestic problems; indeed, they were encouraged to do so and to court popular support for their policies. But the degree of acceptable diversity was never made clear. As James F. Brown has noted, there was always tension between the two criteria of 'cohesion' and 'viability' which Moscow applied to the conduct of the Eastern European regimes — that is, between the requirement of uniformity and Bloc solidarity, on the one hand, and the need for the respective regimes to establish their domestic legitimacy, on the other.[9]

Experiments with economic reform and expanded economic and financial links with the West by Hungary and Poland during the 1970s reflected a determination on the part of their leaders to take maximum advantage of the limited autonomy offered by Brezhnev's system of intra–Bloc relations. As in 1968 with Czechoslovakia, however, increasing Soviet pressure on Poland to reverse the concessions to Solidarity by

Kania and Jaruzelski in 1981, was the ultimate signal throughout the Bloc
that the limits of Moscow's tolerance had been overstepped.

Indeed, it can be argued that every Soviet regime since the formation
of the Eastern European empire in 1945 had to step in from time to time
to specify the mixture of structures and procedures it considered acceptably
'socialist'. The founding of the Cominform in September 1947 was the
first example of this intervention. The process remained a dynamic one,
since the criteria of acceptable diversity and the willingness of the Soviet
Union to pay the economic and political price of enforced uniformity
changed over time. Nevertheless, until the Gorbachev era certain
minimum 'rules of the game' had operated, the actual or potential violation
of which always eventually led to Soviet intervention. These minimum
rules included:

1   the maintenance of the Communist Party's 'leading role', — that is,
     its monopoly of policy–making and of the power to make
     appointments to key positions throughout the system;
2   the maintenance of ideological control, — that is, control over
     education and the media and the preservation of a rigorous system of
     censorship, plus the upholding of certain basic ideological principles
     — most notably state or 'public' ownership of the main means of
     production; and
3   the maintenance of a firm commitment to the Warsaw Pact military
     alliance.

It is the practical abandonment, of the first two of these rules and the
potential modification of the third which underlines the magnitude of the
changes which Gorbachev is fostering in the matrix of Soviet–Eastern
European relations.

Gorbachev's attempted solutions to the problems of the 1980s

At the time of his advent to power Gorbachev confronted a situation in
Eastern Europe that had been conditioned by two recent events: the crisis in
Poland and the increase in East–West tensions over the deployment of
intermediate range nuclear missiles (INF) in Europe. The effect of the two
traumas had been a general tightening of Soviet political and ideological
controls over the region, reflected in a general hiatus in economic and
political reform, despite mounting evidence that reform was imperative.
Under Brezhnev's short–lived successors, Andropov and Chernenko, half–

hearted efforts had been made to revive the moribund integrative and co–ordinating mechanisms of CMEA, but the previously mentioned institutional obstacles to progress in that area had proven to be insuperable.[10]

From the outset Gorbachev made it clear that he contemplated changes in the social, economic and political systems of Soviet socialism that were more far reaching than had ever been attempted in the various reforms and 'social experiments' under Khrushchev and Brezhnev. The success of Deng Xiaoping's economic reforms which had already been underway in China for almost seven years by the time Gorbachev came to power, undoubtedly had a certain influence on his thinking. His reform project went further, however; it involved the refurbishing of the image of socialism itself as a viable alternative world system and entailed an effort to make each socialist country a showcase of efficient social and economic organisation by closely co–ordinating their efforts at modernisation. The course of subsequent events suggests that, although he had a fairly comprehensive understanding of the nature of the problems to be tackled, he did not have anything like a clear blueprint for implementing these goals.

Gorbachev's early programmatic utterances showed, as we have seen in chapter 4, that his policies toward Eastern Europe were strongly influenced by his initial, rather conventionally negative perceptions of the state of East–West relations. Thus, in framing his program of accelerated modernisation of the Soviet and Bloc economies, he professed to wish to rely on the advanced sectors of the Eastern European economies rather than on the West for high–technology imports.[11] In this way he sought to insulate the Bloc's modernisation program as much as possible from the vagaries of East–West relations, and in particular the boycotts and tightened COCOM restrictions which had become a feature of American–led Western responses to perceived Soviet expansionism since the last months of the Carter presidency. Although he had held out the hope of improved East–West relations in his earliest policy statements, Gorbachev did not wish to be dependent on Western goodwill for the success of his 'restructuring' program (*perestroika*).

Recognising the structural obstacles to closer co–ordination of the Bloc economies, Gorbachev undertook a two–fold revamping of the organisation and *modus operandi* of CMEA and the pattern of relations between the Soviet and Eastern European economies. At the 41st (Extraordinary) Session of CMEA in December 1985, at his insistence, the representatives of the Bloc adopted a 'Complex Program of Scientific and Technical Progress of the Member Countries of the Council of Mutual

Economic Assistance up to the Year 2000'.[12] Under the program the central CMEA bureaucracy was significantly reduced in size and deprived of many of its direct administrative responsibilities. Substantively, CMEA was required to adopt virtually the same sectoral priorities for accelerated development as would feature in the Soviet program for domestic development at the 27th CPSU Congress some two months later: namely, the 'electronisation' of the economy, comprehensive automation of production processes (particularly in the area of the machine–tool and engineering industries), the development of nuclear power and other energy sources, the development of new types of composite materials, and biotechnology. These objectives were to be pursued co–operatively by enlisting the participation of enterprises and research and development bodies of the member countries according to their particular strengths in the specified areas. Finally, in a spirit of 'socialist internationalism', the Eastern European members were required to contribute to the accelerated economic development of the non–European members of CMEA — Cuba, Mongolia, and Vietnam — in line with the objective of 'gradual equalising of the levels of economic development'.[13]

The main innovation of the new 'Complex Program', upon which Gorbachev was particularly insistent, was its focus on production co–operation and joint ventures **at the enterprise and institute level**. His strategy was clearly aimed at circumventing the governmental bureaucracies of the respective participating states in order to combat the entrenched autarchic proclivities of the traditional Stalinist economic system. The goal was to integrate the production and technological processes of the Bloc and to operate them under Soviet direction.

But this base–level approach to integration implied a violation of one of the fundamental ideological principles of 'real socialism': 'social ownership' of the means of production; that is, control over the 'appropriation, use and disposition' of the national economic institutions and resources by the state and its agencies in each socialist country.[14] In fact, this important change in the conception of property relations had become conceivable only because analogous changes were under consideration for the Soviet economy, in line with foreshadowed legislation respecting the rights of enterprises, leasing arrangements, an expanded role for co–operatives and so–called 'individual labour activity'. Accordingly, the Soviet Union pressured the member countries to make appropriate changes in their domestic legislation to permit the signing of direct contracts between their own and Soviet enterprises for co–operative work on priority projects in line with bilateral agreements concluded under the Complex Program. In every case of such direct contracts upon which I have information to date, the Soviet institution was cast in the role of the dominant, directing partner.

The entire integration process was publicly justified as a way of achieving technological and economic 'invulnerability' of the Bloc to Western pressure.[15] That logic was more acceptable to some Bloc leaders than to others. Ceausescu evidently considered there to be more danger for his country from vulnerability to the Bloc than to the West, and Romania was the last of the group to sign a bilateral agreement on scientific and technological co–operation with the USSR under the terms of the Complex Program. Indeed, Romania was the only member to decline to endorse a plan in July 1988 to transform CMEA into a common, or 'unified' market.[16] Hungary, under the ostensibly more reformist leadership of Karoly Grosz and Miklos Nemeth, was lukewarm about CMEA integration. Her heavy hard–currency debt burden required the greatest possible freedom of action to unfetter her internal economy and make a start on repaying her debts. Poland, with substantial excess industrial capacity as a result of the economic slowdown during and after martial law, was at first enthusiastic about tying selected enterprises to Soviet–led projects. The results were not very impressive, however, and the eventual decision to undertake negotiations with Solidarity was clear evidence of Jaruzelski's conclusion that this was an unavoidable price for economic reform and the resumption of Western financial aid, without which economic recovery was virtually impossible.

Czechoslovakia and Bulgaria seemingly remained quite comfortable in the Soviet embrace. While paying lip–service to Gorbachev's demands for *perestroika*, the regimes in both countries accomplished little in the way of serious economic, let alone political, reform. They acquiesced in inter-enterprise contracts with Soviet institutions, because that allowed them to avoid the hard choices of going it alone and competing on the world market. In any case, the pace and scope of the implementation of the joint projects were modest enough not to disturb seriously continued central control over their economies. Indeed, Bulgarian leader Todor Zhivkov had pressed ahead so recklessly with *perestroika* in 1987 and 1988 that he had managed to discredit the entire exercise, prompting Moscow to recommend a slowdown — undoubtedly another reason for Gorbachev's evident dislike of the Bulgarian leader.[17]

In East Germany, party and state leader Erich Honecker, although endorsing the idea of economic reform for others, consistently denied its relevance for his country. He continued to do so right up until his forced retirement in mid–October 1989 in the wake of the mass exodus of East German citizens to the Federal Republic of Germany in despair over the total lack of economic and political liberalisation in the GDR. Thanks to its special relationship with the Federal Republic, the GDR had for several years enjoyed sufficient access to Western credits and markets to find the integrated–enterprise model favoured by Gorbachev less than attractive. Thus, despite remaining one of the USSR's primary trading partners, the GDR managed to the end of its 45 years of communist rule to avoid becoming heavily involved in closer forms of productive or technological integration with Moscow or other Bloc states.

Under the self–imposed constraints of his doctrine of 'freedom of choice', Gorbachev was evidently not able to force his own convictions of the imperative nature of *perestroika* on the recalcitrant, orthodox Stalinist Honecker during his visit to East Berlin in October 1989. As in China the previous May, the aroused citizenry of the GDR took advantage of Gorbachev's visit to demonstrate for *perestroika*. Honecker's attempts to raise the spectre of the Beijing massacre to cow the East German demonstrators into submission (incidentally, he had been one of the few Bloc leaders expressly to approve Deng's actions) fortunately proved to be mere rhetoric, and in the end he was forced to resign. According to West German sources, Gorbachev directly influenced his removal in a meeting with SED leaders.[18] Honecker's successor, Egon Krenz, a 52–year–old party functionary in charge of youth and the security apparatus, hardly seemed to possess the sort of reform credentials that would have led Gorbachev to recommend him had he enjoyed the degree of control over Bloc personnel appointments that his predecessors had wielded.[19] Nevertheless, the very fact of Honecker's departure indicated substantial movement in Gorbachev's favour in this bastion of Stalinist orthodoxy. The continuation of popular demonstrations for liberalisation after Krenz's appointment demonstrated the impossibility of maintaining 'business as usual', even if Krenz were inclined to do so. Moscow showed no sign of contemplating moral or material support for the re–establishment of tight party control in East Germany or elsewhere. In any case, Krenz's reign was mercifully short, and he was eventually expelled from the SED. The fact that Honecker, like Vladimir Shcherbitskii at home in the Ukraine, could no longer maintain control over his people removed the last justification for Gorbachev's grudging toleration of his resistance to *perestroika*.

In any case, the reduction in East–West tensions and the unexpectedly speedy opening up of trade opportunities with the West deprived the 'invulnerability' argument of much of its force. It was becoming increasingly clear to the more reform–minded among party leaders, including Gorbachev himself, that the real action in foreign trade and technological modernisation lay outside the CMEA framework. Indeed, it is difficult not to agree with the assessment of a survey of East European developments in 1988:

> Intra–CMEA trade did not fare well, however, and virtually ceased growing. The CMEA itself remained torn between those willing to reform it on market principles and those, like Romania and the GDR, who do not believe in such reform.[20]

By the first half of 1989 it was therefore obvious that the route to Soviet–Eastern European economic integration would be a long and tortuous one, even if the effort to pursue it had continued at a serious level. Even the expediency of trying to do so began to be questioned as a high–priority Soviet objective. An article in the authoritative journal *World Economy and International Relations* placed the whole question of CMEA economic relations in a new context:

> Underrating contemporary world economic realities in the economic strategy of the USSR and the socialist commonwealth as a whole dooms socialism to economic backwardness in relation to capitalism. Attempts to conceal the problem of inadequate structural international economic links by political motives are at the very least short–sighted . . . It is, of course, not a matter of curtailing economic links with the fraternal states — they will deepen in the future as well. At the same time the starting level of participation of the CMEA countries in the world division of labour is still very low and fully allows the combining of progress in socialist economic integration with a rationalisation of the geographic structure of their international economic activity.

The author went on to make the astonishingly disingenuous observation that:

> By asserting the total priority of mutual cooperation, the countries of CMEA are in fact willy nilly subjecting their partners in the capitalist states to real discrimination.[21]

The de–emphasis of economic integration within CMEA implied in this and other analyses,[22] when raised tacitly to the status of official policy, undoubtedly evoked a deep sigh of relief from many Eastern European politicians. Others, however, were not to be quite so happy with the political corollaries of a substantial reduction in the Soviet material commitment to the Bloc. Whatever the level of priority assigned to integration, it was already clear to Soviet leaders by 1990 that the payoff from co–operative transnational ventures involving CMEA partners would be slow and would not contribute much in the short run to the success of *perestroika*. Gorbachev is obviously in a hurry for concrete results; hence Moscow's increasing interest in more direct forms of technological transfer from the West, while continuing to urge better performance from a more selective category of joint ventures with Eastern European partners.[23]

Nevertheless, it is unwise to underrate the degree of economic integration which has emerged in Eastern Europe over the past 45 years. As the tables in the Appendix indicate, most of the members of CMEA are heavily dependent on the USSR for energy, raw materials and markets, and many of them remain heavily indebted to Moscow. As of November 1989, Poland had a debt of nearly 5 billion rubles to the USSR, placing her behind only Cuba (15.5 billion rubles), Mongolia (9.5 billion rubles) and Vietnam (9.1 billion rubles).[24] No short–term shifts in trade towards the West are likely to be able to change this dependence materially. Gorbachev is aware that despite the radical political changes occurring throughout Eastern Europe, the Soviet Union will continue to be able to exert a powerful influence on the policies of the individual countries. This reality is admitted by many observers in the Eastern European countries themselves. A commentator in the Solidarity weekly in Poland argued in February 1990 that, in order to deal with the West, Poland still had to gain the assent of 'the East'; and the only way to break the existing pattern of dependence was to undergo the 'great social sacrifices' entailed in radical market–type economic reforms.[25] In short, trade with the USSR remains a 'soft option' for the East European economies. Until they can wean themselves away from the Soviet economy and eliminate Soviet–type practices in their domestic economies, Moscow will retain substantial leverage over them. By the same token, Soviet reformers see a similar solution for their own economic problems, for economic dependence is increasingly being recognised as a two–way process.[26]

On the political side of *perestroika*, Gorbachev's insistence on *glasnost*, democratisation and freedom of choice throughout the Bloc has had a devastating impact on Eastern Europe and the nature of Soviet relations with the countries of the region. The new orientation meant a definite shift in emphasis, in Brown's terms, from 'cohesion' to 'viability'. The Eastern European leaders were placed on notice that they had to look after themselves, politically as well as economically. The tacit scrapping of the Brezhnev doctrine implicit in the principle of freedom of choice had, by 1988, effectively removed the threat of Soviet intervention as an excuse for not undertaking far– reaching internal reforms.[27] Moreover, deliberate Soviet moves to repair ties with the former 'Eurocommunist' parties of Italy, Spain and elsewhere by admitting past mistakes and endorsing their domestic approaches to social–democratic and other moderate leftist parties had the effect, in addition to legitimising Soviet contacts with an important sector of Western political life, of undermining previous strictures on ideological orthodoxy in Eastern Europe.

Gorbachev's major initiative for a rapprochement with China in the spring of 1989 was obviously intended to send similar signals. In most respects his visit to Beijing in mid–April was a disaster. Although he succeeded in re–establishing formal relations between the CPSU and the CCP, the fact that his presence in Beijing was used by the student demonstrators to pressure the CCP leadership both to extend the Chinese reforms from the economic to the political sphere and to crack down on the rampant, capitalist–type excesses of the economic reform itself was bound to be highly embarrassing to Gorbachev and his hosts. The ensuing vicious repression of the student movement some two weeks after his departure, the subsequent reversion of the CCP leadership under Deng Xiaoping to hardline ideological and political orthodoxy, complete with a purge of erstwhile reformers, and the effective termination of the economic reform itself can only have dismayed Gorbachev, for it played right into the hands of his own domestic conservative opponents.[28] His determination not to allow unfavourable comment on the Chinese events in the Soviet media got him into some difficulty with his liberal supporters, who criticised the immorality of his 'non–interference' in Chinese internal affairs.[29] Nor could Gorbachev have been particularly happy with subsequent Chinese attempts to play the 'Soviet card' by threatening to turn to the USSR for economic assistance if the West continued to apply punitive economic sanctions.[30] The last thing Gorbachev needs at the current stage of his reforms is to link the fragile Soviet economy to a Chinese regime seemingly hell–bent on reverting to centralised command planning and administration. Nevertheless, he evidently remains determined to maintain at least some momentum in the rapprochement with China. In September 1989 a delegation of the USSR Supreme Soviet, led by Gorbachev's parliamentary second–in–command, Anatolii Luk'ianov, travelled to China for a seven–day visit as guest of the Chinese National Assembly. In an affirmation of the refurbished inter–party ties, an invitation was issued by Aleksandr Yakovlev, the head of the CPSU's International Commission, to Deng's hand–picked new CCP General Secretary, Jiang Zemin, to visit the Soviet Union for official talks.[31] In March 1990 Gorbachev himself urged an intensification of Sino–Soviet economic relations to increase the 'dynamism' of the relationship, which had admittedly flagged in the wake of the increasing ideological and political divergence of the two countries since June 1989.

In undertaking his radical changes in the rules of international and domestic communist politics, Gorbachev was, of course, taking a calculated gamble on the Eastern European leaders' instincts and capacity for self-preservation. He was assuming that, despite *glasnost*, democratisation and whatever elements of political pluralism they found it necessary to accept in making their accommodations with domestic social forces and movements, they would be no less careful than he himself has been in the USSR to maintain the 'leading role' of the Communist Party. He purposely left them plenty of leeway to work out the specific content of that role. But he could only have been bemused by the extent to which they have let themselves be forced or manoeuvred into accepting the dismantling of the machinery of Communist Party rule. The various regimes have responded in different ways to the difficult challenge of establishing their 'viability', but the visible demonstration of what was happening in some of them, most notably in Poland and Hungary, without the slightest sign of Soviet intervention, undoubtedly had a cumulative force of its own. Once the dominoes began falling, there was no stopping them, not even at the Soviet border, it would appear.

In Poland and Hungary the dominant reformist elements in the Communist Parties were willing to accept substantial alterations to their conventional monopoly of political power, but events swiftly moved beyond their control, and they soon found themselves fighting for their very survival in the political life of their countries. In Poland a 'round-table' agreement was concluded, in April 1989, to legalise Solidarity and to open up the political structure to various new elements of the emerging civil society. The agreement provided for the establishment of a new upper house of parliament with a wide range of veto powers, based on free, direct elections, and the allowance of a more or less free vote for 35 per cent of the delegates to the dominant lower house.[32]

The elections of 4 June threw all the Communist Party's calculations on limited power sharing into disarray. Virtually all its candidates were defeated at the polls, and General Jaruzelski's choice for the Prime Ministership, the relatively liberal Minister of the Interior, General Czeslaw Kiszczak, found it impossible to form a government in the face of the opposition of the Solidarity majority in the new parliament. Ultimately it fell to a member of Solidarity itself, journalist Tadeusz Mazowiecki, to undertake the task. In the broad coalition he succeeded in putting together in September after weeks of intense negotiations, the communists were allowed only the portfolios of Internal Affairs, Defence and Transportation. Significantly, they were not given control over Media, upon which they had earlier insisted; that went to the prominent Solidarity intellectual, Andrzej Drawicz, who could be relied upon to guarantee that reporting of domestic events would no longer be distorted to reflect Communist Party biases. Gorbachev was subsequently reported to have approved these changes in a meeting with the disgraced former Prime Minister, Mieczyslaw Rakowski, who had dutifully travelled to Moscow in his new capacity as First Secretary of the Polish United Workers' Party to report on the changes in Poland. Gorbachev also endorsed planned alterations to the structure and *modus operandi* of the Polish party, which were said to be similar to those which had recently been introduced in Hungary.[33]   But the Soviets were clearly unhappy over Solidarity's success in 'crowding out' the Communist Party from the centres of Polish political and economic life.[34]   The increasingly demoralised communists tried to salvage what they could from the evolving situation and followed the Hungarian lead by changing the name of their party to the Party of Democratic Socialists in the hope of eventually being able to compete with Solidarity and other emerging political parties in the expected turmoil and social discontent anticipated from Mazowiecki's radical market–centred economic reforms. Gorbachev ultimately found it expedient to accept these changes and to make a virtue of the evolving Polish necessities, by suggesting that the Soviets were closely following the Polish reforms as at least a partial model for their own. In any case, the effects of Polish economic dependence on the Soviet Union, as we have seen, guaranteed the maintenance of a substantial degree of Soviet influence even on a non–communist Polish government.

Gorbachev received little consolation from the changes taking place in Hungary. The original idea of Hungarian party liberals to control the reform movement and to foster the gradual emergence of non–communist parties to compete not only in the electoral process but also in the national parliament for influence on the decision–making process was quickly transcended by events.[35]   The burgeoning of alternative political parties and movements, at first largely encouraged 'from above' by the Hungarian Socialist Workers' Party (HSWP) leadership, demonstrated in several by-elections just how little popularity the HSWP really enjoyed. In response to these signs, in an effort to salvage as much as possible of the party's electoral chances, an Extraordinary Congress of the HSWP was hastily called for early October 1989.

An indication of the nervousness in some Soviet quarters over the impending congress could be gleaned from the questions posed by a *Pravda* correspondent in Budapest during an interview, on the eve of the congress' opening, with the moderate reformist President of the HSWP, Rezso Nyers. The answers were not entirely encouraging, although Nyers gave an impression of commitment to the retention of at least some element of party control over the reform process. Concerning Hungary's future relations with the two main Bloc integrative mechanisms, the WTO and CMEA, Nyers promised to uphold the country's existing international agreements, but he warned that unless significant changes were made in their internal decision–making processes and policy orientation, Hungarian participation would be reduced to a formality.[36]

Events at the HSWP congress quickly rendered even these assurances obsolete. The HSWP was simply abolished and recast as the 'Hungarian Socialist Party' (HSP), which was no longer to be bound by the discipline of 'democratic centralism' and which professed an ideological orientation vaguely combining elements of both social–democracy and communism. Its policies were to be determined by a democratic vote among competing platforms. Current HSWP members were invited to apply for membership in the new HSP before the end of the year. Nyers was elected President of the HSP, and most of the members of the reformist leadership of the HSWP were duly installed in the new party's Presidium. They included Imre Pozsgay, the most prominent communist reformer, who would be the HSP's candidate for President of the Republic, Prime Minister Miklos Nemeth, and Foreign Minister Gyula Horn. Conspicuous by his absence was former HSWP General Secretary Karoly Grosz, who refused to be associated with the new party, but at the same time declined an invitation to join a conservative rump Communist Party being formed around the so–called 'Janos Kadar Society'. At the congress it was conceded that the HSP would be lucky to get 30 per cent of the popular vote for the new parliament scheduled to be elected at the end of November, but that was considered sufficient to give it a decisive influence in a governing coalition, given the expected fragmentation of the non–communist opposition.[37] Other sources suggested that the HSP would win less than 20 per cent,[38] which could place it in a position like that of the Polish party when confronted with genuine electoral competition. In the event, the communists did even worse than expected, polling only 10 per cent of the vote in the first round of elections to the new parliament in March 1990. Moreover, the two largest parties, the Free Democrats and the Democratic Forum, both declared their unwillingness to form a coalition government with the communists.[39] Again, as in Poland, the main hope of the HSP was evidently to serve as the nucleus of an eventual alliance of left–wing forces to compete with economic liberals and nationalists in the difficult period of adjustment to market reforms.

With the Polish and Hungarian examples of the disintegration of Communist Party rule in the fresh air of political competition before him,

Gorbachev might have been expected to regard less negatively the efforts of the remaining orthodox regimes to hold back the pace of reform. That he did not do so suggests two not necessarily incompatible alternative conclusions:

1   that he considered their efforts doomed to failure; or
2   that he actively sought their demise in order to deprive his domestic conservative opponents of potential allies in their effort to retard the pace of reform.

In Bulgaria, the long–serving septuagenarian party and state leader Todor Zhivkov had managed to avoid real political reforms while making seemingly radical, but ultimately only cosmetic, economic reforms. Having effusively endorsed *perestroika*, *glasnost* and democratisation — as Bulgarian leaders inevitably endorse Soviet initiatives — Zhivkov continued to try to eliminate those in his immediate entourage who were genuinely committed to reform.[40] In late September 1989, Gorbachev's close ally Aleksandr Yakovlev chaired a conference of secretaries of ruling Communist Parties responsible for foreign affairs (significantly Hungarian — and Chinese — representatives were absent) in the Bulgarian city of Varna. At the conference Zhivkov seemed to go out of his way to curry Soviet favour. After describing Bulgaria's modest efforts at reform, he hailed the conference's commitment to co–ordinate the foreign policies of the socialist countries and to consolidate the forces of socialism in the world.[41] Bulgaria had been among the most enthusiastic participants in joint ventures with Soviet enterprises under the Complex Program, which must have been a point in Zhivkov's favour.

By December, however, Zhivkov had also fallen before the avalanche of change in Eastern Europe, and he was removed in disgrace under charges of personal arbitrariness and corruption. Unlike in Poland and Hungary, however, the Bulgarian Communist Party subsequently managed to retain firm control of the reform process, which the new party leaders now unreservedly endorsed. They have contrived to grant concessions to political democratisation only when confronted by sporadic mass political pressures and have grudgingly assented to a formal renunciation of the BCP's constitutional 'leading role' in policy–making and administration. Nevertheless, given the general disorganisation of the political opposition in the country, BCP chief and State President Petar Mladenov and Prime Minister Andrej Lukanov — both of whom had been (albeit relatively liberal) members of the Zhivkov entourage — seemed to have a fair prospect of maintaining a dominant role in a freely elected parliament.[42] Opinion polls in March 1990 predicted that the BCP (in the meanwhile renamed the Bulgarian Socialist Party) would get some 40 per cent of the vote in the forthcoming parliamentary elections. In the light of events elsewhere, however, it was unlikely that the BSP's efforts to hold on to power would go unchallenged for very long.

Romania, Czechoslovakia and (until October 1989) the GDR had, with varying degrees of frankness, simply declined to participate in the entire reform exercise. Not surprisingly, Romania's President Nicolae Ceausescu was almost grotesque in denying the relevance of economic and political reforms for his country and in refusing to accept Gorbachev's right to lecture him on the need for change. Ironically, he was taking advantage of the principle of 'freedom of choice' for each Bloc country to devise its own method of strengthening socialism, but his way of doing so clearly rankled Gorbachev and other Bloc reformers.[43] In the wake of the radical developments taking place throughout the communist world, Ceausescu had even appealed to the Chinese, and other unreconstructed hardline parties (the North Koreans, Cubans and Albanians) to set up a new international of 'true' Marxist–Leninists.

Thus it was undoubtedly with little genuine sadness that Gorbachev greeted the forcible removal and swift execution, on Christmas Day, of Ceausescu and his 'royal' consort Elena. Indeed, there was even speculation that the Soviet Union was somehow involved in provoking the unrest and the ensuing military coup which overthrew the Ceausescus.[44] However, subsequent developments in Romania could hardly have been entirely to Gorbachev's liking. The former Communist Party officials at the head of the so–called National Salvation Front, which took power after the coup, proved to be highly resistant to demands from the tenuously organised elements of civil society which began to emerge. Moreover, they soon showed themselves unwilling, or unable, to control the ethnic unrest (mainly directed against the Hungarian minority) which was the direct impetus for the bloody revolution and which has continued to fester in the following months, causing angry recriminations in neighbouring Hungary. It is not likely that Gorbachev approves of the uncontrolled and violent nature of the changes taking place, especially since the population in Soviet Moldavia has begun to manifest considerable interest in the events in post–Ceausescu Romania, which they regard as the homeland from which they were separated as a result of Stalin's conspiracy with Hitler on the eve of the Second World War.

In Czechoslovakia, the replacement as party leader of Brezhnev's crony Gustav Husak by the younger (but not much more liberal) Milos Jakes had very little effect on the process of reform. Although recognising the need for economic liberalisation, Jakes did virtually nothing in that area, and the political situation became, if anything, even more oppressive. Gorbachev contributed materially to the undermining of conservative party forces by repudiating, at a Warsaw Pact meeting in Moscow in early December 1989, the invasion of Czechoslovakia in 1968, at a stroke de–legitimising President Husak and the entire party leadership associated with him. Within two weeks the entire edifice of communist power had collapsed without a fight, and in an exquisite moment of irony, Husak was replaced as President by dissident playwright Vaclav Havel and former Prague Spring party leader Alexander Dubcek became Speaker of parliament. Civil society in Czechoslovakia, which had evidently been waiting in the wings despite years of communist repression, quickly organised itself as the Civic Forum and immediately took over power from the demoralised communists. Under Havel, this 'Velvet Revolution' has seemingly been the most successful example of the transition to the the post–communist formation in all of Eastern Europe. Although it has yet to tackle the difficult business of economic reform, the new government has so far succeeded in gaining a remarkable degree of goodwill in both East and West.

Finally, as we have seen above, the GDR, under Erich Honecker, continued to resist to the end Gorbachev's insistence on economic and political reform. East Germany remained the most important Bloc trading partner of the USSR, especially in the area of industrial technology. Its reliability as a supplier and the exaggerated claims of the healthy state of the GDR economy, thanks largely to its special relationship with West Germany and through it the EEC, seemed to have bought Honecker a good deal of immunity to pressure despite his unconcealed reluctance to involve his country's enterprises and research institutes in direct contractual relations with Soviet firms.[45] In the end, however, it was Honecker's loss of control of the domestic political situation — symbolised by the mass exodus of young people to the West in the autumn of 1989 — that proved his undoing. His successors, Egon Krenz and Hans Modrow, despite attempts to heed the lessons of Honecker's fate by engaging in dialogue with the people and to appear more receptive to reform, ultimately failed to stem the rush towards integration with the FRG. In the parliamentary elections of 18 March 1990, the conservative parties allied with the ruling CDP in the FRG gained a convincing majority. The reconstructed Communist Party received a creditable 16 per cent of the vote, but it was clearly destined for political oblivion in a reunited Germany, at least for the foreseeable future. If it does re–emerge as a political force, it will necessarily be as part of a general coalition of left–wing parties, probably under leadership of the Social–Democratic Party.

The collapse of communism as the dominant political force in Eastern Europe has greatly complicated Gorbachev's relations with the remaining parts of the communist world. Deprived of the traditional guarantee of Soviet economic and political support, some of the communist regimes have followed their Eastern European colleagues and sought to reach accommodation with the rising forces of domestic popular discontent. That has certainly been the case with the Mongolian People's Republic, since 1921 the first Soviet satellite, where the ruling communists have adopted Jaruzelski's 'round table' strategy to broaden the basis of support for inevitable economic and political reforms. The ensuing historical revisions and revelations of repression under the heroes of the communist past make it uncertain whether the reformist party leadership can maintain a vestige of control over the liberalisation process. The Vietnamese have remained virtually silent on Gorbachev's radicalism and its external effects, presumably because of their vulnerability to Soviet economic pressure. They have attempted to isolate their own program of economic reforms from political liberalisation, and political hardliners have succeeded thus far in maintaining their control.[46]

In Nicaragua, the Sandinista regime of Daniel Ortega was constrained by Soviet, as well as Western pressure, to seek peace with its Contra opponents, to dilute the ideological orientation of its policies and to submit to free electoral competition in February 1990 with the reviving non–communist opposition. Ortega's expectations of easy success were rudely disappointed, as the loose coalition of his opponents scored a decisive victory, leaving the Sandinistas with just under 40 per cent of the vote — potentially a considerable political force for the future, but no longer a controlling factor in government. Significantly, the Soviets accepted the people's verdict with equanimity and even offered economic aid to the post–Sandinista government of Mrs Violeta Chamorro.[47]

Gorbachev's relations with Fidel Castro in Cuba and Kim Il Sung in North Korea, both of whom have taken a Honeckerian stance on questions of domestic and international political reform, have grown increasingly tense. Both leaders, although dutifully serving the cause of socialism in the Third World, have eschewed domestic reform in the name of ideological purity and have shown a willingness to pay the price of economic backwardness to keep their countries isolated from the virus of economic and political liberalisation. Castro has actually employed the Maoist euphemism 'rectification' to denote the purges and the political and economic re–centralisation he is currently undertaking in the name of combatting unhealthy capitalist tendencies that had allegedly emerged in an earlier relaxation phase. There are obvious disagreements between Castro and Gorbachev on major issues of policy, but neither regards a public display of antagonism as desirable.[48] Cuba, Mongolia, North Korea and Vietnam stand, along with Poland, at the top of the league table in the magnitude of their ruble debt to the USSR (see Table 3 in the Appendix) and are accordingly in no position to push their relations with Gorbachev to the point of rupture.[49] Nevertheless, Fidel Castro continues to question the ideological legitimacy of the latter's external and domestic policies and remains committed to limiting their impact on Cuba. For Fidel, the lessons of what happened to his close ally Daniel Ortega in the attempt to apply Gorbachevian reformist prescriptions seem to have reinforced the determination to resist pressures for similar actions on his part, although the threat of reductions of Soviet economic aid to Cuba will undoubtedly force him to undertake some type of economic reforms. Kim Il Sung has so far merely ignored what others in the communist world have been doing. One can only speculate on his reactions to the developing Soviet rapprochement with South Korea; but Gorbachev has succeeded in maintaining reasonably good relations with North Korea by continuing to supply it with first–line military hardware, including the state–of–the–art MIG–29. In any case, Gorbachev is probably banking on Kim's departure from the political scene in the foreseeable future and eventual reunification with the more prosperous South. Domination by the South in a unified Korea free of American troops would suit Gorbachev very well.

A new model of Soviet relations with the communist world?

The precise basis of the new model of Soviet relations with what remains of the communist world is necessarily still in the process of elaboration. Much will depend on whether Communist Parties manage to remain in power in one country or another. Ties with countries under Communist Party rule will probably remain closer than in those where the communists are only in a minority, although the Soviets can be expected to continue to try to use local communists to influence their governments in directions favourable to Soviet interests. In many respects Moscow's relations with the Communist Parties of the world will thus revert to the situation prevailing in the interwar period, although it is highly unlikely that any institutionalised central control organisation like the Comintern will be revived.

An interesting recent ideological harbinger of the change in Soviet perspectives is the application of the principle of 'peaceful coexistence' to relations among Communist Party–ruled states.[50] Previously this concept had been considered applicable only to relations with non–communist states. The broader usage implies a recognition that relations among socialist countries might also involve acute conflicts of interest, which should nevertheless not be allowed to develop into active hostility. The principle's most obvious application was to the newly 'normalised' relations with China, where identical views on all international and domestic issues were hardly to be expected. However, the discussion of the concept so far suggests that analogous conflicts were anticipated in relations with and among Eastern European states as well even before the collapse of Communist Party rule.

Some observers, following Gorbachev's visit to Belgrade in March 1988, speculated on the possible 'Yugoslavisation' of Soviet relations with Eastern Europe — that is, a much looser type of relationship based on ideological and structural–political affinities and a mutuality of economic interests.[51] In most cases, such a pattern of relations is no longer applicable, but where Communist Parties manage to hang on to, or eventually return to, power, it does suggest some interesting possibilities. Nevertheless, it would be unwise to underestimate the degree of influence that the Soviet Union, through economic interdependence and treaty commitments, still possesses with respect to the communist world, both in Europe and beyond. The fact that Polish President Jaruzelski found it incumbent to pay a call on Gorbachev immediately after concluding the new agreement with Solidarity and that the then party chief Rakowski sought his approval for the even more dramatic political changes that ensued in September and October, both suggest many elements of continuity in the pattern of Soviet relations with these countries.[52] Even their newly elected non–communist leaders travel regularly to Moscow to gain Gorbachev's assent to their economic and political overtures to the West.

In short, what we seem to be witnessing is a process of 'Finlandisation' of the former countries of the Soviet Bloc: a pattern of relations where the former subordinates enjoy virtually total autonomy in their internal structures and processes of economic and political life, although overt expressions of anti–Soviet sentiment are kept in check, and where their foreign policies are constrained to take account of Soviet interests. Gorbachev or his successors can expect to be able to maintain sufficient leverage to uphold this indirect mode of control as long as the Soviet Union retains a modicum of the existing forms of economic interdependence and as long as the existing bilateral and multilateral security arrangements remain in place. Recent apparently successful efforts by Hungary and Czechoslovakia to obtain agreement for the phased withdrawal of Soviet troops stationed on their territory under the Warsaw Treaty will not materially affect this basic pattern of subordination. It is worth keeping in mind that the patterns of military training and hardware procurements over the past 45 years militate against any sudden diminution of Soviet influence on the military establishments of the Eastern European states. Moreover, the extremely close relations between the Soviet KGB and GRU and their respective intelligence communities — especially in the selection, training and supervision of intelligence professionals — virtually guarantees that the Soviets will continue to enjoy privileged access to information on the thinking of the new post–communist governments.[53] On the other hand, for Czechoslovakia and Poland, if not so much for Hungary, the rise of a reunited Germany with tacit territorial and other claims against the postwar arrangements in Europe has meant that the value of Soviet security guarantees has suddenly acquired new significance. This is especially so because of the elimination of previous forms of direct Soviet control over the domestic political life of these countries. For many of them, 'Finlandisation' represents a decided improvement in their status as autonomous actors on the European scene.

Turning specifically to the military aspects of Soviet–Eastern European relations, it seems clear that virtually all parties favour a lowering of the military profile of East–West interaction in Europe. The most recent spasm of tension over the deployment and counter–deployment of INF weapons in 1983 was very unpopular with even the most loyal regimes in Czechoslovakia, the GDR and Bulgaria.[54] The INF agreement between Washington and Moscow was thus universally hailed throughout the Bloc. Not only had it decreased pressures for conformity and solidarity which Moscow had demanded in response to Andropov's self–generated crisis and removed the prospect of immediate targeting of these countries by virtue of their hosting of Soviet SS–21, SS–22 and SS–23 rockets, but more importantly in the long run, it had made possible a resumption of the promising economic and commercial negotiations which most of the Bloc countries, including the GDR, had been undertaking with Western Europe when the crisis erupted.

Recent Soviet proposals for large conventional and nuclear arms reductions in Europe and the restatement of the once perennial offer to abolish the WTO in return for the dissolution of NATO seem to have been driven by a number of changes in Soviet perspectives on the world situation and the nature of national security. First of all, it is clearly recognised that the threat of aggression from the West is now virtually non–existent and was probably exaggerated in the past because of the almost paranoid conception of Bloc security associated with the classconfrontationist ideology of international realities. Secondly, there is a general acceptance of the proposition that a lowering of defence expenditures will be of substantial benefit to the struggling economies of all the WTO countries, first and foremost among them the Soviet Union itself. Thirdly, there is a growing appreciation in Moscow of the opportunities for the enhancement of Soviet economic and political influence in a substantially disarmed Europe with a correspondingly diminished American presence. Gorbachev's incessant trumpeting of the virtues of the 'common European home' has obviously been designed to prepare the psychological climate for such a change in the pattern of Soviet and American relations with the continent.

On the other hand, the sudden likelihood that a united Germany will become the effective landlord and principal tenant of the 'CEH' has put the entire question of the preservation of some form of American military presence in a new light. Under suitably agreed 'caps' — limits on the total number of troops and categories of weapons — on each side, a united Germany within NATO may well be preferable, in WTO (including Soviet) thinking, to a Europe dominated by a 'neutral' Germany and without a countervailing US and Soviet presence 'on the ground', as it were. The formal structures of NATO and the WTO may perhaps be obsolete, but some type of comprehensive security arrangement involving permanent American (and probably British) forces in Western Europe and Soviet forces in Eastern Europe will have to be devised to take their place.

Conclusions

Gorbachev's new political thinking has perhaps had a greater impact on Soviet relations with the communist world than in any other area, although it is probably pointless to try to view changes in those relations in isolation from the broader issues of East–West relations. With the prospects of enhanced worldwide influence and considerable economic benefits in mind, Gorbachev has obviously been willing to trade most of what had previously counted as 'security of tenure' in Eastern Europe for the opportunity to enter the 'common European home'. The replacement of the Brezhnev Doctrine with what Ministry of Foreign Affairs spokesman Gennady Gerasimov has jokingly called the 'Sinatra Doctrine' — the freedom for the East European countries to 'do things their way' — has opened up possibilities for the Soviet Union not only to operate in Europe as a more or less normal great power but also to shed some of the responsibilities for maintaining an economic and political empire which it no longer considers worth the cost. Similar considerations apply at a somewhat different level of strategic importance to Soviet relations with communist states in other areas of the world as well.

In Europe, as we have seen in chapter 4, the implicit trade–off is based at least partly on a calculation of the growing economic and political antagonism between the EC, the United States and Japan, and on Soviet ability to demonstrate the proposition that the EC needs the Soviet Union as much as the Soviet Union needs it — in order to combat the American and Japanese challenge. The USSR is suggested as a potentially more reliable and secure market for Western European investments and trade. The argument was initially targeted at West Germany in particular, the country correctly viewed as the most crucial, and potentially the most volatile, member of the EC.[55] The tacit Soviet assumption behind the trade–off policy is that the USSR, by virtue of the size of its economy and market and of its resource base, is objectively positioned eventually to dominate such an amalgamation. The collapse of the Soviet economy and the reunification of Germany have substantially altered key elements of the calculation, adding a security dimension to the potential balancing role of the Soviet Union in a united Europe. It remains to be seen just how much Gorbachev's handling of the issue of Lithuanian independence will affect these calculations, particularly on the Western side. While the prospects for Soviet involvement in other parts of the world, such as the Asia–Pacific Region, are not quite so far advanced and the military element is somewhat different, the reasoning behind Gorbachev's trade–off in relations with communist–ruled states and the corollary Soviet diplomatic and commercial offensive is similar.

Whatever their ultimate degree of success, Gorbachev's new policies on relations with the communist world certainly illustrate his impressive talent for 'lateral thinking' and for seeing the 'big picture'. They also demonstrate his willingness to adapt to what he and his advisers see as 'objective tendencies' in the world, including some which he has perhaps unintentionally set in motion himself. It is highly unlikely, for example, that he anticipated the abrupt collapse of friendly communist regimes when he advised them to reform and consolidate their popular political bases. Yet he has shown little inclination to bemoan the fact and has even striven to make a virtue of the necessity to establish new patterns of relations with the successor governments, banking on the latter's good sense in calculating their economic, political and security interests. Few Western politicians can match his combination of tactical skills and strategic consciousness, or, for that matter, his Micawberesque optimism that 'something will turn up' to create benefits out of unanticipated misfortunes. Even without the threat of direct Soviet intervention, he knows that the Soviet Union retains considerable economic, political and intelligence leverage over most of its erstwhile junior partners, particularly in Eastern Europe, if no longer to compel them to follow Soviet dictation, at least to constrain them to consider Soviet interests in formulating their foreign policies. That is the essence of 'Finlandisation', and for most of the post–communist successor regimes it represents a distinct improvement over their previous situation.

Soviet relations with the communist world are thus in an extremely fluid state. Gorbachev has countenanced the dismantling of the once-cherished Soviet 'patrimony' because he has clearly come to believe that it is no longer worth trying to preserve as an isolated enclave in a rapidly changing world that threatens to leave it behind in the march towards social and economic modernisation. He continues to profess that socialism still has a place in broader world processes, but he is no longer sure what that place is or even what the nature of modernised socialism entails. Gorbachev's conservative opponents at home and in communist circles abroad have condemned what they regard as his betrayal of the worldwide 'achievements of socialism'. But few of them probably mourn his disavowal of the Soviet Union's right to prescribe models of socialism and of relations among socialist countries or of the obligations associated with that right.[56] In that sense, the transformation of Soviet relations with the communist world will probably prove irreversible, even if Gorbachev is removed from power. As in the case of *perestroika* of the domestic economy, he has done at least the destructive part of the job of restructuring communist international relations very well indeed.

6 The Soviet Union and the Third World

Introduction

The role of the Third World in Soviet thinking has undergone significant changes in the Gorbachev era. These changes have touched upon such fundamental questions as the position of the Third World in the world revolutionary process, the potential for transformation to socialism in individual Third World countries and the nature of the obligation of the USSR and other socialist states to aid Third World development economically, politically and militarily. While most of the changes are still the subject of lively debate among Soviet ideologists and area specialists, trends in governmental policy under Gorbachev seem to indicate an acceptance of some of the more radical rethinking about Soviet relations with the Third World, not the least of which is its relative down-grading as an arena of intensive Soviet involvement.

That the Third World should have loomed large in Soviet thinking and in East–West relations since the Second World War is not surprising. As Bruce McLaury, President of Washington's renowned Brookings Institution, has pointed out, most crises in Soviet–American relations since the war have resulted from events in the Third World.[1] The nature of Soviet–American rivalry in the Third World in the postwar era has been considerably less direct than in the case of Soviet relations with Western Europe and with capitalist parts of the Asia–Pacific region, discussed in chapter 4, where initial Soviet involvement often required American 'clearance' because of prevailing alliance arrangements. In most parts of the Third World the United States simply did not have such arrangements, either because of lack of interest or through failure to bring them about.

136

For the Soviet Union the Third World was much more important. Traditional Soviet interpretations of international relations, based on Lenin's theory of imperialism (see chapter 1), had regarded revolutions in the colonial and 'semi–colonial' (including Tsarist Russia, in Lenin's view) regions of the world as the key to socialist revolutions in the capitalist heartland. In supporting anti–imperialist revolutions and national–liberation movements in the Third World, the Soviet Union would thus be hastening the collapse of the capitalist world — by removing the source of 'super–profits' and of cheap energy and raw materials, which filled the coffers of international finance capital and fuelled the engines of capitalist production. The East–West rivalry for the Third World was viewed as a zero–sum game in which accretions of newly liberated territories to the socialist camp were a major component of the shift in the 'correlation of forces' in favour of socialism.

As the number of newly liberated countries increased, therefore, considerable attention was devoted to understanding the processes of internal and foreign policy development in these countries and discerning tendencies which, in the framework of Marxist–Leninist ideology, could be considered 'progressive' or reactionary, and hence deserving of support or opposition from the Soviet Union. Whereas Stalin had consistently denied the potential revolutionary significance of national independence in such countries as India and Indonesia, where Communist Parties were not in control of the national–liberation movements, Khrushchev and his colleagues had a much more optimistic view of these movements and were much more willing to devote Soviet resources to assisting them. Hostile Western reactions to Third World developments — for example, the British, French and Israeli attack on Nasserite Egypt in the Suez crisis of 1956 and the US determination to take over from France the fight against North Vietnam after the fall of Dien Bien Phu in 1954 — merely seemed to confirm for Khrushchev that the West was indeed highly sensitive and vulnerable to shifts in political and economic alignment in the Third World. Radical pro–Soviet shifts by nationalist leaders in Ghana, Guinea and Mali in West Africa, and the rapid transition of Fidel Castro from radical nationalism to clear alignment with the Soviet Union on the basis of Marxist–Leninist commitment in the early 1960s, appeared to substantiate Khrushchev's optimistic expectations of the revolutionary potential of national–liberation movements.[2]

These developments proved to be the high–water mark of the revolutionary wave, however. By the mid–1960s there were already signs of complications in the pattern of internal and external development in a number of countries previously considered safely in the Soviet camp.

Some of the pro–Soviet leaders were overthrown and replaced by more neutral or even anti–communist elements. In other cases (Egypt, for example), the radical nationalist leaders showed themselves to be distressingly erratic in their domestic social and economic policies and inclined to external adventures which were not always favourable to Soviet interests. Moreover, Moscow began to realise that its own resources were not unlimited, that aid to Third World regimes could be an expensive proposition and that the payoff from such assistance was not always unambiguous from the standpoint of Soviet foreign policy. The potential for conflict with the United States over the 'local wars' to which radical nationalist regimes seemed susceptible became a matter of increasing concern, particularly in the Middle East. The zero–sum assumptions about East–West rivalry in the Third World came to be called into question as an undue oversimplification of what were proving to be highly complex processes over which the Soviet Union often had very little control.

Still, it was not easy for Moscow to change policy. Assistance for anti–imperialist movements was an article of ideological faith for Soviet leaders, equivalent in some ways to the commitment to human rights espoused by most American administrations. The need for a differentiated approach to various kinds of Third World regimes and movements tended to be more a feature of academic debates than of official Soviet policy. Gradually the ideas initially canvassed in scholarly discourse came to influence official policy as well, particularly after Brezhnev's demise. However, the outlines of a real change in attitudes towards the Third World would occur only with the advent of new political thinking and a new foreign policy team under Gorbachev.

Ideology and policies for the Third World in the 1960s and 1970s

The elaborate body of theory which developed during the Soviet Union's opening towards the Third World under Khrushchev, and which was expanded by his successors, offers useful insights into the pattern of interaction between ideology, theoretical analysis and policy in the post–Stalin era. Almost immediately after Stalin's death, the scope of Soviet policy toward the Third World underwent a noticeable expansion, reflecting a more optimistic perspective on opportunities in the underdeveloped and/or colonial regions. Under Malenkov in late 1953 and 1954 there were already signs of a shift toward a more favourable response to requests for assistance by radical, anti–imperalist movements. For example, arms for the anti–American regime of Jacobo Arbenz in Guatemala, a request which had previously been refused, were by 1954 being shipped, through third parties.[3] Khrushchev provided a rationale for the new, more adventurous policy toward the Third World by reference to the increasingly favourable correlation of economic and military forces at the disposal of the socialist world. In the optimistic picture of the international scene presented in his report to the Twentieth Congress of the CPSU in February 1956, he intimated that the Soviet Union and its allies (especially including China) were now strong enough to offer protection against imperialist interference for national–liberation movements and newly independent states. He depicted the Third World as an area relatively free of the risk of direct superpower confrontation, where the Soviet Union could safely carry on a strategy of limiting Western influence and promoting progress towards socialism.[4]

Khrushchev's optimistic perspective gave rise to an upsurge in theoretical interest in the internal and external dynamics of the Third World. The purpose of most of the scholarly analyses was to provide a new theoretical orientation for Soviet policy and the required ideological legitimation for the abandonment of the rigid two–camp orthodoxy of the late Stalin era, which had categorised all non–communist states and movements as objectively inimical to Soviet interests. One of the principal issues was the nature of the regimes and movements which were leading the national–liberation struggles in the Third World. It was considered necessary to distinguish them from the 'national–bourgeois' leaders of past revolutions in the West which had led to the establishment of capitalism. Wherein did they differ from the latter and thus merit the political and economic support of the socialist countries? Khrushchev himself took the lead in addressing this issue in November 1960 at the Moscow Conference of 81 communist and workers' parties, by coining the concept of the 'national democratic state' to denote those of the new regimes which were anti–imperialist and pro–Soviet in foreign policy, which followed a non–capitalist path of economic development and which adopted progressive social policies domestically.[5]

Perhaps the most significant and potentially the most troublesome effect of the national democracy formula was its relegation of local Communist Parties in the Third World to a secondary, not to say negligible, role. Since, according to the theory, the national democratic leaders were objectively pursuing the same foreign and domestic goals, local Communist Parties could — and indeed should — legitimately serve as subordinate elements of 'united fronts' led by the non–communist national democratic forces. When some of the latter — for example, in

Egypt and Iraq — began to imprison communists, Soviet policy–makers found it expedient to ignore that fact in order to protect their growing economic, military and diplomatic investments in the regimes. Such distressing treatment of communists and the dubious social and economic programs being followed by many of the newly independent national democracies in the late 1950s and early 1960s prompted some of the more conservative Soviet specialists to question the early optimism over the capability of the national democrats to lead their countries to socialism. There were even implicit suggestions of a return to an essentially pre–Leninist 'two–stage' conception of revolution, whereby the eventual struggle for the transition to socialism would ultimately require the leadership of the proletariat (i.e. the Communist Party).[6]

Khrushchev's more optimistic view prevailed, however. Apparently the crucial factor confirming his optimism was the rapid transition of Fidel Castro from 'national–democratic' radicalism to full allegiance to Marxism–Leninism and the Soviet Bloc in 1962. One of the leading Soviet experts on the Third World, Georgii Mirskii, a specialist on Egypt, began arguing at this time that the national bourgeoisie in national democratic states could sometimes transcend their class nature and pursue proletarian goals. In 1963 he adopted the concept of 'revolutionary democrat' to categorise such leaders, who, he said, were capable of transforming the anti–imperialist revolution into an anti–capitalist revolution.[7] This was the line that Khrushchev, now confronted by Mao Zedong with accusations of revisionism for his heterodox policies in the Third World, chose specifically to endorse. In an interview with a Ghanaian newspaper in December 1963, he supported the distinction between revolutionary democrats and the national bourgeoisie. According to one Western observer, the only concession Khrushchev made to his conservative critics was to add an injunction for fairer treatment of local communists to the criteria for considering a given regime as revolutionary democratic.[8]

The removal of Khrushchev in October 1964, the increasing awareness of the high costs of blanket economic assistance to ambitious Third World leaders and the unsatisfactory domestic programs of some revolutionary democratic regimes — indeed the overthrow of such regimes in Algeria, Ghana and Indonesia in 1965 and 1966 — led to a decided cooling of Soviet enthusiasm for Third World adventures. A period of intensive rethinking about the nature of the new regimes and of appropriate policies to deal with them ensued. High on the list of issues raised was the treatment of local communists and the general problem of class relationships in the newly independent states. Virtually none of the protagonists of the debates counselled Soviet withdrawal from the Third World; rather, their concern was to understand more fully just what was taking place in the new states in order to pursue a more rational and differentiated strategy. On the one hand, there was no intention to resile from the heavy commitment to India, the largest single recipient of Soviet aid under Khrushchev. Few had any illusions about the 'socialist' convictions of the Congress Party and its eminent leaders, but the country was too big and potentially too influential in the Third World and beyond to be abandoned on dogmatic ideological grounds. Besides, with the rapid deterioration of Sino–Soviet relations, the at least equally virulent enmity between India and China since their border war of 1962 had made India and the USSR tacit allies, each serving as a counterweight to China in the geo–strategic calculations of the other.

On the other hand, the revolutionary socialist posturing of the leaders of some less prominent Third World countries would no longer be taken at face value in determining the extent of Soviet commitments. Optimists would still argue that the objective conditions of the international situation and the limited opportunities for economic development domestically would drive the bourgeois leaders of revolutionary democracies further along the non–capitalist path, taking them ineluctably towards socialism.[9] Pessimists, led by Nodari Simoniia of the Institute of Oriental Studies, rejected such arguments as wishful thinking, asserting that the transition to socialism could be carried out only by regimes that were already under proletarian leadership; moreover, he accused some national bourgeois leaders of using the socialist world for their own purposes. Simoniia also lamented the fact that Third World countries choosing the capitalist path were commonly developing at a faster rate than those following the socialist path. Nevertheless, he concluded, only genuine revolutionary–democratic vanguard parties could lead these countries to socialism and were deserving of full support.[10]

These were the extreme positions in the debate. Most analysts were not prepared to accept either the unbridled optimism of those who argued for continued blanket support for Third World regimes or the almost totally negative appraisals of the pessimists, who recommended a much more restrictive policy of assistance. The overall result of their analyses, however, was a much more sophisticated investigation of the social and economic processes of the new regimes. One of the important issues were the nature and policy implications of the rise to prominence of military officers in many of the Third World states, often as successors to the revolutionary democrats whom the Soviets had been supporting. The class status of this so–called 'military intelligentsia' was a matter of some concern to Soviet specialists, like Mirskii, who viewed them as an untrustworthy element.   Soviet military officers and other more conservative observers tended to have a more sympathetic attitude, regarding the Third World military as a positive force for organisation and discipline both during and after the national–liberation struggle.[11]

By the middle 1970s, as the complexities of the situation in the various countries and regions of the Third World became generally accepted and earlier optimistic predictions were disappointed, a more sober and less ideologically deterministic policy perspective emerged.   This new perspective was also conditioned by a number of additional factors that were more or less tangential to the issues of the previous debates. One of them was the lowering of the American military profile in the Third World in the wake of the defeat in Vietnam. A second was the increasing arms and force–projection capabilities of the Soviet military, the result of weapons development and procurement decisions made back in the Khrushchev period and subsequently accelerated under Brezhnev. A third was the intensified competition with China for influence in the Third World; Chinese activities had an explicitly anti–Soviet focus and were perceived as especially threatening to Soviet interests after the Sino–US rapprochement in 1972.

These factors, combined with the more sober perspectives derived from the ambiguous experiences of the 1950s and 1960s, produced a strategy that was at once broader in scope yet more selective in its tactical applications.   That is, while attempting to establish its presence everywhere in the Third World — primarily by a variety of diplomatic, commercial and cultural means — Moscow restricted large–scale commitments of military and economic resources to a few countries where the probability of stable success seemed highest. The criteria for these judgements were an amalgam of past formulas: the states and movements considered deserving of Soviet aid commitment were those led by 'revolutionary democrats' heading existing or nascent 'vanguard parties' and displaying a 'socialist orientation' in their plans for economic development. Naturally, they were also unambiguously anti–imperialist and preferably pro–Soviet in foreign policy. To be sure, some relatively well established Soviet clients in the Third World, such as India, Egypt, Syria and Iraq, did not meet all of these criteria, but the geostrategic benefits of the already substantial Soviet economic and military investments in them seemingly outweighed the obvious tenuousness of Moscow's ideological and political influence over their internal policies. In any case, the Soviets could always hope for the emergence of more progressive internal developments in future and could be expected to promote them.

The geographical focus of Soviet activities in the Third World also became at once more universal and more selective in the 1970s. The ubiquitous Chinese challenge and the growing anti-imperialist nationalism in many previously quiescent regions of the world, such as Latin America, the Middle East, Southeast Asia and, of course, Africa, provided increased opportunities for Soviet influence. On the other hand, emerging economic problems at home and the inappropriateness of the types of assistance the Soviet Union was capable of supplying, other than military equipment, limited its ability to take advantage of these opportunities. Furthermore, the expansion of Soviet activities into areas that were particularly sensitive for the West — for example, Latin America (for the United States, with whom Moscow was anxious to maintain a climate of detente) — posed undoubted problems. Recognition of this fact caused the Soviets to limit their actions there and to focus instead on regions where the chances of success were deemed greatest and the risks of confrontation were considered acceptable.[12] In these regions Brezhnev himself ultimately came down on the side of adventurism, tacitly based on the ideological rationale of an alleged 'divisibility of detente'. He argued that agreements with the West like the Declaration of Principles of Soviet Relations with the USA (signed with President Nixon in May 1972) and the Helsinki Agreements of August 1975 had in no way altered the fact of the ongoing class struggle in the Third World or abrogated the Soviet obligation to support it.[13] But even then, the Soviet commitment proved to be highly selective and far from open-ended.

Regional variations in Soviet involvement

Africa and the Middle East have been the areas of heaviest Soviet concentration in the Third World. For a number of reasons, the Middle East in particular once seemed to be the ideal region for Soviet involvement because of several factors: its strategic location and relative propinquity to the USSR; the increasing significance of its petroleum reserves for Western economic and military power, including that of the United States, which was by the 1970s no longer self-sufficient in energy; and the radical, anti-imperialist nationalism of many of its leaders and movements. For a while during the 1950s and 1960s the Soviet Union made rapid progress in establishing close relations with several strategically important Middle East regimes, particularly Nasserite Egypt and Ba'athist Syria and Iraq, all of which received substantial military and economic aid in recognition of Moscow's approval of their 'national-democratic' politics and the 'socialist orientation' of their developmental policies. Embarrassingly for the Soviet leaders, they all tended to treat their local Communist Parties more or less brutally, but all of them seemed well on the road to transforming their ruling political movements into the kinds of 'vanguard parties' that Moscow hoped would become the nuclei for eventual Marxist–Leninist organisations, in which the surviving communists would again regain their influence. The Soviet Union also aspired to unify the radical Arab regimes into a powerful force allied to itself in the struggle against imperialism, utilising their common hatred of Israel and 'Zionism' as a rallying point.

By the mid–1970s virtually all of these expectations had been disappointed. The leaders of the individual regimes had demonstrated that they all had their own agendas, which brought them into bitter conflict with each other and made unity against Israel, or on any other basis, practically impossible. Nor did Moscow's heavy investment in developing their military capacities confer any particular advantage in terms of Soviet influence on their domestic policies. However, their foreign policies were considered sufficiently satisfactory, in an anti–imperialist sense, to render the continuation of Soviet military aid desirable.[14] Nevertheless, the Soviets had few illusions as to the reliability and socialist commitment of their Arab allies. Anwar Sadat's expulsion of Soviet advisors from Egypt in 1976 and Siad Barre's similar action in Somalia a year later amply confirmed this suspicion. The only exception to this generally disappointing picture was the People's Democratic Republic of (South) Yemen, which did have an avowedly Marxist–Leninist vanguard party and which did provide the Soviets with a valuable asset in the form of the former British base at Aden. But the PDRY hardly represented a major accretion to Soviet power or a victory for 'socialist construction' in the Arab world; and success there had its 'opportunity costs' with respect to potential ventures elsewhere in the region.[15] Moscow could hardly have been unduly dismayed, therefore, over the PDRY's decision to amalgamate with the (North) Yemen Arab Republic in May 1990.

Africa seemed somewhat more promising. The collapse of the Portuguese colonial empire and the overthrow of Emperor Haile Salassie in Ethiopia in 1974–75 impelled the Soviets to increase their assistance to the national–democratic movements vying for power in the various successor regimes. Especially in Angola and Mozambique, where there were several competing movements, some supported by the Chinese and/or the Americans, the Soviets materially contributed to the success of what turned out to be the victorious side, at least in the short run. The expansion of the Soviet capacity to deliver arms and the Cuban troops to operate them, together with the realisation that the United States was, for domestic political reasons, unable or unwilling to counter Soviet involvement, emboldened Moscow to push the 'divisibility–of–detente' line in Southern Africa with little fear of effective opposition. Moreover, the intervention of South African troops against pro–Soviet forces in both countries conferred international legitimacy on the use of Cuban troops and Soviet–Bloc advisors, especially for the Organisation of African Unity, which could be expected to support the Soviet activities at the United Nations.[16]

Similar considerations applied in Ethiopia, although there the Soviets were reluctantly forced to sacrifice something tangible as the price for choosing what they considered a strategically and ideologically more promising revolutionary–democratic regime. Namely, they had to give up their existing position in Somalia, which was at war with Ethiopia, and to abandon the important naval base and resupply facilities they had been granted in the Somali port of Berbera. The arms and Cuban troops airlifted by the Soviets into Ethiopia in late 1977 were not as crucial to the victory over the Somali invaders as had been the case earlier in Angola *vis–a–vis* South Africa. However, they were important in consolidating the control of the pro–Soviet regime of Colonel Menghistu and, as Richard Remnek has argued, in influencing the Ethiopians not to expand the war into Somalia.[17]

In all three African countries the Soviets were able to exert a considerable influence over the internal policies of the victorious revolutionary–democratic regimes and to encourage their transition to Marxist–Leninist party–states. But in doing so they stimulated the growth of opposition forces. With eventual Western military support, opposition movements like UNITA in Angola, MNR ('Renamo') in Mozambique and the Tigre and Eritrean National Liberation Fronts in Ethiopia were able to mount effective civil wars which greatly complicated Soviet efforts to achieve long–term stability and to establish solid international legitimacy for the pro–Soviet regimes. Ultimately, the Soviets came to realise that what had once seemed decisive victories for world socialism in a region of great economic and strategic value in fact represented heavy costs in military and economic commitments of indefinite duration, with no guarantee of success and at the price of serious damage to detente with the West. Nevertheless, there were no indications of a willingness to abandon these revolutionary, pro–Soviet regimes, which had come to be considered by Brezhnev as part of the Soviet socialist 'patrimony' in Africa. As in the Middle East, military commitment and control came to epitomise 'proletarian internationalism' in the Soviet perception of relations in the region: a strong Soviet military presence was deemed the most reliable and secure guarantee of stability in the Soviet relationship with a given Third World country.[18]

During the 1970s and early 1980s, the Chinese factor undoubtedly figured as the most salient consideration in Soviet foreign policy thinking toward the developing countries in Asia. Moscow's overtures to various non–communist states in the Asia–Pacific Region, for example the ASEAN countries, were usually oriented, as we saw in chapter 4, towards the long–cherished goal of a general Asian Security System, implicitly directed against China. Moscow's blanket support for Hanoi in expanding its dominance over Laos and Cambodia clearly had an anti–Chinese dimension. Similarly, Soviet acquisition of the former American bases at Camranh Bay and Danang tacitly had an anti–Chinese as well as an anti–American motivation, which helps to explain why the nationally hyper-sensitive Vietnamese were willing to accept this derogation of their sovereignty.[19]

However, by the 1970s the Soviets were already becoming conscious of the great diversity of the non–communist states of the Asia–Pacific region and of their own relatively limited resources, compared with the United States and Japan, to extend their economic influence throughout the region. US President Nixon's Guam Doctrine, which foreshadowed a lowering of the American military profile in the region, seemed to offer an opportunity for greater Soviet involvement, but the resources available to operate effectively were quite limited. Many of the states of the region, to say nothing of Japan, could no longer be considered underdeveloped and, hence, were not susceptible to the kinds of economic and military aid inducements which had proven effective in Africa and the Middle East. Moscow did not possess the hard–currency reserves of commercial and investment capital needed by these states for their industrial development. Soviet purchases of natural rubber from Malaysia and Indonesia in the mid–1970s were loudly hailed as an important demonstration of co–operative economic relations, but they did not amount to much in the total trade of these countries. The value of their trade with China, for example, was consistently twice as great as with the USSR. Soviet efforts to encourage regional moves for transforming the ASEAN region into a 'zone of peace, freedom and neutrality' came to little, particularly once Moscow had declared its unqualified support for Vietnamese expansion, which the ASEAN countries viewed as a clear and present danger to their own security.[20] Nevertheless, the Soviets continued to try to extend their diplomatic and economic presence throughout the region in recognition of its growing importance economically and as a major arena of East–West and Sino–Soviet strategic confrontation. At the same time, while persisting in diplomatic efforts to establish nuclear–free and peace zones throughout the region so as to reduce the freedom of manoeuvre of the still superior US naval forces, the Soviets continued the rapid build–up of their own Pacific Fleet and its associated air and amphibious deployment capabilities.

The relationship with India continued to flourish, despite occasional irritations, even under the right–wing Janata Party government of the late 1970s. The military connection brought benefits to both sides. Although the Soviets were reconciled to the limits of the influence they could exert on Indian domestic policy — and were probably happy enough not to have to share responsibility for India's difficult internal economic and political problems — they were on the whole gratified by the support they received from New Delhi in crucial foreign policy matters. Indian support was far from automatic — for example, on Cambodia and initially on Afghanistan — but it was solid enough when the chips were down to cause Moscow to continue to value highly its long–term investment in India.[21] The Soviets consistently refused to offer encouragement to radical separatist movements in India, such as the Tamils and the Sikhs, or even occasional communist–led regional governments, as in Kerala, which might have offered them the prospect of a more ideologically reliable base of operations on the subcontinent.[22] On the other hand, they supported similar separatist movements among the Baluchis of Iran and Pakistan during the same period, which seemed to underline the special nature of the relationship with India despite its admittedly 'bourgeois–democratic' regime. Strategic considerations of mutual Soviet and Indian interests in the Indian Ocean and the southern flank of China, discussed in chapter 4, undoubtedly explain much of the strength of Soviet commitment to India in the 1970s and subsequently. Ideological considerations obviously took a back seat.

The Afghanistan adventure, by contrast, represented a curious amalgam of the various factors we have been discussing here: ideological and military–strategic as well as the blatantly opportunistic. Indeed, Afghanistan marked the culmination of the Brezhnevian fascination with the possibilities of decisive military intervention in low–risk situations in support of ideologically congenial, pro–Soviet regimes. Soviet relations with the often unstable, traditional royalist regimes in Afghanistan had been quite good ever since the early 1920s. The main objective of Soviet policy had always been to keep Afghanistan out of British hands, and to that end Moscow had occasionally sent in clandestine armed bands to support one side or another in the incessant tribal and dynastic conflicts in the country. From the mid–1950s, Soviet support took a more organised and systematic form in competing with the West (mainly the United States) for economic and military aid to the relatively stable Kabul regime of King Zahir Shah. By the early 1970s the Soviets were clearly winning this competition, and the United States had effectively withdrawn from the field. Nevertheless, in 1973, when the opportunity of a pro–Soviet coup by military officers trained in the USSR and led by the King's pro–Soviet cousin, Mohammed Daoud, arose, Moscow gave its tacit endorsement. Daoud at first pursued a policy of close alignment with Soviet interests, especially with regard to Pakistan and the West, but he was soon confronted with internal problems created by the former of the two main wings (the Khalq and Parcham factions) of the nascent Communist Party, which wanted him to pursue a more radical program of domestic social and economic transformation.[23] Rising traditional opposition to their radical anti–Islamic policies emboldened Daoud to resist the Khalqis and prompted him to accept support from the Shah of Iran to follow a less pro–Soviet line. The overthrow and execution of Daoud by the Khalq, led by Nur Mohammad Taraki and Hafizullah Amin, in the coup of April 1978 was, accordingly, warmly greeted by Moscow, which poured in arms and military advisers to support the Khalq in the growing civil war with the traditional Islamic forces that became known in the West as the Mujahideen. Soviet diplomatic and military personnel deployed in Afghanistan soon became involved in the internal politics of the Khalq and supported Taraki in an ill–fated coup to remove Hafizullah Amin in September 1979. The victory of the latter posed Moscow with the problem of association with an unpredictably radical regime of dubious loyalty to itself and clearly incapable of reconciling the various contending elements in Afghan society.

The decision to intervene with massive, direct Soviet military force to replace Amin with the more moderate Babrak Karmal, leader of the Parcham faction, in December 1979, proved to be a turning point in the history of Soviet policy towards the Third World and indeed of Soviet foreign policy in general. It has since been revealed that the decision was taken by a minority in the Politburo comprising Brezhnev, Defence Minister Dmitrii Ustinov, hard–line ideologist Mikhail Suslov and Foreign Minister Andrei Gromyko, against the advice of the Chief of the General Staff, Marshal Nikolai Ogarkov, and other military experts, as well as KGB Chief Yuri Andropov. According to Boris Yel'tsin, the radical gadfly of contemporary Soviet politics, the other members of the Politburo were not even consulted on the decision.[24] The fateful order to intervene was taken against the background of the astonishingly ineffectual

American response to the Iranian hostage crisis — the Khomeini regime's seizure of US diplomatic personnel in Teheran — in the fall of 1979, which convinced Brezhnev that he had little to fear in the way of an American military reaction. The invasion promised substantial benefits for Moscow. A major advantage was the establishment of an ideologically reliable buffer state on the Soviet border to quarantine the Islamic radicalism emanating from Iran, which threatened to engulf the USSR's own Central Asian population. Another was a speedy and dramatic improvement in the Soviet Union's geostrategic position *vis–a–vis* China and the West. In reality, the entire exercise steadily deteriorated into an endless drain on Soviet military and economic resources, as the West reacted with increasingly effective support for the Mujahideen. Eventually it became a nagging source of domestic popular discontent. It also helped to consolidate the US rapprochement with the Chinese and isolated the USSR from most of its traditional supporters in the Third World, with the signal exception of India. The Soviets faced a similar outcome from their support for the Vietnamese in Cambodia. The negative results of the more aggressive turn in their activities in the Asia–Pacific region had, by the end of the Brezhnev era, led the Soviets to re–examine the entire thrust of their policy towards the Third World.

Soviet relations with Latin America were significantly less intensive than those with Africa and Asia, yet a similar complex of ideological, military and opportunistic factors ultimately coalesced to increase Moscow's involvement there as well, further exacerbating relations with the United States. Soviet foreign policy in Latin America was traditionally conditioned by distance and by Washington's sensitivity to events in what it considered its own backyard, as expressed in the Monroe Doctrine. The Comintern had succeeded in establishing Communist Parties in most Latin American states, and in some they operated legally — a tendency that accelerated in the 1960s and 1970s, as the number of party members in the region substantially increased.[25]

Under Khrushchev Soviet policy became more adventurous, in line with evidence of a rising tide of anti–Yankee nationalism among the bourgeois–democratic and military–oligarchic regimes of the area. The overall Soviet strategy was to encourage local Communist Parties, where legal, to participate in such regimes and to try to influence them to adopt an anti–imperialist orientation, a restrictive stance toward foreign capital and progressive domestic social measures. Soviet specialists on Latin America were fully conscious of the broad gradations in the levels of development in the region and of the dominant position of foreign, transnational capital. Many of them applied Western 'dependency theory' in analysing the prospects for Soviet involvement. Pessimists among them saw very limited opportunities for the Soviet Union to replace Western sources of development capital and concentrated rather on encouragement of the growth of national consciousness and progressive social policies within the framework of the existing order. Optimists, by contrast, regarded 'dependence', and the distorted patterns of economic development generated by it, as promising fuel for revolutionary social conflagration in the region.[26] But the policy adopted was to work with existing governments, regardless of their political colouration, and to influence them, where possible, with or without the assistance of local communists, to adopt a more independent position in international relations.

Paradoxically, the accession of Fidel Castro to the Soviet Bloc in the early 1960s merely complicated Soviet policy in Latin America. Especially after the assembly of Third World radicals at the Tricontinental Congress in Havana in January 1966, Castro began actively pursuing his own, quite different line in Latin America. He ridiculed both the policy of working with existing regimes and the accommodatory role of local Communist Parties as fruitless and demanded direct support for violent revolutionary activity. Moreover, he had begun purging pro–Moscow elements from the Communist Party of Cuba which he had recently undertaken to reconstitute for his own purposes. By thus radicalising Latin American communism and committing it to revolution, Castro succeeded mainly in alarming non–communist political forces and undermining Soviet diplomatic efforts throughout the region.[27] In the context of increasing Chinese diplomatic and ideological competition in Latin America, the Soviet response was to accede tacitly to Castro's urgings and adopt a more aggressive policy, albeit with reservations.

The tensions in Soviet relations with Cuba lessened considerably after the failure of Castro's 'great leap forward' adventure with the sugar harvest of 1970, when the need for Soviet economic aid became imperative. Cuba joined CMEA in 1972, and agreed in future to co–ordinate policy more closely with Moscow. The setback to the more aggressive Soviet–Cuban involvement resulting from the overthrow of the communist–backed Allende government in Chile in September 1973 evoked acrimonious debates among Soviet Bloc analysts. Some argued that Allende had been too radical in his domestic policies; others, following Castro, contended that he had not been radical enough. For a time Moscow reverted to a more cautious, pragmatic strategy in the region.

However, in the heady atmosphere surrounding the successful Soviet–Cuban joint venture in 'revolutionary' military activity in Africa in the middle and late 1970s, and the indecisive response by Washington, Moscow became more assertive in seeking out similar opportunities in Latin America, principally in Central America and the Caribbean, where radical nationalism was particularly rife. Cuba took responsibility, as in Africa, for the overtly military side of things, although large numbers of Cuban combat troops were not in evidence, presumably for fear of arousing a dangerous North American response. The immediate result was a broad expansion of Soviet involvement in a region of vital American concern, specifically in Nicaragua, Guyana, Jamaica and Grenada, with secondary support for national–liberation movements in neighboring states. Washington's eventual reply, under the Reagan administration, took the form of an outright invasion of Grenada, in October 1983, and extensive assistance to anti–communist movements in Nicaragua and El Salvador: a clear signal to the Soviet Union that it had over–extended itself in Latin America as well.

Gorbachev's new political thinking on the Third World

The main thrust of Gorbachev's policy toward the Third World has been to de–emphasise this third 'stream' of the world anti–imperialist torrent (the other two, it will be recalled, are the socialist countries and the working class of the capitalist world). It would be going too far to assert that Moscow has abandoned the Third World. As Jerry Hough has pointed out, support for independence movements is an article of faith for Soviet communists.[28] Nevertheless, the change in tactics being applied to maintain Soviet influence there is in keeping with the strategic perspective of the downgrading of class struggle as the fundamental feature of international relations between the world of socialism and the world of capitalism. Detente is now recognised as 'indivisible', and the benefits of unstable gains in individual Third World countries are increasingly seen as not worth the costs of confrontation with the West. Accordingly, pro–Soviet revolutionary–democratic regimes are being urged to make their peace with the imperialists and their domestic opponents, and Moscow is providing substantial diplomatic assistance in arranging the necessary accommodations.

The new approach has entailed some fundamental rethinking of the nature and indeed the desirability of economic interdependence between the Third World and the world capitalist market system. As late as the autumn of 1983, Soviet commentators were still arguing that the only solution to the economic exploitation of the Third World lay in self–reliance and 'alliance with world socialism';[29] less than four years later some had begun talking of the possibility of creating, on the basis of the mutual long–term interests of the capitalist West, the developing countries and the socialist countries, a 'universal program of action and a universal strategy of cooperation in the solution of the most acute contemporary global problems'.[30] To be sure, there were few illusions as to the nature of capitalist relations with Third World economies. Nonetheless, there were equally few illusions about the capacity of the socialist world to provide a viable alternative. Interdependence affected it as well, and the main issue was for the USSR, as well as the Third World, to become involved in world market processes as fully and as speedily as possible.

The translation of the ideas of the more innovative Soviet Third World specialists to practical policy was far from instantaneous, although Gorbachev was known to be highly receptive to their assessments. Even if he fully accepted their views, which is not at all certain, he was not entirely a free agent, especially with Gromyko still in charge of the foreign policy machinery. The May Day slogans published soon after his accession to power in the (northern) spring of 1985, for example, continued in the traditional vein of full support for the anti–imperialist struggle of the newly independent states, with individual slogans for Africa, the Middle East and Latin America.[31] In his first major speech, at a Plenary Session of the CPSU Central Committee on 23 April 1985, he repeated the customary attacks on the United States and other imperialist states for threatening the independence of Third World countries. (He particularly mentioned Nicaragua and Grenada.) He also subjected the 'plundering role of transnational corporations' and discriminatory Western trade practices to scathing condemnation for disrupting the world economy and exploiting the former colonial countries.[32]

The same themes were repeated in his major 'Political Report' to the XXVIIth CPSU Congress in February 1986, where the problems of exploitation and the mounting debt of the Third World countries continued to figure prominently in his account of international problems. However, for perhaps the first time, he acknowledged the inability of individual or groups of (read: 'socialist') countries to solve these increasingly global problems.[33] Despite this, the new version of the party program adopted by the Congress reverted to the old formulas on the importance of the anti–imperialist struggle of the newly independent states for the world revolutionary process and repeated the commitment to provide material support especially for those states which had chosen the 'path of socialist orientation' and were led by 'revolutionary–democratic parties'.[34] Official statements still hailed the crisis of world capitalism and imperialism and the growing economic and military might of world socialism as the main features of the epoch, which made the continuation of an assertive Soviet policy toward the Third World seem unobjectionable. By the time of completion of Gorbachev's manuscript for his book *Perestroika* in the middle of 1987, there were already signs of a change in his attitude, although his presentation of prescriptions for appropriate policies by Third World countries and their capitalist exploiters still contained much of the old bravado.[35]

A year later, however, the world and the place of the Soviet Union in it evidently seemed far different from the way they had appeared at the beginning of his reign. By the middle of 1988, with almost three years of *perestroika* and *glasnost* and the successful conclusion of the INF agreement with the United States under his belt, Gorbachev knew that the economic position of the Soviet Union was much worse than he had originally suspected. He had also come to realise that advantageous arrangements with the capitalist world were possible if he could convince the West of the sincerity of his commitment to change. In his report to the special 19th Party Conference in June 1988, Gorbachev emphasised the need for 'realism' in the conception of Soviet foreign, as well as domestic, policy. He gave full expression to the priority of 'common human values' over class considerations in international relations and to the principle of 'freedom of choice' of all peoples in fashioning their economic and political systems. While he pledged 'consistently to carry out the line of deepening . . . relations with the developing states and with the nonaligned movement', the main thrust of his remarks was clearly directed towards broadening the spectrum of potential partners to work in co–operation for the solution of global problems.[36] That is, the fact of a 'socialist orientation' by individual Third World states, was no longer considered a matter of cardinal importance. In fact, commitments to the survival of such regimes had become something of an embarrassment for Gorbachev, impeding Soviet efforts to demonstrate its *bona fides* as a constructive, responsible member of the international community.

A continuing problem for Gorbachev towards the end of the 1980s has therefore been to distance the Soviet Union from these radical regimes and their uncertain fate without appearing to abandon them entirely, thus giving rise to accusations of betrayal by his conservative domestic and international communist critics. Some Soviet academic writers have continued to debate the merits of the concepts of socialist orientation, vanguard parties, states of national democracy and 'people's democracy'.[37] As David Albright has shown, even the conservative critics of Gorbachev's policies have succeeded in clothing their arguments in the garments of the new political thinking[38] — surely one of the pitfalls for the Western analyst of Soviet writings in the era of *glasnost*.

An interesting example of the gamesmanship involved in the policy debates was the publication in September 1989 in the party's main theoretical journal, *Kommunist*, of an article which cleverly linked two seemingly unconnected issues in the search for economic savings to pay for domestic *perestroika*: arms reduction and a withdrawal from ill-conceived adventures in the Third World. The author, Igor' Malashenko, Scientific Secretary of the Institute of the USA and Canada of the USSR Academy of Sciences, condemned both the quest for 'mirror–image' military parity with the United States and a concentration in foreign policy on expanding Soviet influence in regions of the world 'having a secondary significance from the standpoint of national security'.[39] The narrowness of the circle of foreign–policy decision–makers had led to the rise of what Malashenko calls 'geopolitical' thinking, which tended to blur genuine considerations of national interests. Stereotyped ideological modes of situational perception and choice among alternative policies resulted in decisions which were often unwise and unnecessarily costly:

> For decades we, in essence, linked our security to the victory of socialism on an international scale, and the greater the number of countries that set out on the socialist path of development, the more secure the position of the Soviet Union in the world seemed. In practice, however, this ideological approach became combined with the growth of geopolitical considerations in our policy . . .
>
>   The combination of ideology and geopolitics bore queer results. In the dormant years, stagnation within the country was combined with heightened activity in the world arena, the globalisation of the influence of the USSR. But in the sphere of foreign policy a 'gross' [*valovoi*] approach predominated; behind the impressive figures the main thing was lost sight of: do the national interests of the USSR really require participation in the solution of all questions, in all barely significant regional conflicts? For this is fraught with great political costs and swallows up huge material resources.[40]

Malashenko was thus calling for a drastic withdrawal from Third World adventures as well as a substantial cut in defence expenditures, governed not by the weaponry choices and national security conceptions of the United States, but by the Soviet Union's own views of its defence requirements. Somewhat reminiscent of the arguments of the 'little–Englanders' of nineteenth century Britain, he contended that the USSR could do itself and its friends more good by concentrating on improving its domestic economic and social performance than by engaging in expansionist ventures abroad. The zero–sum–game thinking of the Brezhnev era was no longer appropriate and probably never had been.

The publication of Malashenko's views in so authoritative a place was certainly no accident. The article set forth a highly provocative liberal position to counter the equally extreme conservative position which maintained the traditional views of the sources and uses of Soviet power and which sought, among other things, to retain commitments to deserving Third World clients and to enlarge their number wherever possible. This juxtaposition of the extremes left Gorbachev clear title to the middle ground, where he clearly felt most comfortable.

Gorbachev has attempted to manage the dilemma between disassociation from and continued support for Third World nations by a two–pronged strategy for changing the 'rules of engagement', so to speak. The first prong is the strategy of 'national reconciliation' under which pro–Soviet, 'vanguard–party'–ruled countries involved in armed conflicts with Western–assisted anti–communist movements are encouraged to form governments of national unity with their enemies. To make reconciliation possible the 'revolutionary–democratic', 'people's–democratic' or Communist Party regimes are pressed to abandon radical socialist social and economic programs and institutions (such as collectivised agriculture, the prohibition on private industry and trade and pressure against organised religion) and to enlist the support of non–communist individuals, groups and public associations. This strategy has been applied in each of the Third World regions we have been discussing, most notably in Afghanistan, Angola, Cambodia and Nicaragua. The important thing to note is that, unlike the case of the United States in Vietnam during the period of 'Vietnamisation' from 1972–75, the Soviets have continued to provide ample military, economic and diplomatic support to their client party–regimes to enable them to survive in the unfamiliar circumstances of economic and (limited) political competition. The regimes have not been pressured to give up power, merely to share it with elements that have little capacity to govern in their own right, although that, too, could change in time.[41] The fact that the Soviets have been willing to countenance the effective dismantling of Communist Party rule in such core countries as Poland, Czechoslovakia and East Germany suggests that they would accept a similar outcome if their Third World clients proved unable to maintain themselves in power in a more or less democratic electoral contest. Nicaragua is certainly a case in point. In the meantime, they are supplied with sufficient military support to ensure that they are not defeated on the field of battle. The only relevant country where this strategy has apparently not yet been applied with much determination is Ethiopia, where the military and domestic political situations are so grim as to incapacitate the regime for making a credible offer of a coalition solution.

The ingenuity of the national reconciliation strategy lies in the diplomatic pressure the Soviets have been able to exert, through formal processes of agreements involving the United States, to ensure that the latter is unable to continue to supply its clients with sufficient military means to win the ongoing guerilla struggles. They have succeeded beyond most Western expectations in Afghanistan and seemed, until the electoral surprise in February 1990, to be having a similar effect in Nicaragua, where their suport for the Contadora process essentially precluded Washington from maintaining its aid to the Contras. There are prospects for an analogous outcome in Angola, where the UNITA forces of Jonas Savimbi have been hard pressed to maintain a presence in the political settlement following the withdrawal of Cuban troops because of internal pressures in the US to give the negotiated solution a chance. In Cambodia the diplomatic processes for an agreement to establish a national–reconciliation coalition were not consummated, not so much because of American intransigence, but mainly because the Chinese were unwilling to abandon their Khmer Rouge allies and accept the pro–Vietnamese and hence pro–Muscovite regime of Hun Sen as the leader of a coalition government. Nevertheless, by creating an atmosphere of reasonableness and diplomatic rectitude around the negotiation process, the Soviets have succeeded in exercising enough international restraint on the supply of the anti–government forces to give Hun Sen an excellent chance of survival. Even without major Vietnamese military support, government forces have been able to fight their combined opponents to a standstill. There are already signs of a split in ASEAN over attitudes toward the Hun Sen regime now that the Vietnamese have seemingly completed their withdrawal.

As has been the case in Afghanistan, the anti–Soviet coalition appears to have poorer prospects for victory without the presence of the occupying 'fraternal' troops than with them. Gorbachev has been astute enough to understand this apparent paradox; by distancing itself from the embattled regimes the Soviet Union not only seems to be able to help them at much lower cost, but it is much less vulnerable to harmful domestic and international fallout if the client regimes ultimately fail. These regimes generally enjoy considerable sympathy in organised Third World bodies, such as the Organisation of African Unity and the Nonaligned Movement, although the presence of Soviet (or Cuban or Vietnamese) troops tends to dilute that sympathy to a certain extent. Military disengagement thus allows Moscow to take greater advantage of their support in pressing the case for the survival of its clients against direct and indirect Western interference.

Elsewhere in the Third World, despite their strictures on disarmament and the wastefulness of military expenditures, the Soviets continue to be a large–scale and reliable supplier of military equipment to a gradually increasing number of countries.[42] Third World countries like Syria and India have been recipients of the latest Soviet technology — such as the MIG–29 fighter aircraft, which is generally considered to be on a par with the best available in the West, and which has not yet been supplied even to most of Moscow's Warsaw Pact allies. The Soviets have few illusions by now about the policy influence the sale of these arms procures for them, although, in addition to being a source of foreign currency, they do represent a visible symbol of friendship and trust toward the regimes in question, as well as an entry to their military establishments. As long as Third World countries continue to seek modern arms, the Soviets are no more likely than the United States, or other developed Western or industrialising countries like Brazil or Israel, to foresake the commercial opportunities and the lowering of unit production costs they represent for their own domestic military needs.

The other prong of Gorbachev's strategy of 'constructive disengagement' in the Third World lies on the higher moral plane of championing of Third World interests in the so–called 'New International Economic Order'. In his address to the UN General Assembly in December 1988, Gorbachev, in addition to his highly publicised proposal for unilateral Soviet arms reductions, devoted considerable attention to the Third World debt problem and the responsibility of the capitalist West to make up for its past exploitation of the colonies. His solution was to 'internationalise' the debt problem by establishing a co–ordinated program among the creditor nations to relieve the debt burden on countries with little prospect of ever being able to repay in full. He announced that the Soviet Union was prepared to accept a hundred–year moratorium on Third World debts owed to it (predominantly denominated in non–hard currencies) and to write them off completely 'in a whole number of cases'.[43] (See Table 3 in the Appendix for selected Third World country debts to the USSR). At present it is still too early to assess the prospects for success of this part of his strategy. What he evidently has in mind is involving the Soviet Union from the outset in this particular component of the international financial system (the USSR has been unsuccessful so far in its attempts to enter the main institutions), thus gaining a foothold in its operational machinery from which to be able to influence policy on trade and aid with the Third World. Soviet specialists have been writing pessimistically about the fate of the so–called 'North–South Dialogue' since the early 1980s. Now, Gorbachev is seeking to build on the experience of individuals like Willi Brandt, who have attempted to address the deteriorating debt situation and to create permanent mechanisms for dealing with it. It cannot have escaped Gorbachev's attention that the Soviet Union itself, not to mention some of its more heavily indebted partners (e.g. Poland and Hungary), may well find itself in an analogous situation in the course of reforming its economy with the aid of foreign capital and credits. By getting in on the ground floor of a more universal, perhaps UN–centred, financial assistance mechanism, the Soviet Union could thus hope to exert substantial 'democratising' influence on the terms of financial aid, and avoid the restrictive conditions currently imposed by the existing capitalist–dominated agencies. Such activity would certainly enhance Soviet influence as a champion of the less fortunate nations in a much more tangible fashion than the customary ideological and political methods of the past. The problem is to obtain the capital necessary to fund the prospective new institution. For the foreseeable future, only the Western countries are likely to be in a position to supply it, and they have shown themselves to be unenthusiastic about such proposals. It is perhaps significant that Gorbachev avoided any mention of the New International Economic Order in his UN address. At this stage he presumably wishes to avoid frightening the West until a substantial international constituency can be created to press for the establishment of the necessary machinery.

Conclusions

Soviet policy toward the Third World has in some respects come full circle since the Stalinist period. From an attitude of malign neglect of non–communist anti–colonial regimes and movements during the postwar years under Stalin, Soviet policies under Khrushchev and Brezhnev came to reflect the belief that the Third World was the most important arena of international class struggle, where the greatest advances were to be made in changing the 'correlation of forces' in favour of world socialism. Disappointment over the behaviour of the majority of national–liberation movements once they gained power and the growing availability of 'projectable' military power led to a more selective, but more intensive, focusing of Soviet military, political and economic assistance on so–called 'revolutionary–democratic' or 'people's–democratic' regimes, committed to the socialist path of development. By the time Gorbachev had come to power in 1985, however, it was already clear that this policy had been a costly failure, not only in creating viable socialist states, but also by raising the level of East–West confrontation. The result has been a tacit disengagement from particularly difficult situations and a general lowering of the priority of the Third World in Soviet foreign policy.

This has by no means entailed a reversion to the isolationism of the Stalin period, however. Over the past four decades the Soviet Union has established firm relations throughout the Third World, and the latter has become a significant source of support for Soviet diplomacy in the international arena. In the United Nations and its associated bodies, for example, these countries almost invariably side with the Soviet Union against the United States on contentious issues. Gorbachev's express commitment to upgrading the status of the UN and the Nonaligned Movement suggests an intention to continue courting the favour of Third World countries. Indeed, the message of his speeches in Vladivostok and Krasnoyarsk is that he intends to expand the Soviet presence in areas of the world, such as the Western Pacific region, where it has previously largely been lacking.

However, the nature of that presence will be primarily diplomatic and commercial, rather than military, as it would have been under Brezhnev. Given the current state of the Soviet economy, it is likely that commercial involvement will remain modest in terms of hard–currency expenditures and opportunistic in the commodities and countries that are targeted. The main thrust of Gorbachev's policies in the APR and elsewhere in the Third World is thus toward the establishment of an ubiquitous Soviet presence. He seeks to establish bases for diplomatic and intelligence operations in order to influence the policies of regional governments to lessen their involvement in Western security arrangements and to increase their receptivity to Soviet economic and political interests.

Gorbachev's carefully orchestrated disengagement from major points of confrontation, such as Afghanistan, Angola and Cambodia, under the strategy of national reconciliation, is part of the general scaling down of Soviet material involvement in the Third World. In addition to its symbolic value as a symbol of Moscow's acceptance of the norms of peaceful international behaviour, this strategy reflects a fundamental change in Soviet priorities. Whereas, under Brezhnev, domestic development was consciously sacrificed to extend the scope of Soviet goals in foreign policy, primarily in the Third World, now, under Gorbachev, foreign expansion is being sacrificed — or rather, basically modified in its express goals and the strategies for attaining them — to the radical restructuring of the domestic economy and society. Although Soviet threats to existing Western security interests will continue to be a cause of concern, especially in the smaller Third World countries, the significance of this shift in Soviet priorities can hardly be exaggerated.

7 Conclusions

The perils of writing a book on 'Soviet Foreign Policy Today' in the Gorbachev era are self-evident. Things are changing so rapidly in Soviet foreign and domestic affairs that there is a very real danger that conclusions applicable 'today' have a high probability of no longer being relevant tomorrow. To avoid leaving the book entirely hostage to the vagaries of Kremlin politics or other possible sources of change, I have tried to locate Gorbachev's new political thinking and the policies associated with it in the broader context of the evolution of Soviet foreign policy, particularly in the Brezhnev era, when the institutional and ideological parameters with which Gorbachev has had to operate were largely established. This approach admittedly has its dangers. Concentrating too heavily on bygone institutions and practices may leave the observer unprepared for or skeptical of the magnitude of the changes — the sharp breaks with the past — that Gorbachev has boldly sought to introduce. On the other hand, it does help to put those changes into perspective, by examining what it is he has been trying to change and why he has failed in his attempts to do so.

One advantage of the method of historical comparison is the opportunity it presents to address the important question of whether Gorbachev's new approach to foreign policy really differs from the traditional Soviet practice of seeking a temporary 'breathing space' (*peredyshka*) to consolidate gains or confront weaknesses in the country's internal and external situation when opportunities for further advances are perceived to have been exhausted. As we have seen, Lenin's introduction of NEP and the declaration of the 'temporary stabilisation of capitalism' in the early 1920s were examples of the search for a 'breathing space'. The popular front period of the latter 1930s and the wartime accommodation with the Western allies were others, as were the periods of 'peaceful coexistence' under Khrushchev following Stalin's death and detente under Brezhnev after the WTO invasion of Czechoslovakia. In each case, however, the quest for breathing space was ideologically rationalised as being merely temporary, and the qualification was always added that the international 'class struggle' continued, albeit by more peaceful means. Even then, opportunities for further advance in areas peripheral to the main arena of East–West confrontation were still to be acted upon. That was the essence of the conception of the 'divisibility of detente' under Brezhnev, but it had always been implicit in the breathing–space policies of every Soviet leader before Gorbachev.

The question is whether Gorbachev's new political thinking has really broken this cycle of advance and consolidation. The evidence suggests that it has. Nevertheless, a certain amount of caution is still obviously warranted. On the positive side, Gorbachev has officially abandoned the notion of class struggle as the ineluctable essence of international relations in the era of imperialism. Survival in the nuclear age, uneven economic development in the framework of universal economic interdependence, and problems of the environment are now said to transcend class struggle as issues of interstate relations, and a rational accommodation of mutual and conflicting interests, he believes, can now obviate previous tendencies towards armed conflict. On the other hand, Gorbachev has not eschewed the goal of creating a reconstructed form of socialism as an alternative world system to compete with capitalism for addressing the common problems and aspirations of mankind. That project is obviously a very long–term one indeed, and in the meantime, his evolving model of a 'possible socialism' may come to look very much like welfare capitalism.

A greater cause of concern on the negative side, perhaps, is the still immense military power at Moscow's disposal. Facile Western conclusions that the Soviet Union is no longer effectively a superpower in either a military or a political and economic sense are most certainly premature, if not entirely mistaken. Gorbachev clearly has no intention of rendering his country militarily impotent, or even of materially weakening its defence capabilities. If anything, available evidence suggests a continuing effort to upgrade the qualitative characteristics of the Soviet Army, albeit in line with a new emphasis on a 'defensive doctrine'. This is apparently part of the deal he has made with the Soviet military establishment for their general endorsement of his programs. Also, it is worth remembering that for economic reasons (and probably political reasons as well), the Soviet Union remains the world's number one purveyor of military hardware.

Consequently, until we have more conclusive proof of the genuineness of Gorbachev's commitment to democratic methods, 'freedom of choice' and the peaceful settlement of contentious issues — and his handling of the demands for independence by the Baltic Republics may seem rather worrying to some in this regard — and given the constant features of the USSR's geopolitical situation, it would be unwise to conclude that the current radical changes in Soviet foreign policy are irreversible or that what we are witnessing is more than a prolonged breathing space. Gorbachev's ideological innovations would seem to militate against a simple reversion to past forms of expansion, if he eventually does decide to terminate the present hiatus, and in that sense the old cycle would still have been broken. But this would mean only that the West would have to be prepared for a more traditional pattern of international big–power rivalry — this time with nuclear weapons. Let us hope that more effective means could be devised to manage potential conflicts from such rivalry than in the past.

It is clear by now, more than five years after his accession to power, that Gorbachev has been considerably more successful in the basically negative exercise of destroying old institutions and ideological shibboleths than he has in the positive task of fashioning new ones. He has demonstrated a remarkable ability not only to formulate goals and recognise needs of Soviet society appropriate for his vision of socialism in the modern world, but also to identify realistically the domestic and international obstacles to their attainment. He has also shown himself courageous enough to adopt radical policies to remove them, regardless of the cost in traditional Soviet political and ideological values. But, like Khrushchev before him, he has not thus far been quite so adept in devising strategies and programs to bring his visions to fruition. Also, like Khrushchev, he has acquired many enemies in the course of trying to implement his policies.

These conclusions underline just how much the Gorbachevian reforms at home and abroad have been a one–man show. I have argued elsewhere that all Soviet–type systems and their derivatives, such as Yugoslavia's 'self–managing socialism', ultimately depend on the authority of a single individual, namely the general secretary (or, as in Tito's case, the President) of the ruling Communist Party.[1] As self–consciously ideological systems, they require authoritative, legitimising definitions of policy for their machinery of implementation to be put into operation, that is, for the officials of the appropriate arms of the bureaucracy to be constrained to take the necessary action. This is especially true under the conditions of *glasnost, perestroika* and democratisation, where much of the old machinery of government and administration has been dismantled and where the number of contending opinions and policy proposals is virtually unlimited. From time to time Gorbachev has had to intervene to indicate just what official policy is on a given issue. Meanwhile, he and his closest colleagues and advisors have been trying to revise the ideological foundations of the system to conform to the new, more liberal conditions and to provide guidelines, or at least a general orientation, for policies at home and in relations with allied socialist countries. Thus far, it is clear that no acceptable ideological framework has yet emerged, and personalised intervention remains the order of the day on almost every issue. Gorbachev's imposition of a French–style executive Presidency, with himself as the incumbent, reflects his recognition of this fact and his determination to possess the formal power to act decisively and effectively. Time will tell whether institutional change alone is sufficient to bring about substantive reform.

Nowhere is this pattern of increasingly institutionalised, one–person rule more apparent than in the area of foreign policy. To act upon his 'new political thinking' Gorbachev has had to dismantle much of the old Soviet foreign policy establishment. He has also had to make significant changes in the personnel and relative power positions of the Soviet Army and the KGB in the decision–making hierarchy in order to acquire the requisite freedom of manoeuvre for his new initiatives. Gorbachev obvious believes that the creation of a favourable international climate is essential to the success of his domestic reforms, not only to permit the transfer of scarce resources from military to civilian uses and enlist the participation of foreign capital and technology in modernising the Soviet economy, but also to overcome the siege mentality which had for so long justified the maintenance of the inefficient, highly politicised command system of national economic management. His already legendary new initiatives on arms control and other confidence–building measures have been designed precisely to foster a benign image of the USSR as a worthy partner in international politics and the world economy. So far, he has been remarkably successful in obtaining a favourable response from the once–feared and detested centres of 'world imperialism': the United States and her allies. He has managed to inject his own concepts, such as 'international economic security', 'the common European home', 'freedom of choice' and 'national reconciliation' into the lexicon of international discourse. In the process of clearing the way for accommodations with erstwhile enemies he has also succeeded in eliminating or defusing a number of points of friction in the Third World which had severely encumbered Soviet relations with the West and China.

There is no doubt that by his new initiatives and methods in the conduct of Soviet foreign policy Gorbachev has compelled the United States and its allies to rethink their own worldview and modes of interacting with the world. As former US Secretary of State Henry Kissinger has warned in connection with the impending changes in Europe, Western policy–makers must quickly develop a comprehensive conception of their own long–term interests and expectations to meet the Soviet challenge to existing institutional and cognitional patterns, which have served the West well in the era of confrontation, but are likely to be increasingly less relevant in the future.[2] Third World observers, too, are showing some anxiety over the changes in the international climate which will no longer encourage individual states to play one superpower off against the other in the hope of selling influence for economic and military assistance. Nor can Third World leaders continue to justify the maintenance of dictatorial rule by the need to combat imperialism or communism.[3] In short, in the relatively brief period he has been in power Gorbachev has had an amazingly transformatory impact on international relations.

Yet, paradoxically, in his own bailiwick, the world of socialism, the effect of Gorbachev's radical reforms has, from a traditional Soviet perspective, been mainly destructive. His success in imposing *perestroika*, *glasnost* and democratisation on his reluctant Communist Party colleagues at home and in Eastern Europe has resulted in a wave of previously suppressed anti–Muscovite and anti–communist sentiment which has ended in the dismantling of the Communist Party's monopoly of political and economic power. It is doubtful whether Gorbachev expected things to go so far. Ironically, in his sponsorship of the principle of freedom of choice as the hallmark of his initiatives in foreign policy and as the key to his new–found acceptability in the West, he has mortgaged his ability to intervene to reverse the process of disintegration in the East. In the negative sense of destroying the apparatus of traditional Stalinist power, he has certainly succeeded in his effort to make *perestroika* irreversible. As the Chinese gerontocrats around Deng Xiaoping have demonstrated since early June 1989, the loss of Communist Party domination is never entirely irreversible in a brute, physical sense. However, as long as Gorbachev remains at the helm, the likelihood of so complete a turnabout is probably excluded in the Soviet Union and Eastern Europe. Such a development would certainly mean the end of his visions of such things as a 'common European home', agreements on radical arms reductions with the United States and the establishment of a firm Soviet presence throughout the Third World. Indeed, Gorbachev has seemed almost to relish the changes taking place in Eastern Europe. In a television appearance in Washington in late October 1989, Gennady Gerasimov, the Soviet Foreign Ministry's chief press spokesperson, announced with a whimsical touch that the Brezhnev Doctrine had been replaced with what he termed the 'Frank Sinatra Doctrine' — the East Europeans, he said, 'can do it their way'. This change was formalised by Foreign Minister Shevardnadze at a conference of Warsaw Pact foreign ministers a few days later, where the right to employ foreign troops to suppress domestic unrest in the member states was officially repudiated.[4] In this area of foreign policy, too, Gorbachev appeared to be intent on making a reversion to the past at least formally impossible. In any case, the extent of the dependence of the Eastern European economies on Soviet raw materials, energy and markets for their finished goods and the continuing military and security linkages guarantee that he will be able to exert substantial influence on their policies for the indefinite future, even in the absence of the 'leading role' of the local Communist Parties. There is evidence that the Mazowiecki government in Poland is operating under the realisation that Poland still needs the Soviet Union considerably more than the Soviet Union needs it and will probably continue to do so for the foreseeable future. This dependency factor undoubtedly represents an element of stability in Soviet relations with Eastern Europe and with the West as well, giving Gorbachev a degree of confidence in dealing with his Western negotiating partners that a superficial examination of the situation would not lead one to expect. Gorbachev's foreign–policy position is not quite so vulnerable to the vagaries of change as it evidently appears to many Western observers; so far, at least, he has little reason to want to alter its basic directions.

If, on the other hand, his more conservative, less cool–headed opponents were to succeed in overthrowing him, which seems increasingly unlikely at this point, the basic parameters of Soviet foreign policy would inevitably change. Relations with the West, although perhaps not returning to the acrimony of the Cold War period, would probably remain frozen at something less favourable than the present level. His successors would be unlikely to continue to make the military and diplomatic concessions upon which progress towards international reconciliation has so far depended. Moreover, irrespective of formal arrangements, they could be expected to exert considerably greater economic and political pressure on their Warsaw Pact allies to check any tendencies to disregard Moscow's interests in international relations.

Even if Gorbachev remains in power, however, it is likely that he will take steps to tighten discipline at home and possibly in some areas of alliance politics as well. He clearly must do something to deal with the growing domestic manifestations of both popular and elite discontent over the failure of his reform programs to produce tangible results.[5] In his crackdown on the efforts of the Baltic Republics to push ahead for independence Gorbachev is already evincing signs of toughening his position. He is also showing increasing testiness in his attitude towards the criticism which some of the more radical elements in the Soviet media are levelling at him under the banner of *glasnost*. Indeed, the editor of the liberal large–circulation weekly *Argumenty i fakty*, Vladislav Starkov, whom Gorbachev tried unsuccessfully to force into retirement, has claimed that the real struggle in Soviet politics today is not between liberals and conservatives, but is located to a considerable extent 'inside Gorbachev's head': 'It's Gorbachev battling Gorbachev,' he says. Starkov depicts Gorbachev as a veteran Communist Party bureaucrat who, having set off a series of revolutionary reforms, is now dismayed at the turbulent results. In Starkov's quaint phrase, 'He cooked the *kasha* [traditional Russian buckwheat cereal], and it didn't turn out the way he expected.'[6]

Thus it is possible that Gorbachev himself will change the direction of *perestroika* at home. There are already clear signs that he is seeking to reintroduce greater political control over ethnic and industrial unrest. Ostensibly these are to be only temporary measures until his liberalising economic reforms have had a chance to bear fruit and the more democratic legislative and administrative institutions he has established have had time to settle down into a less frenetic, less self–destructively critical routine. This limited reversal would, in fact, probably help Gorbachev to ward off a challenge by his conservative opponents. The danger, however, is that he will hesitate to return to a consistent program of liberalisation once the crisis has passed — or, alternatively, that *perestroika* will fail, that the crisis will not pass and that he will become accustomed to semi–authoritarian methods of rule.

In either case, the effects on Soviet foreign policy could be harmful, for the aura of trust and of commitment to common values that has been a major element of his public relations success in the West will have at least partially dissipated. In the end, everything depends on him: the persistence of his dedication to reform, the strength of his personality and, of course, the viability of his programs. The West can do some things to assist in the last of these, but the scope for outside influence is relatively limited, given the sheer magnitude of the requirements of the Soviet economy and the fundamentally conservative nature of the system and its political culture. Strong individual leaders have always exerted a decisive influence in shaping the Russian/Soviet system and its foreign and domestic policies. Gorbachev has demonstrated that it takes an extremely forceful and visionary individual even to attempt to change them. The tragedy is that the system itself, and its people, may, after 70 years of Bolshevik rule, have become impervious to radical change. In that case we shall all be the losers. One can only hope that in demolishing the myths and antipathies of the past, Gorbachev will have made it impossible for his successors, or indeed himself, to revert to earlier images of the Soviet Union and its place in the world.

Appendix

Table 1 Share of Total Soviet and East European Imports (1) from European Comecon Countries and (2) from European Market Economies Plus Japan 1970-1984 (in %)

		1970	1971	1972	1973	1974	1975	1976	1977	1978	1979	1980	1981	1982	1983	1984*
USSR	(1)	56	58	58	52	46	42	43	46	49	46	43	46	43	46	48
	(2)	26	25	28	30	35	38	39	35	34	37	38	39	37	34	33
Eastern Europe Total	(1)	63	63	62	58	51	56	55	58	58	56	55	58	61	63	63
	(2)	28	29	31	35	40	36	36	33	32	33	32	30	27	26	26
Bulgaria	(1)	73	74	77	75	65	69	73	77	78	77	75	72	74	77	76
	(2)	21	18	16	17	25	25	20	17	16	17	19	21	18	15	15
Czechoslovakia	(1)	63	63	68	63	59	64	65	66	67	66	65	67	70	73	75
	(2)	27	28	26	28	31	28	28	26	26	27	28	26	23	21	18
GDR	(1)	66	65	63	61	56	63	68	65	65	61	59	62	64	62	63
	(2)	28	29	33	34	36	31	26	28	28	33	33	32	30	31	31
Hungary	(1)	62	63	63	60	54	63	51	50	49	50	47	47	49	48	48
	(2)	29	30	30	31	37	28	38	39	40	40	42	43	39	38	38
Poland	(1)	65	56	58	49	42	43	45	50	51	51	53	62	58	59	55
	(2)	27	29	35	45	52	50	50	44	42	39	36	30	33	31	33
Romania	(1)	48	46	45	40	32	37	40	42	37	34	31	31	37	43	38
	(2)	41	42	44	46	51	45	38	38	40	37	33	33	25	19	20

Source: Calculated from Totals expressed in current $US based on national foreign Trade statistics published by Secretariat of UN Economic Commission for Europe, presented in Peter Knirsch, 'Economic Relations Between the Soviet Union and Eastern Europe and Their Implications for East-West Relations', in Kinya Niiseki (ed.) *The Soviet Union in Transition*, Boulder, Col.: Westview Press, 1987, pp.122-5

* Data for 1984 are preliminary

Table 2 Share of Total Soviet and East European Exports (1) to European Comecon Countries and (2) to European Market Economies Plus Japan 1970-1984 (in %)

		1970	1971	1972	1973	1974	1975	1976	1977	1978	1979	1980	1981	1982	1983	1984*
USSR	(1)	53	52	53	47	42	49	47	46	47	44	42	43	42	43	44
	(2)	22	23	22	26	34	29	31	30	28	34	37	35	34	33	34
Eastern Europe Total	(1)	64	64	65	63	56	63	61	62	62	59	56	56	56	58	57
	(2)	26	26	26	28	32	27	28	27	27	29	30	28	28	29	29
Bulgaria	(1)	76	75	76	76	71	75	76	76	74	70	66	65	68	73	72
	(2)	16	16	15	15	14	12	13	12	12	17	18	16	13	12	10
Czechoslovakia	(1)	64	64	66	65	61	65	68	68	68	66	63	64	67	68	69
	(2)	24	24	23	25	28	24	22	22	22	24	26	24	22	21	20
GDR	(1)	68	69	71	69	64	68	66	69	69	68	64	61	59	60	61
	(2)	24	24	23	25	30	25	27	23	22	23	26	30	31	32	31
Hungary	(1)	62	65	65	64	63	68	55	56	54	52	50	53	52	49	49
	(2)	30	27	27	29	29	24	34	34	35	37	38	33	33	36	38
Poland	(1)	60	59	60	58	53	57	57	57	57	57	52	56	49	50	48
	(2)	31	32	32	36	38	34	34	34	34	33	36	32	36	36	37
Romania	(1)	50	48	47	45	36	38	38	42	41	36	37	30	32	34	26
	(2)	36	38	37	39	46	38	39	34	37	40	39	37	34	37	46

Source: Calculated from Totals expressed in current $US based on national foreign Trade statistics published by Secretariat of UN Economic Commission for Europe, presented in Peter Knirsch, 'Economic Relations Between the Soviet Union and Eastern Europe and Their Implications for East-West Relations', in Kinya Niiseki (ed.) *The Soviet Union in Transition*, Boulder, Col.: Westview Press, 1987, pp.122-5

* Data for 1984 are preliminary

Table 3   Outstanding debt owed to the USSR by selected
socialist and developing countries as of 1 November 1989
(in million rubles)

	Total	Principal	Written off	Rescheduled
Socialist countries				
Albania	127.8	80.3	19.6	–
Bulgaria	433.6	433.6	–	–
Hungary	622.5	622.5	–	–
East Germany	110.0	110.0	–	–
Poland	4 955	4 952.1	–	3 157.7
Yugoslavia	394.0	375.6	–	–
Vietnam	9 131.2	8 856.1	406.4	1 568.7
North Korea	2 234.1	2 234.1	–	417.6
China	6.2	6.2	–	–
Cuba	15 490.6	15 092.0	–	2 360.4
Laos	758.2	758.2	–	49.8
Mongolia	9 542.7	8 981.3	57.2	2 031.5
Total	43 805.9	42 502.0	483.2	9 585.7
Developing countries (selected)				
Algeria	2 519.3	2 447.7	–	560.0
Angola	2 028.9	1 930.2	–	768.0
Afghanistan	3 055.0	2 898.6	–	624.0
Egypt	1 711.3	1 711.3	–	8.2
India	8 907.5	8 907.4	–	–
Indonesia	404.5	330.9	–	–
Iraq	3 795.6	3 514.5	–	1 414.8
Cambodia	714.8	714.5	–	29.8
South Yemen	1 847.6	1 835.7	0.8	581.2
Mozambique	808.6	722.6	–	363.0
Nicaragua	917.3	837.6	–	473.0
Syria	6 742.6	6 514.6	1.7	992.7
Ethiopia	2 860.5	2 849.7	51.7	854.9
Total of all developing countries	42,039.7	40,587.9	61.9	7,812.5

Source: *Izvestiia* 1 March 1990, p. 3

Notes

Chapter 1

1   Originally published under the pseudonym of 'X' as 'The Sources of Soviet Conduct' in *Foreign Affairs* Vol. XXV, No. 4 (July 1947), pp. 566–82.

2   See, for example, Franz Borkenau *European Communism* London: Faber and Faber, Ltd, 1953.

3   Hugh Seton–Watson 'The Historical Roots' in Curtis Keeble (ed.) *The Soviet State: The Domestic Roots of Soviet Foreign Policy* Aldershot, Harts: Gower Publishing Company, 1985, p. 21.

4   David W. Minar *Ideas and Politics: The American Experience* Homewood, Ill.: Dorsey Press, 1964, p. 7. For an extended treatment of ideology in its various aspects, particularly Marxism and Marxism–Leninism, see John Plamenatz *Ideology* in the series 'Key Concepts in Political Science', London: Macmillan, 1970.

5   V. Afanasyev *Marxist Philosophy: A Popular Outline* (Leo Lampert, trans.) Moscow: Foreign Languages Publishing House, 1964, pp. 354–5.

6   ibid., pp. 360–61.

7   Minar *Ideas and Politics*, pp. 7–8.

8   Evidence for this assertion can be found in the address by one of today's leading party ideologists, Politburo member Aleksandr N. Yakovlev, to the Social Sciences Division of the USSR Academy of Sciences in April 1987, where he reiterated the 'scientific validity' of the ideology as a tool for understanding the world, but demanded that Soviet social scientists remove the 'ossified' accretions to the doctrine that had left the prevailing 'theoretical consciousness . . . still at the

level of the 1930s'. Aleksandr N. Yakovlev 'Achieving qualitative
change in Soviet society: the role of the social sciences', translation
reprinted in the *International Social Science Journal* no. 115 (February
1988), pp. 149, 152.

9   This point is emphasised by the Polish sociologist Andrzej Flis in his
article 'Crisis and Political Ritual in Postwar Poland' *Problems of
Communism* vol. XXXVII, no. 3–4 (May–August 1988), pp. 43–54.

10 The best known formulation of this process is, of course, *The
Manifesto of the Communist Party* by Karl Marx and Friedrich
Engels, New York: International Publishers, 1948.

11 The English liberal economist J. A. Hobson had been among the first
to outline the international financial concentration of capitalism in his
book *Imperialism*, published in London in 1902. Further elaboration
of the the theory of finance capital was presented by the German
Marxist economist Rudolf Hilferding in *Das Finanzkapital* Vienna,
1910.

12 V. I. Lenin *Imperialism, The Highest Stage of Capitalism* New
York: International Publishers, 1939.

13 'Lenin and Imperialism' in Victor Serge *From Lenin to Stalin,*
translated from the French by Ralph Manheim, New York: Monad
Press, 1973, p. 127.

14 Perhaps the most brazen statement of the Stalinist formulation of the
ideological, political and economic issues involved in the struggle for
power in the 1920s is in the official history of the party prepared
under his auspices, *History of the Communist Party of the Soviet
Union (Bolsheviks): Short Course* (first published in 1938) Sydney:
Current Book Distributors, 1942, esp. pp. 273–5.

15 For a good account of the current historical debates in the USSR see
Heinz Timmermann 'Gorbatschow — ein Bucharinist?: Zur
Neubewertung der NEP–Periode in Moskau' Cologne: Berichte des
Bundesinstituts fur ostwissenschafliche und internationale Studien,
1988, Report no. 15/1988.   See especially the section on
'International implications' pp. 18–25.

16 'Conditions of Admission to the Communist International' Approved
by the Second Comintern Congress, 6 August, 1920, in Alvin Z.
Rubinstein (ed.) *The Foreign Policy of the Soviet Union* 2nd edn,
New York: Random House, 1966, pp. 72–6.

17 Victor Serge *From Lenin to Stalin* p. 38.   That many of the
survivors in the late 1930s still maintained their commitment and
loyalty to the Comintern, even in the face of the mounting evidence of
Stalin's criminal duplicity, is well illustrated in the Serbian writer

Dobrica Cosic's novel *Gresnik* (The Sinner) Belgrade: BIGZ, 1986. One of the justifications for such continued loyalty on the part of relatively intelligent persons was, of course, the rise of Nazism and Fascism and the failure of the Western democracies to take a principled stand against them.

18   Cited by Adam B. Ulam in *Expansion and Coexistence: The History of Soviet Foreign Policy, 1917–1967* New York: Frederick A. Praeger Publishers, 1968, p. 121.

19   Robert C. Tucker *The Marxian Revolutionary Idea* New York: W. W. Norton & Co. Inc., 1969, p. 139.

20   Discussed in Robert G. Wesson *Soviet Foreign Policy in Perspective* Homewood, Ill.: The Dorsey Press, 1969, pp. 224–5.

21   Authoritative references to the doctrine of 'developed socialism' may be found in an article by the prominent ideological apparatchik Vadim Zagladin, 'Istoricheskaia missiia rabochego klassa i sovremennoe rabochee dvizhenie' *Kommunist* no. 11 (July 1978) pp. 66–80, and in the report of the then chief ideologist Mikhail A. Suslov to an All-Union Conference of Ideological Workers in October 1979, 'Delo vsei partii' *Kommunist* no. 15 (October 1979) pp. 22–43.

22   For one view of the background to the tightening of the military purse–strings which culminated in the removal, almost two years after Brezhnev's death, of Marshal Nikolai V. Ogarkov, Chief of the Soviet General Staff, for continuing to push increases in military spending see Michael MccGwire *Military Objectives in Soviet Foreign Policy* Washington, D.C.: The Brookings Institution, 1987, pp. 311–12.

Chapter 2

1   Leon Trotsky, 'What now?' in *The Third International After Lenin* New York: Pathfinder Press, 1970, p. 256.

2   Quoted in E.H. Carr *The Bolshevik Revolution, 1917–1923*, vol. 3, Baltimore, Md.: Penguin Books, 1966, p. 28.

3   On Bukharin's position see the recently published archives of the party Central Committee in *Izvestiia TsK KPSS* no. 2 (February 1989), especially the message by Bukharin on 22 February 1918 on p. 188.

4   In 1921 the Foreign Department of the Cheka–GPU was established under spymaster M. A. Trilisser. Astrid von Borcke *KGB: Die Machte im Untergrund* Neuhausen–Stuttgart: Hanssler–Verlag, 1987, pp. 26–7.

5   Perhaps the most insightful short account of Soviet diplomacy at Genoa and Rapallo is by George F. Kennan *Soviet Foreign Policy, 1917–1941* Princeton: Van Nostrand, Anvil edn, 1960, pp. 38–53.

6   Carr *The Bolshevik Revolution*, vol. 3, pp. 335–8. Carr observes (p. 335), quoting Levi, that 'the first impulse to this action in the form which it took did not come from the German side'.

7   Trotsky *The Third International After Lenin*, pp. 91–7.

8   See, for example, the recent Soviet reassessment of the events of 1928–32 by Heinz Timmerman, 'Die Geschichte der Kommunistischen Internationale in neuen Licht: Ansatze zu einer Umwertung in Moskau', Cologne: Berichte des Bundesinstituts fur ostwissenschaftliche und internationale Studien, 1988, Report no. 54/1988, pp. 15–16; see also the same author's 'Gorbatschow — ein Bucharinist?', pp. 20–22.

9   Ulam *Expansion and Coexistence*, p. 183.

10 On the experiments in Czechoslovakia see M. Stefaniak 'Novye usloviia, poiski novykh reshenii', in B. M. Leibzon (ed.) *Iz istorii Kominterna* Moscow:"Mysl'", 1970, pp. 128–9.

11 'The Soviet View of Munich', in Rubinstein (ed.) *The Foreign Policy of the Soviet Union*, pp. 143–5.

12 See Stalin's Report to the Eighteenth Congress of the All–Union Communist Party (Bolsheviks) on 10 March 1939 in ibid., pp. 145–9.

13 It is interesting to note in this connection that Tito, whose contact with and instruction from the USSR during the war were by radio to the Comintern in Moscow, continued to have exchanges with the Comintern as late as November 1943. See Vladimir Dedijer *Novi prilozi za biografiju Josipa Broza Tita*, vol. 2, Rijeka: GRO 'Liburnija', 1981, p. 1046.

14 For a good brief analysis of the speech and its implications see Joseph L. Nogee and Robert H. Donaldson *Soviet Foreign Policy Since World War II* 2nd edn, New York: Pergamon Press, 1984, pp. 74–5.

15 The relations between Moscow and an important group of Communist Parties involved in the resistance movement during the war are discussed with some interesting reinterpretations of the role of the Comintern in the essays in Tony Judt (ed.) *Resistance and Revolution in Mediterranean Europe, 1939–1948* London: Routledge, 1989. See, especially Mark Wheeler 'Pariahs to partisans to power: the Communist Party of Yugoslavia', pp. 110–56.

16 Stalin allegedly chose this title in order to compel Western media to make a pro–Soviet propaganda statement every time they cited the journal by name. Ulam *Expansion and Coexistence*, p. 460.

17 For the terms of the negotiations see A. Doak Barnett 'The Sino–Soviet Alliance' in Franz Schurmann and Orville Schell (eds)

Communist China: Revolutionary Reconstruction and International Confrontation, 1949 to the Present New York: Vintage Books, 1967, pp. 259–61.

18   For a general assessment of the politics of the Khrushchev era see T. H. Rigby 'Khrushchev and the Rules of the Game' in R. F. Miller and Ferenc Feher (eds) *Khrushchev and the Communist World* London: Croom Helm, 1984.

19   N. S. Khrushchev 'Some Fundamental Questions of Present–day International Development — Report of the Central Committee of the CPSU to the Twentieth Party Congress, February 1956' in Rubinstein *The Foreign Policy of the Soviet Union* 3rd edn, pp. 28–33.

20   ibid. See also his speech to the Higher Party School of the Institute of Marxism–Leninism of the CC CPSU on 6 January 1961, in ibid., pp. 266–9.

21   On the details of the Yugoslav reaction see Robert F. Miller 'Khrushchev and Tito' in R. F. Miller and F. Feher *Khrushchev and the Communist World*, pp. 189–209.

22   Palmiro Togliatti '9 Domande sulla Stalinismo' in *Nuovi Argomenti*, no. 20 (16 June 1956), translated in The Russian Institute, Columbia University (ed.) *The Anti–Stalin Campaign and International Communism* New York: Columbia University Press, 1956, p. 139.

23   For an authoritative statement of the doctrine soon after the event see S. Kovalev 'Suverenitet i internatsional'nye obiazannosti sotsialisticheskikh stran' *Pravda* 26 September 1968, p. 4.

24   For a recent discussion of the evolution, strengths and weaknesses of these defensive arrangements, see Marko Milivojevic, John B. Allcock and Pierre Maurer (eds) *Yugoslavia's Security Dilemmas: Armed Forces, National Defence and Foreign Policy* Oxford: Berg, 1988.

25   For contemporary speculation on these issues, see Harrison E. Salisbury *War Between Russia and China* New York: Bantam Books, 1970, pp. 152–8.

26   Robert F. Miller, 'Eurocommunism and the Quest for Legitimacy' in T. H. Rigby and Ferenc Feher (eds) *Political Legitimation in Communist States* London: Macmillan, 1982, pp. 126–45.

27   Nogee and Donaldson *Soviet Foreign Policy*, p. 241.

Chapter 3

1   I refer here to the expulsions of Soviet and Czechoslovakian diplomats and correspondents from the UK in May 1989. 'Soviet spies "sweeping the world" for secrets' *The Australian* 29 May 1989, p. 7. See also the recent book on Soviet electronic espionage by Desmond

Ball *Soviet Signals Intelligence (SIGINT)* Canberra, Australia: Strategic and Defence Studies Centre, Research School of Pacific Studies, The Australian National University, 1989.

2   Louis Fischer *The Soviets in World Affairs: A history of the relations between the Soviet Union and the rest of the world, 1917–1929* New York: Vintage Books, 1951, pp. 461–8.

3   Max Beloff *The Foreign Policy of Soviet Russia, 1929–1941*, vol. 1, 1929–1936, pp. 48–55.

4   From 1934 to 1939 the membership of the CPUSA, for example, increased from 25 000 to 75 000. K. Shirinia 'Politika narodnogo fronta' in B. M. Leibzon (ed.) *Iz istorii kominterna* Moscow: "Mysl'", 1970, p. 168.

5   William L. Shirer *The Rise and Fall of the Third Reich: A History of Nazi Germany* New York: Simon and Schuster, 1960, pp. 804–11.

6   Milovan Djilas *Conversations with Stalin* New York: Harcourt, Brace & World, Inc., 1962 (Harvest edn), pp. 114–15.

7   E. H. Carr *The Bolshevik Revolution, 1917–1923*, vol. 3, pp. 397–400.

8   Leon Trotsky *The Third International After Lenin* New York: Pathfinder Press Inc., 1970, pp. 224–7.

9   For an assessment of the Pact's demoralising effects in the West European Communist Parties themselves, see Joan Barth Urban *Moscow and the Italian Communist Party, From Togliatti to Berlinguer* Ithaca: Cornell University Press, 1986, pp. 151–2.

10 For good analyses of the impact of leadership of the resistance on the political perspectives of local communist leaders, see the chapters on France, Italy and Greece by Lynne Taylor, David Travis and Haris Vlavianos, respectively, in Tony Judt (ed.) *Resistance and Revolution in Mediterranean Europe, 1939–1948* London: Routledge, 1989.

11 Amirah Inglis *Amirah: An un–Australian Childhood* Melbourne: William Heinemann, 1989 (paperback), pp. 42–3, 135.

12 Louis Fischer *The Soviets in World Affairs*, pp. 504–10.

13 The publication of a forged letter purportedly from Comintern President Zinoviev to the British Communist Party by the Conservative press in October 1924 had been a major factor in the Tory victory in the general elections of 29 October. See ibid., pp. 364–5.

14 For accounts of the connections of these bodies with Soviet political and intelligence institutions see John Barron *KGB Today: The Hidden Hand* London: Hodder & Stoughton, 1984; also J. A. Emerson Vermaat 'Moscow Fronts and the European Peace Movement'

Problems of Communism vol. XXXI, no. 6 (November/December 1982), pp. 43–56.

15   Cited in Vermaat ' Moscow Fronts', p. 44.

16   Barron *The KGB Today*, p. 262 n.

17   Richard F. Rosser *An Introduction to Soviet Foreign Policy* Englewood Cliffs, N.J.: Prentice–Hall Inc., 1969, p. 265.

18   Barron, *The KGB Today*, p. 271.

19   ibid., p. 264.

20   On the links between the KGB and other intelligence services of the socialist countries with the international terrorist 'fraternity', see Uri Ra'anan, Robert L. Pfaltzgraff Jr, Richard H. Schultz, Ernst Halperin and Igor Lukes (eds) *Hydra of Carnage: The International Linkages of Terrorism. The Witnesses Speak* Lexington, Mass.: Lexington Books, 1986.

21   This point is made by Alexander Rahr in 'Winds of Change Hit Foreign Ministry' *Radio Liberty Research* RL 274/86, 16 July 1986.

22   ibid. Only a brief report of the meeting appeared in the Soviet press (*Pravda*, 24 May 1986).

23   Rahr 'Winds of Change'.

24   A good example is the agreement in July 1989 of the Greek Communist Party, under the hard–line, Moscow–oriented leadership of Harilaos Florakis, to enter a coalition with the right–wing New Democratic Party. 'Communists join Right to rule Greece' *The Australian* 3 July 1989, p. 9.

25   See, for example, Desmond Ball 'How Moscow steals ASEAN's secrets' *Pacific Defence Reporter* vol. XV, no. 12 (June 1989), pp. 8–14.

26   See the short biography of Kryuchkov in *Pravda*, 22 September 1989, p. 1. Kryuchkov is identified by Amy W. Knight as a *protégé* of Yuri Andropov, like Gorbachev, which suggests an additional reason for the evident closeness of the two and for his selection to replace Chebrikov in the Politburo as the person in general charge of the KGB. Amy W. Knight *The KGB: Police and Politics in the Soviet Union* Boston: Unwin Hyman, 1988, p. 123.

Chapter 4

1   'Text of President Reagan's Address to Parliament on Promoting Democracy' *New York Times* 9 June 1982, p. A16. See also Reagan's speech to the UN General Assembly on 17 June 1982, *New York Times* 18 June 1982, p. A16. Reagan first used the phrase 'evil empire', appropriately enough, in an address to a convention of the

National Association of Evangelists in Orlando Florida on 8 March 1983. *Keesing's Contemporary Archives*, vol. XXXI, no. 1 (January 1985), p. 33347.

2 'Aktual'nye voprosy ideologicheskoi, massovo–politicheskoi raboty partii': Doklad chlena Politbiuro TsK KPSS tovarishcha K.U. Chernenko *Kommunist* no. 9 (June 1983), pp. 30–31.

3 '"Aktual'nye voprosy ideologicheskoi, massovo–politicheskoi raboty partii", Postanovlenie Plenuma TsK KPSS, 15 iunia 1983 goda' *Kommunist* no. 9 (June 1983), p. 40.

4 *New York Times* 7 January 1984, p. 3.

5 One of the most famous of these diagnoses was the eminent sociologist, Tat'iana Zaslavskaia's 'Novosibirsk Report', delivered in Moscow in April 1983 and subsequently circulated in *samizdat* and leaked to the West. 'Doklad o neobkhodimosti bolee uglublennogo izucheniia v SSSR sotsial'nogo mekhanizma razvitiia ekonomiki' ('Report on the Need for a More Thorough Study of the Social Mechanism of the Development of the Economy') Radio Free Europe/Radio Liberty *Materialy samizdata*, Issue no. 35/83, 26 August 1983.

6 For a discussion of Gorbachev's early ambivalence toward the abolition of the central control machinery see R. F. Miller 'The Soviet Economy: Problems and Solutions in the Gorbachev View' in R. F. Miller, J. H. Miller and T. H. Rigby (eds) *Gorbachev at the Helm: A New Era in Soviet Politics?* London: Croom Helm, 1987, pp. 109–35.

7 See, for example, the exhortation to Soviet social scientists by Aleksandr Yakovlev in an address to the Social Sciences Section of the USSR Academy of Sciences in April 1987, abridged as 'Dostizhenie kachestvenno novogo sostoianiia sovetskogo obshchestva i obshchestvnnye nauki' in *Kommunist* no. 8 (May 1987), pp. 3–22; also the editorial article 'Obshchestvennye nauki — perestoike: Bogatstvo teoreticheskogo znaniiia dolzhno sluzhit' narodu' *Pravda* 27 July 1988, p. 1.

8 George Soros, an American businessman who pioneered the establishment of Western–type cultural foundations in Eastern Europe and set up the 'Cultural Initiative' foundation in Moscow in 1987 to fund various social, economic, cultural and ecological projects, was among the first to understand the implications of Gorbachev's attempt to use the opening to the West to influence Soviet domestic developments along modern, non–dogmatic lines. See his article 'The

Gorbachev Prospect' in *New York Review of Books* vol. XXXVI, no. 9 (1 June 1989), pp. 16–19.

9   'Doklad General'nogo sekretaria TsK KPSS M.S. Gorbacheva na Plenume TsK KPSS 23 aprelia 1985 goda' *Kommunist* no. 7 (May 1985), pp. 16–17.

10   'U.S. Says Soviet Naval Force Is Training in Central Pacific' *New York Times* 15 May 1985, p. 2.

11   For a comprehensive, if somewhat controversial, analysis of the basically offensive thrust of the nominally 'defensive' Soviet military doctrine see Michael MccGwire *Military Objectives in Soviet Foreign Policy* Washington, D.C.: The Brookings Institution, 1987, especially pp. 13–35.

12   On these changes see Robert F. Miller 'Seapower as an instrument of foreign policy' *Pacific Defence Reporter* vol. XV, no. 8 (February 1988), pp. 35–6.

13   *Pravda* 26 February 1986.

14   On Yakovlev's anti-Americanism, see Douglas Clarke 'The Soviet Military and the Changes in Moscow' *Radio Free Europe Research* RAD Background Report/203 (Military Affairs) 7 October 1988.

15   Dobrynin was retired in Gorbachev's massive shakeup of the Central Committee apparatus in September 1988, but he was kept on as one of Gorbachev's team of special advisers, which also includes Marshal Sergei Akhromeev, who was replaced as Chief of the General Staff by another outsider (like Yazov, from the Far Eastern Military District), Colonel General Mikhail Moiseev. Akhromeev continues to serve as one of Gorbachev's principal advisers on arms control and disarmament issues. Sergei Zamashchikov 'Virtual Unknown to Head General Staff' *Report on the USSR*, vol. 1, no. 3 (20 January 1989), pp. 14–17.

16   Bernard Weinraub 'Reagan Reported to Invite Gorbachev to Talks in U.S. with Goal of Arms Accord' *New York Times* 13 March 1985, p. 1.

17   *New York Times* 22 March 1985, p. 3.

18   'Doklad General'nogo sekretaria TsK KPSS M.S. Gorbacheva na Plenume TsK KPSS 23 aprelia 1985 goda' *Kommunist* no. 7 (May 1985), p. 16.

19   ibid., p. 17.

20   *New York Times* 2 April 1985, p. 3.

21   ibid., 3 April 1985, p. 9.

22   ibid., 8 April 1985, p. 1.

23   ibid., 12 April 1985, p. 3.

24   *Keesing's Contemporary Archives*, vol. XXXI, no. 10 (October 1985), pp. 33928–9.

25   ibid.

26   ibid., p. 33927.

27   ibid., p. 33929.

28   *Pravda* 26 February 1986.

29   *Keesing's Record of World Events*, vol. XXXIII, no. 2 (February 1987), p. 34971. As he left the final session of the Reykjavik talks, Reagan, obviously miffed, was quoted as accusing Gorbachev of not really wanting a summit. To the latter's rejoinder that 'there's still time', Reagan replied, 'No, there isn't.' Bernard Weinraub, 'How Grim Ending in Iceland Followed Hard–Won Gains' *New York Times* 14 October 1986, p. 1.

30   Soviet officials were alleged to have considered Reagan's ultimate refusal to include SDI in the Reykjavik deal a 'public relations victory for Moscow'. Cited by Philip Taubman 'Talkative Russian Officials Sense Diplomatic Windfall' *New York Times* 14 October 1986, p. 12.

31   Philip Taubman 'Domestic Issues a Topic of Soviet News Briefing' *New York Times* 11 October 1986, p. 6.

32   'Domestic sources of Soviet foreign policy', interview of Foreign Minister Eduard Shevardnadze by staff writer Galina Sidorova, *New Times* no. 28 (July 11–17, 1989), p.9.

33   Despite Gorbachev's assertions to the contrary in his book *Perestroika: New Thinking for Our Country and the World* London: Collins, 1987, p. 250. The book was published before the INF treaty and before the series of unilateral Soviet initiatives on nuclear and conventional weapons, which have greatly accelerated the pace of US–Soviet negotiations on security.

34   ibid., pp. 210–52 *passim*.

35   Georgi Shakhnazarov 'Governability of the World' *International Affairs* no. 3 (March 1988), p. 23.

36   The most famous example was the letter by the Leningrad chemistry professor, Nina Andreeva, whose article 'I Cannot Give Up My Principles' ('Ne mogu postupatsia printsipami') was published in edited form in *Sovetskaia Rossiia* on 13 March 1988. Gorbachev himself ordered a detailed official rejoinder in *Pravda* on 5 April 1988, under the title 'The Principles of Perestroika: Revolutionary Qualities in Thought and Actions' ('Prtintsipy perestroiki: revoliutsionnost' myshleniia i desitstvii') attacking Andreeva and the Politburo conservatives behind the publication of her letter, presumably headed by his second–in–command, 'Second Secretary' Yegor Ligachev. See,

for example, the speculation by Christopher Walker, of the *Times* of London, 'Gorbachev in serious trouble over reforms' *The Australian* 22 April 1988, p. 7.

37 *Keesing's Record of World Events* vol. XXXIV, no. 3 (March 1988), p. 35804.

38 Paul H. Nitze 'Security Challenges Facing NATO in the 1990s' *Department of State Bulletin* vol. 89, no. 2145 (April 1989), pp. 45–6.

39 ibid., p. 46.

40 Genrikh Trofimenko 'Towards a New Quality of Soviet–American Relations' *International Affairs* no. 12 (December 1988), p. 18.

41 'Moscow wary of arms plan' *The Australian* 27 July 1989, p. 10.

42 V. Pankov 'West European Integration on Social–Reformism Models' *International Affairs* no. 3 (March 1979), p. 79.

43 ibid., p. 81.

44 For a good summary of the provisions of the Final Act see *Keesing's Contemporary Archive*, vol. XXI (1975), pp. 27301–09.

45 ibid., p. 27308.

46 For a representative article on Soviet economic and political expectations *vis–a–vis* West Germany see Sh. Sanakoyev, 'USSR and FRG: Developing Cooperation' *International Affairs* no. 7 (July 1978), pp. 3–11; with Italy, A. Ivanchenko, 'Soviet–Italian Economic Cooperation', ibid., no. 8 (August 1978), pp. 105–12. In both cases the prognosis is regarded as basically positive, despite the 'pernicious' political influence of NATO and, above all, the USA.

47 *New York Times* 24 February 1978, p. 3.

48 *Keesing's Contemporary Archives*, vol. XXV (1979), pp. 29753–4.

49 For a good summary of the complex West German attitudes on the NATO deployments see *Keesing's Contemporary Archives*, vol. XXVII (1981), pp. 31098–100. The leader of the left wing of the SPD, Herbert Wehner, had consistently argued that Soviet military deployments were basically defensive — a position later discarded by the Soviets themselves.

50 Report in *Die Welt*, cited in *Keesing's Contemporary Archives*, vol. XXVI (1980), p. 30471.

51 The *Financial Times* 26 April 1983 reported that 62 Soviet agents had been expelled in the first four months of 1983, as compared with 49 in all of 1982 and 27 in 1981, cited in *Keesing's*, vol. XXIX (1983), pp. 32219–22.

52 'Rech' General'nogo sekretaria TsK KPSS tovarishcha Iu.V. Andropova' *Kommunist* no. 9 (June 1983), p. 15.

53 ibid.
54 For an example of contemporary Western assessments, see Bohdan Nahaylo, 'Soviet Foreign Policy Since Gorbachev Took Over' *Radio Liberty Research* RL 202/85, 25 June 1989.
55 A. Bykov, 'New Stage of STR [Scientific and Technical Revolution — RFM] and East–West Economic Ties' *International Affairs* no. 1 (January 1986), p. 88.
56 ibid., p. 92.
57 For an excellent comprehensive discussion of the evolution of Gorbachev's thinking on Western European political and security issues see Eberhard Schulz 'Das "neue politische Denken" und die Deutschen' Cologne: Berichte des Bundesinstituts fur ostwissenschaftliche und internationale Studien, 1989, no. 15–1989.
58 For a discussion of the changes in Gorbachev's negotiating strategy, with special reference to arms control issues — but not limited to the latter, in my opinion — see George G. Weickhardt 'New Soviet Style in Arms Control Negotiations' *Report on the USSR* vol. 1, no. 29 (21 July 1989), pp. 6–9. Weickhardt dates the appearance of the new style in the latter half of 1988.
59 See, for example, 'Eduard Shevardnadze in Denmark' *Moscow News* no. 42 (16 October 1988), Supplement, p. 5; on relations with Spain, see V. Vernikov's interview with the MFA's arms control and disarmament chief, V. P. Karpov, 'Vzaimnye konsul'tatsii: dialog ravnykh' *Izvestiia* 12 May 1988, p. 5; on the importance of 'dialogue' for the general improvement of Soviet relations with Western Europe, see the account of Shevardnadze's meeting with the diplomats of the twelve West European EEC countries accredited to Moscow on 7 February 1989, 'Novoe kachestvo dialoga' *Izvestiia* 8 February 1989, p. 5.
60 John Barron *KGB Today: The Hidden Hand* London: Hodder & Stoughton, 1983, p. 265.
61 See, for example, the article co–authored by V. Zhurkin, S. Karaganov and A. Kortunov, 'Vyzovy bezopasnosti — starye i novye' *Kommunist* no. 1 (January 1988), pp. 42–50. The article is actually a rather disappointingly heavy–handed appeal for the Soviet Union not to let itself be provoked into competing in the arms race, which the US is manipulating in order to bankrupt the Soviet economy. In itself, this article does not augur well for the approach of the new Institute, although it may only be a reflection of the still inchoate state of the new political thinking at that stage (the end of 1987) and

the continuing need at the time to justify changes in approach in terms reminiscent of the old–style, hard–headed anti–imperialist rhetoric.

62   See, for example, A. Rassadin, 'Zapadnoevropeiskaia voennaia integratsiia — perspektivy i vozmozhnye posledstviia' *MEiMO* no. 2 (February 1989), pp. 104–15.

63   ibid., pp. 113–14.

64   Hella Pick 'France backs summit quest' *The Sydney Morning Herald* 6 July 1989, p. 11. The likely continuation of US links to Western Europe on various levels is even discussed in an approving manner by G. Vorontsov in 'Ot Hel'sinki k "obshcheevropeiskomu domu"' *MEiMO* no. 9 (September) 1988, p. 44.

65   Schulz *Das "neue politische Denken"*, pp. 35–45.

66   V. Vernikov 'Vzaimnye konsul'tatsii: dialog ravnykh' *Izvestiia* 12 May 1988, p. 5.

67   See, for example, Gorbachev's letter in July 1989 to French President Mitterand as host of the 'G–7' Western economic summit, calling for the inclusion of the European socialist countries in the economic integration process. Andrew Clark 'Gorbachev letter to Summit calls for world integration' *Australian Financial Review* 18 July 1989, p. 13; see also the account of his message by N. I. Maslennikov 'Shans dlia Evropy' *Kommunist* no. 12 (August 1989), p. 115.

68   'Evropeiskoe soobshchestvo segodnia. Tezisy Instituta mirovoi ekonomiki i mezhdunarodnykh otnoshenii AN SSSR' *MEiMO* no. 12 (December 1988), p. 18.

69   See, for example, S. Shibaev and A. Rubtsov, 'Nauchno–proizvodstvennaia kooperatsiia SSSR so stranami Zapadnoi Evropy' *MEiMO* no. 7 (July 1988), pp. 106–11; and V. Spendarian and N. Shmelev 'Problemy povysheniia effektivnosti vneshneekonomicheskikh sviazei SSSR' *MEiMO* no. 8 (August 1988), pp. 10–25.

70   Terence Hunt 'Bush welcomes G–7 plea by Gorbachev' *The Australian* 18 July 1989, p. 12; also, 'USSR "not ready to join"' *Canberra Times* 18 July 1989, p. 12.

71   Spandarian and Shmelev 'Problemy', p. 10.

72   See his remarks at a joint press conference with Gorbachev at the end of the latter's visit to Paris in July 1989, 'Press–konferentsiia v Parizhe' *Pravda* 7 July 1989, p. 3.

73   'Soviets import food for miners' *The Australian* 5 September 1989, p. 12.

74   See, for example, the favourable analysis of the draft program of the West German Social–Democratic Party 'O proekte programmy SDPG'

Kommunist no. 9 (June 1989), pp. 107–15; also, the tacit endorsement of the current line of the Italian Communist Party which, for the CPSU, is now a model of the kind of opening to West European social–democracy it seeks for itself, in L. Popov 'Tribuna marksistskoi mysli IKP. Po stranitsam zhurnala "Rinashita"' *Kommunist* no. 4 (March 1989), pp. 118–22; and Aleksandr Yakovlev's address to the XVIII Congress of the CPI in Rome on 20 March 1989, where he stressed the cultural linkages between the USSR and the European left: 'Evropeiskaia tsivilizatsiia i sovremennoe politicheskoe myshlenie' *Izvestiia* 21 March 1989, p. 4.

75 ibid.

76 'Soviets approve of union: Kohl' *The Sydney Morning Herald* 12 February 1990, p. 9.

77 Shevardnadze's exploratory hints are noted in Ian Murray and Andrew McEwen 'NATO's foundations shake' *The Weekend Australian* 24–25 March 1990, p. 18.

78 Richard Vines 'Call for EC pact to replace NATO' *The Australian* 22 March 1990, p. 12.

79 Soviet Foreign Minister Andrei Gromyko referred to the proposal in a speech to the USSR Supreme Soviet in July 1969. 'Gromyko "We want relations with the United States to be friendly"' *The Times* (London) 11 July 1969, p. 10. For an analysis of Soviet intentions see 'Soviet plan to encircle China' *The Times* 3 July 1969, p. 6.

80 Basil Gingell 'Russia sets up distant sea bases' *The Times* 18 December 1969, p. 6.

81 For a Soviet view of the course of negotiations on these issues see N. Nikolayev 'For Good–Neighborliness and Cooperation Between the USSR and Japan' *International Affairs* no. 2 (February 1978), pp. 46–50.

82 Myles L. C. Robertson, Soviet Policy Towards Japan: An Analysis of Trends in the 1970s and 1980s, PhD Thesis, Department of International Relations, Research School of Pacific Studies, The Australian National University, 1987, especially pp. 113–19.

83 ibid., Table 10, p. 127b.

84 See, for example, S. Agafonov 'Pochemu ne podpisan kontrakt' *Izvestiia* 21 April 1989, p. 5, where the writer complains of the continuing Japanese tendency to link economic relations with political conditions, namely the 'territorial question'.

85 In late 1978 Soviet commentators were still depicting socialist 'victories' in Angola, Mozambique, Ethiopia, Afghanistan and Vietnam as an inspiration to 'national liberation movements'

throughout the Third World. A. Iskenderov 'Unity of the World Revolutionary Process — A Factor of Stronger Peace' *International Affairs* no. 12 (December 1978), p. 70.

86 See, for example, the unsigned article 'Peking: Against Peace and Socialism' *International Affairs* no. 1 (January 1978), p. 55.

87 Quoted in Robertson *Soviet Policy Towards Japan*, p. 30.

88 'Rech' tovarishcha Gorbacheva M.S.' *Pravda* 29 July 1986, pp. 1–3.

89 See, for example, the extravagant claims for the Declaration by Iu, Lugovskoi 'Vyrazhaia voliu narodov' ('Expressing the will of the peoples') *Izvestiia* 23 December 1986, p. 3; and also the analysis, some seven months later by the noted Soviet area specialist M. Kapitsa 'Aziia i Tikhii okean: ot konfrontatisii k sotrudnichestvu' *Izvestiia* 28 July 1987, p. 5. Gorbachev clearly sought to build on the relationship established by the 1986 Declaration during his next major visit to India in November 1988. See, for example, his reference to the teachings of the Buddha in a speech in reply to Indian President R. Venkataraman, 'Otnosheniia SSSR i Indii nabiraiut silu' *Pravda* 19 November 1988, p. 2.

90 'Vremia deistvii, vremia prakticheskoi raboty: Vystuplenie M.S. Gorbacheva v Krasnoiarske' *Pravda* 18 September 1988, p. 2.

91 ibid. For a critical analysis of the proposals see Milan Hauner 'Gorbachev in Krasnoyarsk: New Soviet Disarmament Proposals for Asia' *Radio Liberty Research* RL 426/88, 17 September 1988.

92 ibid.

93 'Australia–Soviet fisheries deal will boost trade' *The Canberra Times* 9 February 1990, p. 4.

94 Desmond Ball *Soviet Signals Intelligence (SIGINT)* Canberra: Strategic and Defence Studies Centre, Research School of Pacific Studies, The Australian National University, Canberra Papers on Strategy and Defence no. 47, 1989, especially chapter 4. It is interesting to note that as the time approached for the establishment of a Soviet diplomatic mission in Port Moresby, the government of Papua New Guinea requested Australian help in the upgrading of its National Intelligence Organisation to monitor the expected upsurge in Soviet 'extra–curricular activities'. See Rowan Callick 'PNG consulate opens in Irian Jaya' *Australian Financial Review* 19 September 1989, p. 12.

95 These developments are assessed in Denis Warner 'Overview: Peace hath her victories' *Pacific Defence Reporter* 1989 Annual Reference Edition, vol. XV, no. 6/7 (December 1988/January 1989), pp. 4–6.

96   For a discussion of current Soviet thinking see Milan Hauner 'Does the Soviet Far East Have a Future?' *Report on the USSR* 3 March 1989, pp. 5–7.

97   On this and related problems see V. Ivanov and A. Minakir 'O roli vneshneekonomicheskikh sviazei v razvitii tikhookeanskikh raionov SSSR' *MEiMO* no. 5 (May 1988), pp. 64–7.

98   For the difficulties experienced by the Australian company CSR in negotiating a deal to establish a timber milling complex near Khabarovsk see Sue Neales, 'Prospects abound — as do the hurdles' *Australian Financial Review* 10 May 1989, p. 15.

99   See the interview with Yazov in 'V interesakh obshchei bezopasnosti i mira' *Izvestiia* 27 February 1989, p. 2.

100 'Gotovnost' k konstruktivnomu obsuzhdeniiu' *Pravda* 28 May 1989, p. 4.

101 Robert Y. Horiguchi 'Japan: Careful footsteps in Communist quicksands' *Pacific Defence Reporter* vol. XVI, no. 2 (August 1989), pp. 35–8.

102 See the interview with Singapore's Prime Minister Lee Kwan Yew on the 'Limits to Sino–Soviet rapprochement' *Pacific Defence Reporter* vol. XVI, no. 1 (July 1989), pp. 24–5.

103 'Vstrecha M.S. Gorbacheva s S. Uno' *Izvestiia* 6 May 1989, p. 1.

104 For a reference to the report, which was published in *US News and World Report*, see the AFP dispatch in *The Australian* 7 August 1989, p. 6; for the denial see *Report on the USSR* 18 August 1989, p. 31.

105 'Japanese Socialists seek curbs on arms' *The Age* 11 September 1989, p. 9.

106 Ivor Ries 'Russia, Japan in $4bn deal' *The Australian Financial Review* 14 August 1989, pp. 1,4.

107 Mary–Louise O'Callaghan 'Soviet fishing deal feeler finds favour with Forum' *The Sydney Morning Herald* 3 April 1989, p. 13.

108 The Soviet campaigns were serious enough for a leading American diplomat in the region to warn his government of the threat to US strategic interests. Davendra Sharma 'US concern at "other powers" in S. Pacific' *Canberra Times* 18 August 1989, p. 6.

109 Bryan McManus 'Suharto visit boosts ties with Kremlin' *The Weekend Australian* 9/10 September 1989, p. 14.

110 See, for example, Shevardnadze's message to the 22nd Conference of ASEAN foreign ministers in Brunei in July 'Privetstvennoe poslanie' *Izvestiia* 5 July 1989, p. 5.

111 Denis Warner's interview with Lee 'Limits to Sino–Soviet

rapprochement' *Pacific Defence Reporter* vol. XVI, no. 1 (July 1989), p. 24.

Chapter 5

1 Many of Amalrik's foreign policy predictions were, of course, incorrect, but an amazing number of his domestic forecasts were amazingly accurate. Andrei Amalrik *Will the Soviet Union Survive Until 1984?* New York: Harper and Row, 1970.
2 That is, they maintained close control over the pattern of consumption expenditures and tied them most closely to the capacity of the domestic economy to satisfy this structured demand. For an elaboration of the concept, see Ferenc Feher, Agnes Heller and Gyorgy Markus *The Dictatorship over Needs: An Analysis of Soviet Societies* Oxford: Basil Blackwell, 1983.
3 That is convincingly shown by Vladimir Sobell in 'Eastern Europe's Debts: Heavy Burden, Little Benefit' *Radio Free Europe Research* RAD Background Report/50 (Eastern Europe), 22 March 1988.
4 See, for example, Roger Kanet 'East–West Trade and the Limits of Western Influence' in Charles Gati (ed.) *The International Politics of Eastern Europe* New York: Praeger Publishers, 1976, p. 209.
5 'Comrades in arms but not in trade' *The Sydney Morning Herald* 5 January 1989, p. 4.
6 For a good brief analysis of these difficulties see Peter Knirsch 'Economic Relations Between the Soviet Union and Eastern Europe and Their Implications for East–West Relations' in Kinya Niiseki (ed.) *The Soviet Union in Transition* Boulder: Westview Press, 1987, pp. 104–29; for a more detailed analysis see Franklyn D. Holzman *The Economics of Soviet Bloc Trade and Finance* Boulder: Westview Press, 1987, especially chapters 4 and 8. The political dimensions of the autarchic impulse are cogently discussed by a young Yugoslav economist, O. Golubovic in SEV — zajednica planskih privreda, unpublished MA thesis, Belgrade: Economics Faculty, Belgrade University, 1983.
7 For example, the meeting of WTO party leaders in Warsaw on 15–16 July 1988, after making a statement on conventional disarmament in Europe, also passed a resolution on ecology. See Vladimir V. Kusin 'An evaluation of the Warsaw Pact's summit's nonmilitary aspects' *Radio Free Europe Research* RAD Background Report/138 (Eastern Europe), 20 July 1988. For a good analysis of the various structures and functions of the WTO see Robin Alison Remington *The Warsaw*

Pact: Case Studies in Communist Conflict Resolution Cambridge, Mass.: The MIT Press, 1971.

8 Alec Nove, in the autumn of 1980, was already questioning the ability of the Soviet Union to continue to bail out its WTO allies because of the mounting evidence of economic difficulties in the USSR itself. 'The security complex of the Soviet Union' *The Times Higher Education Supplement* 17 October 1980, pp. 11–12.

9 James F. Brown 'Relations Between the Soviet Union and Its East European Allies: A Survey' *RAND Report R–1742–PR*, 1975, cited by Andrzej Korbonski 'Eastern Europe' in Robert F. Byrnes (ed.) *After Brezhnev : The Sources of Soviet Conduct in the 1980s* Bloomington, Ind.: Indiana University Press, 1983, p. 303, n. 6.

10 For a comprehensive summary of the renewed efforts at military–strategic, political and economic co–ordination of the Bloc during the Andropov–Chernenko interregnum see Wolfgang Berner, Christian Meier, Dieter Bingen, Gyula Jozsa, Fred Oldenburg and Wolff Oschlies 'Sowjetische Vormachtpolitik und Autoritatskrise in Osteuropa' in Heinz Timmermann (chief ed.) *Sowjetunion 1984/85: Ereignisse, Probleme, Perspektiven* Munich: Carl Hanser Verlag, 1985, pp. 279–303.

11 See Gorbachev's speech at the April (1985) Plenum of the CPSU Central Committee *Kommunist* no. 7 (May 1985), pp. 16–18. He further elaborated on this theme in his Political Report to the 27th Congress of the CPSU in February 1986. *Izvestiia* 26 February 1986.

12 *Sotsialisticheskaia industriia* 19 December 1985, pp. 1–3.

13 ibid., p. 3.

14 I have discussed the salience of contemporary property relations for economic and political reform in socialist countries in Robert F. Miller 'Theoretical and Ideological Issues of Reform in Socialist Systems: Some Yugoslav and Soviet Examples' *Soviet Studies* vol. XLI, no. 3 (July 1989), pp. 430–48.

15 The strategy of 'invulnerability' through integration is discussed in Robert F. Miller 'The Soviet Union and Eastern Europe: Genuine Integration at Last?' in R. F. Miller, J. H. Miller and T. H. Rigby (eds) *Gorbachev at the Helm: A New Era in Soviet Politics?* London: Croom Helm, 1987, pp. 214–44.

16 'Eastern Europe in 1988' *Radio Free Europe Research* vol. 13, no. 52, 251/88, 30 December 1988, p. 45.

17 ibid., pp. 11–12.

18 '"Push from Gorbachev" forced Honecker out' *The Australian Financial Review* 24 October 1989, p. 11.

19   'Honecker's choice keeps his powder dry' *The Canberra Times* 20 October 1989, p. 8.

20   'Eastern Europe in 1988', p. 3.

21   A. Kunitsyn 'Sotsializm: vybor mirokhoziaistvennoi strategii' *MEiMO* no. 1 (January 1989), p. 55.

22   Of particular note is the article by the well known 'perestroishchiki' V. Spandarian and N. Shmelev, 'Problemy povysheniia effektivnosti vneshneekonomicheskikh sviazei SSSR' *MEiMO* no. 8 (August 1988), pp. 10–25.

23   See, for example, Leonid Chausov 'Vremia ne zhdet' *Pravda* 10 November 1988, p. 5; and the analysis by Vlad Sobell 'The reshaping of the CMEA's scientific program' *Radio Free Europe Research* RAD Background Report/164 (Economics) 23 August 1988.

24   'Unikal'nyi dokument' *Izvestiia* 1 March 1990, p. 3.

25   Maciej Zalewski 'Impuls niemiecki' *Tygodnik Solidarnosc* no. 8 (75), 23 February 1990, p. 3.

26   See, for example, the decision to abolish two of the main functions of CMEA — multilateral co–operation and co–ordination of plans — at a meeting of the organisation's top officials in Prague in late March 1990. 'Eastern trade Group takes on lesser role' *The Sydney Morning Herald* 29 March 1990, p. 13.

27   See the statement by Soviet Foreign Ministry spokesman Gennadii Gerasimov in an interview in Washington cited in Radio Liberty RL 492/87, 4 December 1987, p. 12; on the other hand, see George Schoepflin, 'The Brezhnev Doctrine after Twenty Years' Radio Liberty *Report on the USSR*, vol. 1, no. 4, 27 January 1989, pp. 1–3, where it is argued that no Soviet leader could explicitly repudiate the doctrine.

28   That the reform is indeed in retreat, despite official Chinese statements to the contrary, is evident, for example, in the collapse of joint ventures with Western firms in the automotive industry. 'Foreign carmakers in crisis as paralysis grips policy' *The Australian Financial Review* 20 October 1989, p. 16.

29   Thomas Sherlock, citing two Soviet authors, in 'Emerging Criticism of Gorbachev's Foreign Policy' *Report on the USSR* vol. 1, no. 36 (8 September 1989), pp. 18–19.

30   David Chen 'Beijing flexes its Soviet muscles' *The Australian* 18 October 1989, p. 11.

31   'Chinese party chief invited to Moscow' *The Sydney Morning Herald* 13 September 1989, p. 6.

32   'Poland set for free elections' *The Age*, 7 April 1989, p. 7.

33 'Party ready to break the mould' *The Sydney Morning Herald*, 13 October 1989, p. 12.

34 See, for example, the comments of the *Pravda* correspondent in Warsaw, A. Starukhin 'V tiskakh problem' *Pravda* 2 October 1989, p. 6.

35 Imre Karacs, 'Ready, steady, go for media free–for–all' *The Australian* 14 April 1989, p. 8.

36 'Trudnoe vremia obnovleniia' *Pravda* 4 October 1989, p. 4.

37 The best account of the congress is by the veteran Yugoslav journalist Tomislav Butorac 'Zbogom zloglasenom komunizmu' in the Croatian weekly *Danas* 17 October 1989, pp. 47–9.

38 Andrew Clark 'Hungary cannot turn back the tide of reform' *The Australian Financial Review* 19 October 1989, p. 15.

39 Mark Coultan 'Communists come in from the cold' *The Sydney Morning Herald* 31 March 1990, p. 21. Coultan oddly accepted the Hungarian communists' claim to be 'delighted' with this result, since it guaranteed them substantial representation in parliament!

40 The most striking example was his removal of Chudomir Aleksandrov, his supposed heir apparent. Stephen Ashley 'BCP Plenum Ousts Chudomir Aleksandrov' *Radio Free Europe Research*, Bulgarian SR/7, 29 July 1988.

41 'Zavershilos' soveshchanie' *Pravda* 29 September 1989, p. 5.

42 Coultan 'Communists come in from the cold'.

43 See, for example, Gorbachev's blunt criticism of Romanian economic policies during Ceausescu's visit to Moscow in October 1988: 'Gorbachev hits out at Romanian leader' *The Age* 7 October 1988, p. 8.

44 These unproven allegations are recounted in Andrew Clark 'Who was behind Romania revolt?' *The Australian Financial Review* 4 January 1990, p. 1.

45 'Eastern Europe in 1988', pp. 15–18, 24–5.

46 See, for example, the report of a recent party central committee plenum at which leading reformer Tran Xuan Bach was expelled from the Politburo and other positions of influence, by Alan Boyd 'Vietnam's hardliners put brake on reform', *The Australian* 3 April 1990, p. 8.

47 Evg. Bai and M. Kozhukhov 'Sandinisty perekhodiat v oppozitsiiu' *Izvestiia* 27 February 1990, p. 4; 'Moscow Offers to Help New Nicaraguan Government' (TASS commentary on statement by Soviet Foreign Ministry spokesman) *Report on the USSR* vol. 2, no. 10 (9 March 1990), p. 31.

48 These disagreements are evident in the report of Shevardnadze's conversations with Castro in Havana in early October 1989. 'Obmen mneniiami' *Pravda* 7 October 1989, p. 5.

49 'Unikal'nyi dokument' *Izvestiia* 1 March 1990, p. 3.

50 See, for example, Aleksandr Bovin 'Mirnoe sosushchestvovanie i mirovaia sistema sotsializma' *MEiMO* no. 7 (July 1988), pp. 5–15. The specific application of this principle to relations with China was recommended on the eve of Gorbachev's visit to that country by the authoritative Pravda correspondent Vsevolod Ovchinnikov, 'Otkryt' budushchee' *Pravda* 15 May 1989, p. 5.

51 Vladimir V. Kusin 'The "Yugoslavization" of Soviet–East European Relations?' *Radio Free Europe Research*, RAD Background Report/57 (Eastern Europe) 29 March 1988.

52 'Druzheskaia vstrecha' *Pravda*, 29 April 1989, pp. 1,3.

53 See, for example, the report of an interview with a Hungarian intelligence officer in *Magyar Hirlap* by Agence France Presse on 6 February 1990, in 'Hungarian Intelligence Continues to Cooperate with KGB' *Report on the USSR* vol. 2, no. 7 (16 February 1990), p. 35; see also the analysis by Vladimir V. Kusin 'The Secret Police: Disliked and Weakened, But Not Beaten Yet' *Report on Eastern Europe* vol. 1, no. 6 (9 February 1990), pp. 36–9.

54 Berner, Meier et al. in *Sowjetunion 1984/85*, pp. 283, 295–7.

55 See, for example, S. Shibaev and A. Rubtsov 'Nauchno-proizvodstvennaia kooperatsiia SSSR so stranami Zapadnoi Evropy' *MEiMO* no. 7 (July 1988), pp. 106–111; and M. Maksimova 'Raskryt' potentsial sotrudnichestva' *MEiMO* no. 10 (October 1988), pp. 61–6.

56 Gorbachev made this point emphatically during his visit to Beijing, where he declared that the attempt to prescribe models in the past had been the cause of 'many difficulties in the development of world socialism'. 'We are not the model: Gorbachev' *The Age* 18 May 1989, p. 7.

Chapter 6

1 In his Foreword to the book by Jerry F. Hough *The Struggle for the Third World:Soviet Debates and American Options* Washington, D.C.: The Brookings Institution, 1986, p. v.

2 This point is made by Hough in ibid., p. 157.

3 The Polish freighter *Stefan Batory*, with a consignment of arms, was intercepted off the Guatemalan coast by a US warship in 1954.

(Personal communication to the author by a US Navy officer who had served on the intercepting destroyer).

4 W. Raymond Duncan 'Introduction: Soviet Policy in Developing Countries' in Duncan (ed.) *Soviet Policy in Developing Countries* Waltham, Mass.: Ginn–Blaisdell, 1970, p. 2.

5 The criteria were set forth rigorously in the Statement of the Eighty–One Communist Parties in December 1960, quoted in ibid., p. 6.

6 For a good analysis of the skeptical conservative arguments see Hough *The Struggle for the Third World*, pp. 152–5.

7 Ishwer C. Ojha 'The Kremlin and the Third World Leadership: Closing the Circle?' Duncan (ed.) *Soviet Policy in Developing Countries*, p. 17.

8 Ojha, ibid., p. 18. According to Ojha this prescription merely entailed letting communists 'out of jail so that they could dissolve themselves and join the leading party as individuals'.

9 For example, Viktor Tiagunenko, a leading Soviet Third World expert, and Rostislav Ul'ianovskii, a specialist on these regions in the International Department of the CPSU Central Committee — both cited in Hough *The Struggle for the Third World*, pp. 59–60, 83–4; also in Ojha 'The Kremlin and Third World Leadership', p. 20.

10 ibid., p. 23.

11 The various positions during this period are discussed in Galia Golan *The Soviet Union and National Liberation Movements in the Third World* Boston: Unwin Hyman, 1988, pp. 57–9.

12 Prominent Soviet Third World specialists, such as Vitalii Zhurkin and Evgenii Primakov, warned in the early 1970s against the dangers of confrontation by violent involvement in these regions and the opportunities of detente for longer–term Soviet gains. Others, however, argued for a more aggressive posture, for example in Chile in support of the Allende regime. Cited in ibid., pp. 163–6.

13 See his report to the 25th Congress of the CPSU, *Pravda* 25 February 1976.

14 For a good overview of Soviet efforts in the Middle East, see Alvin Z. Rubinstein 'Soviet Policy in the Middle East: Perspectives from Three Capitals' in Robert H. Donaldson (ed.) *The Soviet Union in the Third World: Successes and Failures* Boulder, Col.: Westview Press, 1981, pp. 150–60; on the case of Soviet relations with Iraq see Robert O. Freedman 'Soviet Policy Toward Ba'athist Iraq, 1968–1979' in ibid., pp. 161–91.

15 Only the Soviet military saw progressive tendencies in the PDRY. Golan *The Soviet Union and the National Liberation Movements*, pp. 232–3.

16 For a good account of the development of Soviet policy in Angola, see Arthur Jay Klinghoffer 'The Soviet Union and Angola' in Duncan (ed.) *The Soviet Union in the Third World*, pp. 97–124.

17 Richard B. Remnek 'Soviet Policy in the Horn of Africa: The Decision to Intervene' in ibid., pp. 139–40.

18 This point is stressed by David E. Albright in 'Gauging Soviet Success in Africa and the Middle East: A Commentary' in ibid., p. 213.

19 For a comprehensive analysis of Soviet–Vietnamese relations and their ramifications in ASEAN, see Leszek Buszynski *Soviet Foreign Policy and Southeast Asia* London: Croom Helm, 1986.

20 Thomas L. Wilborn 'The Soviet Union and ASEAN' in Duncan (ed.) *The Soviet Union in the Third World*, pp. 271, 282–4.

21 For a treatment which stresses Indian disappointment of Soviet expectations see M. Rajan Menon 'The Military and Security Dimensions of Soviet–Indian Relations' in ibid., pp. 232–50, especially pp. 244–6.

22 Golan *The Soviet Union and National Liberation Movements*, p. 9.

23 This account relies on the discussion by Amin Saikal and William Maley 'Introduction' in Saikal and Maley (eds) *The Soviet Withdrawal from Afghanistan* Cambridge: Cambridge University Press, 1989, pp. 2–5; and Shirin Tahir–Kheli 'The Soviet Union and Afghanistan: Benefits and Costs' in Donaldson (ed.) *The Soviet Union in the Third World*, pp. 219–26.

24 'Article Says General Staff Opposed Afghan Intervention' *Report on the USSR* 31 March 1989, p. 34.

25 W. Raymond Duncan 'Soviet Power in Latin America: Success or Failure?' in Donaldson (ed.) *The Soviet Union in the Third World*, p. 8.

26 Some of these debates are recounted in Hough *The Struggle for the Third World*, pp. 89–91.

27 These effects of Castro's radicalism in the late 1960s are discussed in W. Raymond Duncan 'Moscow and Cuban Radical Nationalism' in Duncan (ed.) *Soviet Policy in Developing Countries*, pp. 118–20.

28 Jerry Hough *The Struggle for the Third World*, p. 261.

29 Iu. Osipov 'Problemy perestroiki mezhdunarodnoi valiutnoi sistemy i razvivaiushchiesia strany' *MEiMO* no. 11 (November 1983), p. 72.

30 N. Shmelev '"Tretii mir" i mezhdunarodnye ekonomicheskie ontnosheniia' *MEiMO* no. 9 (September 1987), p. 24.

31 'Prizyvy TsK KPSS k 1 Maia 1985 goda' *Pravda* 13 April 1985, p. 1.

32 'O sozyve ocherednogo XVII s"ezda KPSS i zadachakh, sviazannykh s ego podgotovkoi i provedeniem' *Kommunist* no. 7 (May 1985), p. 17.

33 'Politicheskii doklad Tsentral'nogo Komiteta KPSS XVII s"ezdu Kommunisticheskoi partii Sovetskogo Soiuza' *Kommunist* no. 4 (March 1986), pp. 16–18.

34 'Programma Kommunisticheskoi partii Sovetskogo Soiuza: Novaia redaktsiia' ibid., pp. 110–11, 142.

35 See, for example, his pledge to continue to support the national liberation struggle in southern Africa and his encouragement of greater independence on the part of the member states of ASEAN, in Gorbachev *Perestroika*, pp. 182–3, 187.

36 'O khode realizatsii reshenii XXVII s"ezda KPSS i zadachakh po uglubleniiu perestroiki' *Kommunist* No 10 (July 1988), pp. 19–23.

37 See, for example, the article by the alleged liberal G. Mirskii 'K voprosu o vybore puti i orientatsii razvivaiushchikhsia stran' *MEiMO* no. 5 (May 1987), especially p. 78.

38 David E. Albright 'The USSR and the Third World in the 1980s' *Problems of Communism* vol. XXXVIII, no. 2–3 (March–June 1989), p. 68.

39 I. Malashenko 'Interesy strany: mnimye i real'nye' *Kommunist* no. 13 (September 1989), p. 117.

40 ibid., pp. 119–20.

41 See, for example, the description of the national reconciliation program in Cambodia by two Soviet observers of the scene on the eve of the Vietnamese troop withdrawals. S. Kolesnikov and E. Shashkov 'Istselenie' *Kommunist* no. 13 (September 1989), pp. 102–13.

42 Albright sees no signs of a decline in Soviet arms deliveries to the Third World. 'The USSR and the Third World in the 1980s', p. 65.

43 'Speech by Mikhail Gorbachev at the UN General Assembly' Supplement to *Moscow News* no. 51 (3351) 1988.

Chapter 7

1 Robert F. Miller, Perestroika Yugoslav Style: Some Lessons for Other Reforming Communist Systems, (unpublished paper presented in the Department of International Relations, Research School of Pacific Studies, The Australian National University, August 1989), pp. 6–8.

2 Henry Kissinger 'The new dangers of the new Europe' *The Weekend Australian* 14–15 October 1989, p. 23.

3 See, for example, Rajni Kothari 'Minorities to be squeezed now by major powers' *The Canberra Times* 11 September 1989, p. 9.

4 'East bloc "can do it their way"' *The Australian* 27 October 1989, p. 7.

5 See, for example, the results of opinion polls in the USSR and Poland, which show popular disenchantment with the respective reform programs in the two countries and a loss of popular support for their Communist Parties. 'Perestroika getting us nowhere: opinion polls' *The Australian* 24 October 1989, p. 10.

6 Quoted in 'Editor hits back at Gorbachev' *The Sydney Morning Herald* 24 October 1989, p. 8.

Index